FRACTAL DREAMS
New Media in Social Context

FRACTAL DREAMS

New Media in Social Context

edited by
Jon Dovey

LAWRENCE & WISHART
LONDON

Lawrence & Wishart Limited
99a Wallis Road
London E9 5LN

First published 1996 by Lawrence & Wishart, 1996
Collection © Lawrence & Wishart, 1996
Each Essay © the author(s), 1996

ISBN 0 85315 800 2

British Library Cataloguing in Publication Data.
A catalogue record for this title is available from
the British Library.

Photoset in Garamond by
Derek Doyle & Associates, Mold, Clwyd
Printed and bound in Great Britain by
Redwood Books, Trowbridge, Wiltshire

Contents

For my father

Acknowledgements

Thanks to Roshanak Nedjad and other staff at the Cinevideo Festival for giving me the opportunity to develop these ideas; also to the British Council in Munich. Thanks also to Vicky Grut and Ruth Borthwick at Lawrence & Wishart for their forbearance and support. Also to Martin Lister of Gwent College of Higher Education for being a generous colleague and to all the students who have given me feedback, especially Jo Castro for use of bits of her research. Finally, thanks to all the contributors who squeezed the necessary time out of their busy schedules to make this book happen.

Introduction

To begin, talking of the future with a story from the past. An experience that evokes much of what this book will discuss: my first encounter with Virtual Reality (VR), in Berlin, in 1991 at the Film Festival.

The former Academie der Kunste of the old East Germany, a beautiful neo-classical edifice redolent with the authority of the Stalinist state. The Academy had been taken over by the international video art community as the site of the Berlin Video Festival. The poor Ossis to the fatcats of the Film Festival proper. Here on the first landing of the sweeping marble staircase is a VR installation, punters are lining up to participate in this new game sensation.

The first thing I am struck by is how the participants in the helmet and glove, the VR voyagers, are immediately rendered blind by the technology. Arm out ahead, head covered, they look like blindfolded victims in a medieval dance of death. The impact of this sight is not lost on the spectators; they laugh and giggle as the poor unfortunate stumbles around the stage, getting stuck in impossible corners, only to be rescued by the beautiful assistant in the white suit. O yes, I forgot an essential fact, the installation is sponsored by Phillip Morris tobaccos, the white suits are the company acolytes.

When my turn comes I strap myself into the heavy gear and set off on my voyage to the future. I see a rather poor graphic of a lobby. Moving my hand moves a silly hovering hand that has popped up in the bottom left hand of my frame. Using the hand as direction pointer I appear to move through the lobby, confronting a set of double doors and managing to pick up a smart card that waits. (No mean feat when your hand is encased in a medieval gauntlet.) Having inserted the image of the credit card into the image of the slot, the doors open – I find I am staring into deep space. From the depths of the star pattern tiny dots appear to rush toward me as they get bigger.

They turn out not to be stars but tiny packs of Marlboro. I try to reach out to catch them as they hurtle by. It was hard, perhaps I wasn't supposed to do that, perhaps I was supposed to plunge off into deep space flying like Superman. I tried, I fell down. It was then that I discovered that the programme would continue to run despite my prostrate form. So much for interactivity.

Berlin 1991, no more belief systems, only technology and corporate capital. My first taste of the new Renaissance promised by the enthusiastic celebrants of New Media, just another bad sales pitch for more cancer.

This is a book for people who don't believe the hype, for the reader who wants to question the surprisingly persistent myth that technology will set us free. It is a myth driven by relentlessly optimistic media coverage. Each onslaught of hyperactive technobabble becomes more tedious than the last, until at last we become just plain bored by global capitalism's latest manifestation. We should make no mistake that this is indeed what is emerging. The realm of the digital offers the media/finance/military power bloc an opportunity to reorganise and consolidate its power.

One of the rhetorical characteristics of popular writing about New Media is a profusion of terms and claims that seek to transcend rather than define. So what exactly are we talking about here?

Centrally this book is concerned with those technologies that extend our image-making potential from the analogue representations produced by photomechanical means of production – photography, cinema, analogue video – to the digital production of images. From analogue to binary digits. These linked developments are manifesting themselves primarily in three fields of technology. Multimedia, Virtual Reality and computer networking. Again these separate fields are often conflated together in reference to their effects on mass media by use of the term 'the information superhighway', so that image-making becomes further subsumed within electronic media. A common and fundamental quality of these emerging technologies is the diminution of the significance of the carrier medium, or substrate (the celluloid, paper or videotape), in preference for the 'live' electronic state, often referred to as 'Cyberspace'. The essays that follow seek to examine the cultural impacts of such developments by placing them into an historical and political context.

The seemingly exponential rate of technological developments makes the precise definition of what is occurring difficult to delimit. The problem is to know where to stop, how to draw the lines that would give us a frame to examine the process. Are we merely experiencing a further dose of the vertiginous effects of progress which characterised modernism, or is this something else again? One thing we can observe with certainty is that these technologies are having a significant quantitative impact. More texts get made faster.

What about qualitative impact? Does more equal better? Does faster equal more useful, or more beautiful? Or more interesting? The concept of interactivity is often used to describe the kinds of qualitative changes brought about by New Media technologies. The ability of the user to interact with information and image, to change, reformulate or tailor the data to suit his or her own ends.

However, what I hope this book will begin to do is to question the precise nature of the qualitative changes claimed for new media. These claims are pervasive, both within the 'serious' media and within critical and art theory. Many of the contributors to *Fractal Dreams* have chosen to begin their pieces with an assessment of the Utopian rhetoric of technological determinism as it currently manifests itself. Such writing often seems to owe more to science fiction than critical discourse. (A similarity to which we will return.) The essays in *Fractal Dreams* start by defining themselves in opposition to this rhetoric. They seek to analyse this discourse and recontextualise it within the culture and power structures which will determine the eventual outcomes of digitisation. We are living through the utopian moment that accompanies all new media technologies. In this moment the dominant discourse is constructed as optimistic, full of potential, hope, pregnant with possibility limited only by megabyte capacity. Transcendence is a key concept, transcending the body bound realities of the unpleasant world that we live in for a massive interactive cyber fun park of creativity, simulation and shopping. A park in which difference, and definition, is dissolved through the incantation of the spell of 'interactivity'.

Fractal Dreams sets out to ask a number of key questions of this dominant discourse. How does such a Utopian rhetoric account for the ways in which all recent democratic media possibilities have been co-opted into the apparent democracy of the spectacle? How can we reinscribe a sense of the power relations of the image within the practices of the new technologies of vision? It appears that the lure of the technology is so strong that we are in danger of erasing our own cultural histories. It is a lure which partakes of our unconscious desires for a future which we want to be better – a libidinous view which is strong enough to blind us to the material developments of history. In an attempt to explore these developments, this collection looks centrally at the issue of access to the technology. How much will it cost? How far will its use be circumscribed by its design? Where will the primary markets be? Who gets to write the software? What kind of value systems will they replicate?

Information and representation have always been a site of struggle. Contending forces within the culture have fought over control of the Bible, painting, photography, the press, cinema, radio and television. Propaganda and counter-propaganda. Representation has political significance. In a period of transition new cultural forms will emerge, they will be articulated and institutionalised. In the absence of either constructive critical debate or patterns of political organisation these new forms will be given over to the forces of the market and the needs of multinational capital. By default they will simply be part of the profit production process at the expense of some of the democratic, creative, and educational possibilities that they undoubtedly *do* possess.

The essays in *Fractal Dreams* will seek to articulate these possibilities. They will attempt to mark out the territory of the new mediasphere which is emerging and to distinguish between what is actual and what is virtual in these new worlds. They also stake some claims for a radical media practice, a practice which addresses all those with a stake in using media to promote democratic diversities rather than homogenised consumers. *Fractal Dreams* is an attempt to create and appropriate some alternative territories before the borders of the new map become too tightly closed.

Since beginning this project in 1992, developments have continued apace. In particular the much trumpeted charms of Virtual Reality have receded as the actual reality of the technology has asserted itself. Technical problems suggest that it is likely to be another ten years (or so!) before we can enjoy fully immersive, hi-resolution, fully interactive worlds. However, multimedia is by now a well established and rapidly developing market, with CD-ROM emerging as the consumer platform of the next decade. The growth of public awareness and subscription to the various computer networks that make up the Internet has also exploded over the past year. The critical writing about these technologies has moved out of the journals devoted to art, science, and education into the broadsheet press. Media, culture and lifestyle pages are suffused with netsurfers, cyberpunks and prognoses of 500 channel fibre optic TV. Science and computer pages continue to pour out ever more excitable responses to the possibilities offered in the latest set of manufacturers' press releases. The utopian rhetoric has established itself as part of the culture which shapes consumer attitudes towards the new technologies. Such writing begins to look more and more like PR for the media multinationals whose horizontal integration controls the global flow of information in an ever tightening grip.

Against this background the publication of this collection

looks even more timely. The need for another space in which to explore the new worlds that are opening up is even more pressing. I hope this book will be one contribution to such a space. In particular I hope it will be a useful starting point for many students of media and design, who are even now being recruited in the gadarene rush to the future without any body of critical thought to help them avoid a career in the new digital sweatshops.

The collection opens with a number of essays which consider some of the theoretical implications of digital media. These pieces acknowledge the excitements offered by technologies which appear to offer technological expression to structuralist and post-structuralist critical thought. In particular these pieces explore the relationship between changing notions of identity and their social contexts. Kevin Robins' contribution opens the collection by mounting a comprehensive critique of the utopian rhetoric of Virtual worlds, acknowledging the notion of the fractured self but placing it firmly back within the realm of the social and political. His authoritative review of the literature argues for a discourse which is rooted in the world that still exists when we 'jack out' of the system. Through a review of popular culture, especially cinema, as a site of consumption for ideas about past, present, and future, Sean Cubitt argues for a 'negative utopia'. His piece also highlights the crisis of individuality and suggests a future based on the dissolution of self in a radically contradictory and ultimately ecological open system.

Nickianne Moody's piece concentrates on the implications of digital technologies for the relationship between self · and memory. Drawing parallels between medieval allegory and computer-gaming she deconstructs the idea of interactivity by showing how it is rooted in simulation and hyperreality, 'painting by numbers'; her essay argues for forms of interactive computer art that release the contemplative and creative rather than reproduce the passive consumer. The two essays in the middle of the book use the recent cultural history of independent film and video as a paradigm for thinking about how a political agenda for New Media could be approached. Fred Johnson's *Cyberpunks In the White House* reviews developments around the information superhighway in the US. In particular, he mounts a critique of government policy, and recounts how coalitions are forming to set up a public interest agenda for the forthcoming digital networks. His piece opens up a debate which has barely begun to occur in the UK, and one which should become increasingly significant as we too have to grapple with how we can inscribe ideas of the civic space and public service into the emergent media networks.

My own contribution to the book comes at New Media through looking at video practice. By disinterring the utopian moment of video culture in the late 1960s and contrasting it with the current reality of camcorder culture, it explores models of cultural prediction. I hope that by looking at camcorder culture in the context of voyeurism and surveillance it may alert us to what a 'tabloid' digital culture might look like.

There follow three contributions that deal with artists' use of New Media. Ailsa Barry provides a very useful introduction to the field, drawing our attention to the many pitfalls that confront the artist wishing to participate in the fairy tale of infinite digital creativity. Beryl Graham's piece provides an excellent review of a number of artists' work, making a major contribution to defining the work that is getting made, especially in its relationship to audience. The transition from audience to player, and the precise status of the player in the artwork are here articulated for the first time. The Canadian artist Catherine Richards has provided a lucid account of her own practice as an artist working around the issues of VR. Her work returns to the concerns with the self and the body explored in the opening of the book, here reformulated by an artist taking contemporary and feminist notions of identity and reworking them in technologically based artworks. Her piece is based around descriptions of work she has produced set into a context of theoretical movements which have informed her practice.

Finally, Judith Squires has written an important critique of cyberfeminism, using the works of Shulamith Firestone, Donna Haraway and Sadie Plant. Her essay argues that cyberfeminism is in danger of becoming a new orthodoxy in the technolibertarian hallucinations which serve corporate capital. She places the current crisis of self within a history of the Enlightenment, demanding that we attend to Haraway's original description of cyberfeminism as 'an ironic political myth' rather than a manifesto.

The collection as a whole offers a variety of inflections in the way it traverses the field, from academic and theoretical through to agit and personal. I have consciously tried to avoid homogeneity in the hope that readers will be able to find what they are looking for in this combination of approaches.

Cyberspace and the World We Live In

Kevin Robins

The idea of an Earthly Paradise was composed of all the elements incompatible with History, with the space in which the negative states flourish.

E.M. Cioran

And what Freud calls all the time reality, and the problem of reality, is always social reality. It is the problem of the other or the others, and it is never, never, never physical reality ... The problem is always the difficulty or the impossibility of coping with or recognizing social reality, that is, human reality, the reality of other humans, the reality, of course, of institutions, laws, values, norms, etc.

Cornelius Castoriadis

Cyberspace is, according to the guruesque William Gibson, a 'consensual hallucination'. The contemporary debate on cyberspace and virtual reality is something of a consensual hallucination, too. There is a common vision of a future that will be different from the present, of a space or a reality that is more desirable than the mundane one that presently surrounds and contains us. It is a tunnel vision. It has turned a blind eye on the world we live in.

You might think of cyberspace as a utopian vision for postmodern times. Utopia is nowhere (*outopia*) and, at the same time, it is also somewhere good (*eutopia*). Cyberspace is projected as the same kind of 'nowhere-somewhere'. Nicole Stenger tells us that 'cyberspace is like Oz – it is, we get there, but it has no location'; it 'opens up a space for collective restoration, and for peace ... our future can only take on a

1

luminous dimension!'[1] In their account of virtual reality, Barrie Sherman and Phil Judkins describe it as 'truly the technology of miracles and dreams'. Virtual reality allows us 'to play God':

> We can make water solid, and solids fluid; we can imbue inanimate objects (chairs, lamps, engines) with an intelligent life of their own. We can invent animals, singing textures, clever colours or fairies.

With charmless wit (or perhaps banal gravity, I cannot tell which), they suggest that 'some of us may be tempted to hide in VR; after all, we cannot make of our real world whatever we wish to make of it. Virtual Reality may turn out to be a great deal more comfortable than our own imperfect reality.'[2] All this is driven by a feverish belief in transcendence; a faith that, this time round, a new technology will finally and truly deliver us from the limitations and the frustrations of this imperfect world. Sherman and Judkins are intoxicated by it all. Virtual reality, they say, 'is the hope for the next century. It may indeed afford glimpses of heaven.'[3] When I read this, I can hardly believe my eyes. We must consider what these spectacular flights of fantasy are all about.

But utopia is surely about more than a new pleasure domain? Krishan Kumar reminds us that it is also 'a story of what it is to encounter and experience the good society'.[4] In this respect, too, the self-proclaiming visionaries tell us they have good news and great expectations. The utopian space – the Net, the Matrix – will be a nowhere-somewhere in which we shall be able to recover the meaning and the experience of community. Recognising 'the need for rebuilding community in the face of America's loss of a sense of a social commons', wishful Howard Rheingold believes that we have 'access to a tool that could bring conviviality and understanding into our lives and might help revitalise the public sphere.'[5] We shall be able to rebuild the neighbourhood community and the small-town public sphere, and, in a world in which every citizen is networked to every other citizen, we can expand this ideal (or myth) to the scale of the global village. 'Virtual communities,' says Rheingold, 'are social aggregations that emerge from the Net when enough people carry on [electronically-mediated] public discussions long enough, with sufficient human feeling, to form webs of personal relationships in cyberspace.'[6] Communication translates directly into communion and community. It is a familiar dogma, and there is good reason to be sceptical about its technological realisation. But we should also consider the worth of this vision of electronic community as the 'good society'.

In the following discussion, I shall be concerned with these utopian aspirations and sentiments. But I shall not accept them on their own terms: my interest is in their discursive status and significance in the world we presently inhabit. The propagandists of the virtual technological revolution tend to speak as if there really were a new and alternative reality; they would have us believe that we could actually leave behind our present world and migrate for this better domain. It is as if we could simply transcend the frustrating and disappointing imperfection of the here and now. This is the utopian temptation:

> Men can, in short, become gods (if not God). What need then for 'politics', understood as the power struggles of a materially straitened and socially divided world? The frequently noted contempt for politics in utopian theory is the logical complement of its belief in perfectibility.[7]

I think we should urgently set about dis-illusioning ourselves. There is no alternative and more perfect future world of cyberspace and virtual reality. We are living in a real world, and we must recognise that it is indeed the case that we cannot make of it whatever we wish. The institutions developing and promoting the new technologies exist solidly in this world. We should make sense of them in terms of its social and political realities, and it is in this context that we must assess their significance. Because it is a materially straitened and socially divided world, we should remember how much we remain in need of politics.

The prophets of cyberspace and virtual reality are immersed

3

in the technological imaginary. What concern them are the big questions of ontology and metaphysics:

> What does it mean to be *human* in today's world? What has stayed the same and what has changed? How has technology changed the answers we supply to such questions? And what does all this suggest about the future we will inhabit?[8]

This opens up a whole domain of speculation on disembodied rationality, tele-existence, the pleasures of the interface, cyborg identity, and so on. Of course, these issues are not without interest. But, at the same time, there is the exclusion of a whole set of other issues that also pertain to what it is to be human now and what future humans can look forward to. It is as if the social and political turbulence of our time – ethnic conflict, resurgent nationalism, urban fragmentation – had nothing at all to do with virtual space. As if they were happening in a different world. I think it is time that this real world broke in on the virtual one. Consider the cyberspace vision in the context of the new world disorder and disruption. The technological imaginary is driven by the fantasy of rational mastery of humans over nature and their own nature. Let us consider these fantasies of mastery and control in the context of what Cornelius Castoriadis has called the 'dilapidation of the West', involving a crisis of the political and the erosion of the social fabric.[9] In looking at cyberspace and virtual reality from this different vertex, we can try to re-socialise and re-politicise what has been posed in an abstract, philosophical sense as the question of technology and what it means to be human in today's world.

Cyberspace and Self-Identity

Let us first consider the question of self-identity, which has become a pervasive theme in all discourses on cyberspace and virtual reality. In this new techno-reality, it is suggested, identity will be a matter of freedom and choice:

4

> In the ultimate artificial reality, physical appearance will be completely composable. You might choose on one occasion to be tall and beautiful; on another you might wish to be short and plain. It would be instructive to see how changed physical attributes altered your interactions with other people. Not only might people treat you differently, but you might find yourself treating them differently as well.[10]

Identities are composable in so far as the constraints of the real world and real-world body are overcome in the artificial domain. The exhilaration of virtual existence and experience comes from the sense of transcendence and liberation from the material and embodied world. Cultural conditions now 'make physicality seem a better state to be from than to inhabit':

> In a world despoiled by overdevelopment, overpopulation, and time-release environmental poisons, it is comforting to think that physical forms can recover their pristine purity by being reconstituted as informational patterns in a multidimensional computer space. A cyberspace body, like a cyberspace landscape, is immune to blight and corruption.[11]

In cyberspace, 'subjectivity is dispersed throughout the cybernetic circuit ..: the boundaries of self are defined less by the skin than by the feedback loops connecting body and simulation in a techno-bio-integrated circuit.'[12] In this accommodating reality, the self is reconstituted as a fluid and polymorphous entity. Identities can be selected or discarded almost at will, as in a game or a fiction.

This question of technology and identity has been taken up in quite different ways, and we should take good care to distinguish them. At the banal end of the spectrum are invocations of a new world of fantasy and imagination. When they suggest that 'in VR we can choose to represent ourselves as anything we wish', Sherman and Judkins have in mind the idea that we might want to represent ourselves as 'a lobster or a book-end, a drumstick or Saturn'.[13] The guru of the Virtual Reality industry, Timothy Leary, has similar powers of imagination. In the electronic domain, he says, 'anything you

5

can think of, dream of, hallucinate can be created. And communicated electronically. As Jimmy Hendrix sang, "I'm a million miles away and I'm right here in your windowpane as Photon the Clown with a 95-foot-long triple penis made of marshmallows." '[14] In less grandiose fashion, Howard Rheingold describes how electronic networks 'dissolve boundaries of identity':

> I know a person who spends hours of his day as a fantasy character who resembles 'a cross between Thorin Oakenshield and the Little Prince', and is an architect and educator and bit of a magician aboard an imaginary space colony. By day, David is an energy economist in Boulder, Colorado, father of three; at night he's Spark of Cyberion City – a place where I'm known only as Pollenator.[15]

New identities, mobile identities, exploratory identities – but, it seems, also banal identities. Only the technology is new: in the games and encounters in cyberspace, it seems, there is little that is new or surprising. Rheingold believes that they have their roots 'deep in that part of human nature that delights in storytelling and playng "let's pretend".'[16] Michael Benedikt develops the same point:

> Cyberspace's inherent immateriality and malleability of content provides the most tempting stage for the acting out of mythic realities, realities once 'confined' to drug-enhanced ritual, to theatre, painting books, and to such media that are always, in themselves, somehow less than what they reach for, mere gateways. Cyberspace can be seen as an extension, some might say an inevitable extension, of our age-old capacity and need to dwell in fiction, to dwell empowered or enlightened on other, mythic planes.[17]

All this rhetoric of 'age-old' dreams and desires – which is quite common among the cyber-visionaries – is unspeakably vacuous and devoid of inspiration. It is a familiar old appeal to an imaginative space in which we can occupy new identities and create new experiences to transcend the limitations of our mundane lives. It is the aesthetic of fantasy-gaming; the fag-end of a Romantic sensibility.

The imagination is dead: only the technology is new. The visions are bereft (lobsters and drumsticks), but the point is that the technology will, supposedly, let us experience them *as if they were real*. Another self-styled seer, Jaron Lanier, reveals why the technology is the crucial element. Which particular identity one inhabits is of less importance than what is common to all identities in virtual existence. As we grow up in the physical world, Lanier argues, we have to submit to the dictates of its constraining and frustrating reality. We discover 'that not only are we forced to live inside the physical world, we are made of it and we are almost powerless in it':

> We are actually extremely limited. We can't get to our food easily, we need help. The earlier back into my childhood I remember, the more I remember an internal feeling of an infinite possibility for sensation and perception and form and the frustration of reconciling this with the physical world outside which was very very fixed, very dull, and very frustrating – really something like a prison.[18]

The new technology promises to deliver its user from the constraints and defeats of physical reality and the physical body. It provides the opportunity to go back and to explore what might have been, if we had been able to sustain the infantile experience of power and infinite possibility. Virtual reality is, or is imagined as, 'a combination of the objectivity of the physical world with the unlimitedness and the uncensored content normally associated with dreams or imagination.'[19] The technology is invested with omnipotence phantasies. In the virtual world, it is suggested, we shall receive all the gratifications that we are entitled to, but have been deprived of; in this world, we can reclaim the (infantile) illusion of magical creative power.

All this appears rather familiar and unexceptional. Familiar and unexceptional, because this discourse on virtual futures constitutes no more than a mundane, commonsense re-formulation of the (Kantian) transcendental imagination, 'rooted in a coherent and unified subjectivity, in the unity of mind and body, the "transcendental synthesis" of our sensible and intelligible experience.'[20] *Plus ça change* ... There are more radical and challenging encounters with cyberspace, however. These other discourses can no longer accept the ontological status of the subject, and take as their premise the fractured, plural, decentred condition of contemporary subjectivity. They take very seriously the argument that the postmodern condition is one of fragmentation and dissolution of the subject. Continuing belief, or faith, in the essential unity and coherence of the personal self is held to be ideological, illusionary and nostalgic. In the postmodern scheme of things, there is no longer any place for the Kantian (even less the Cartesian) anthropology. Virtual technology is welcomed as the nemesis of the transcendental ego and its imagination. In cyberspace, there are possibilities for exploring the complexities of self-identity, including the relation between mental space and the bodily other. We are provided with a virtual laboratory for analysing the postmodern – and perhaps post-human – condition.

Weaving together a blend of post-structuralist theory and cyberpunk fiction, this other discourse charts the emergence of cyborg identities. In the new world order, old and trusted boundaries – between human and machine, self and other, body and mind, hallucination and reality – are dissolved and deconstructed. With the erosion of clear distinctions, the emphasis is on interfaces, combinations and altered states. David Tomas writes of the 'technologising' of ethnic and individual identities: 'The continuous manipulation ... of the body's ectodermic surface and the constant exchange of organic and synthetic body parts can produce rewritings of the body's social and cultural form that are directly related to the reconstitution of social identities.'[21] In an already hybrid world, it introduces 'another *technologically* creolised cultural laminate with a different set of ethnic-type rules of social bonding.' But, more than this, through the configurations of electronic and virtual space, 'it presents an all-encompassing sensorial ecology that presents opportunities for alternative dematerialised identity

8

compositions.'[22] In its most sustained form – a kind of cyborg schizoanalysis – the collapse of boundary and order is linked to the deconstruction of ego and identity and the praise of bodily disorganisation, primary processes and libidinal sensation.[23]

This critical and oppositional discourse on cyberspace and virtual reality has been developed to great effect within a feminist perspective and agenda. The imaginative project was initiated by Donna Haraway in her manifesto for cyborgs as 'an effort to contribute to a socialist-feminist culture and theory in a post-modernist, non-naturalist mode, and in the utopian tradition of imagining a world without gender.' Cyborg identity represented an 'imaginative resource' in developing an argument for *pleasure* in the confusion of boundaries and for *responsibility* in their construction.'[24] Subsequent cyberfeminists have tended to place the emphasis on the moment of pleasure and confusion. Claudia Springer draws attention to the 'thrill of escape from the confines of the body': 'Transgressed boundaries, in fact, define the cyborg, making it the consummate postmodern concept ... It involves transforming the self into something entirely new, combining technological with human identity.'[25] Virtual reality environments allow their users 'to choose their disguises and assume alternative identities', Sadie Plant argues, 'and off-the-shelf identity is an exciting new adventure ... Women, who know all about disguise, are already familiar with this trip.' In this context, engagement with identity is a strategic intervention, intent on subverting masculine fantasies; it is 'a disturbance of human identity far more profound than pointed ears, or even gender bending, or becoming a sentient octopus.'[26]

This political edge is not always sustained, however, and it is not all that there is to cyborg feminism. It is accompanied by other desires and sentiments, reminiscent of – though not entirely the same as – the phantasies of omnipotent gratification evoked by Jaron Lanier. Cyberspace is imagined as a zone of unlimited freedom, 'a grid reference for free experimentation, an atmosphere in which there are no barriers, no restrictions on how far it is possible to go'; it is a place that allows women's desire 'to flow in the dense tapestries and complex depth of the

9

computer image.'[27] Claudia Springer evokes 'a microelectronic imaginary where our bodies are obliterated and our consciousness integrated into the matrix.' Observing that the word 'matrix' derives from the Latin '*mater*', meaning both 'mother' and 'womb', she suggests that 'computers in popular culture's cyborg imagery extend to us the thrill of metaphoric escape into the comforting security of the mother's womb.'[28] There is an idealisation of the electronic matrix as a facilitating and containing environment. Like the original, maternal matrix, 'the silently active containing space in which psychological and bodily experience occur', this other, technological, matrix seems to offer the space for unconstrained, omnipotent experience, as well as providing a 'protective shield' affording 'insulation from external reality.'[29]

It is time that we let this reality intrude into the discussion again. We should consider these various, and conflicting, discourses on cyberspace and self-identity in the context of wider debates on identity and identity crisis in the real world.[30] It is, of course, in accounts of the 'postmodern condition' that the question of identity has been problematised, with the idea of a central and coherent self challenged and exposed as a fiction. The argument, as Stephen Frosh observes, is that 'if the reality of modernity is one of fragmentation and the dissolution of the self, then belief in the integrity of the personal self is ideological, imaginary, fantastic ... whatever illusions we may choose to employ to make ourselves feel better, they remain illusory, deceptive and false.'[31] No longer stable and continuous, identity becomes uncertain and problematical. Carlo Mongardini takes note of the inconsistency of the ego-image in the postmodern era, and of the disturbing consequences of that inconsistency:

> A capacity for resistance in the individual is what is lacking here and above all *a historical consciousness which would permit him to interpret and thus control reality*. The individual becomes a mere fraction of himself, and loses the sense of being an actor in the processes of change.[32]

The loss of coherence and continuity in identity is associated with the loss of control over reality.

This crisis of self-identity is, then, more than a personal (that is, psychological) crisis. As Christopher Lasch has argued, it registers a significant transformation in the relationship between the self and the social world outside. It is associated with 'the waning of the old sense of a life as a life-history or narrative – a way of understanding identity that depended on the belief in a durable public world, reassuring in its solidity, which outlasts an individual life and passes some sort of judgement on it.'[33] This important cultural shift involves a loss of social meaning, and a consequent retreat from moral engagement. Mongardini observes a loss of the ethical dimension of life, which requires precisely continuity and stability of individual identity and social reality. There is now, he argues,

> a greater sense of alienation that makes it increasingly difficult to have relationships that demand more of the personality, such as love, friendship, generosity, forms of identification ... The loss of ability to give meaning to reality is also the product of psychic protection, the desire of the individual not to put himself at risk by exposing himself to the stimulus of a reality he can no longer interpret.[34]

There is dissociation and disengagement, withdrawal and solipsism. 'Change acts like a drug', argues Mongardini. 'It leads individuals to give up the unity and coherence of their own identity, both on the psychological and social level.'[35]

In the discourses on cyberspace and identity, however, things do not appear so problematical or bad. This is because the technological realm offers precisely a form of psychic protection against the defeating stimulus of reality. Techno-reality is where identity crisis can be denied or disavowed, and coherence sustained through the fiction of protean imagination; or it is where the stressful and distressing consequences of fragmentation can be neutralised, and the condition experienced in terms of perverse pleasure and play. Cyberspace and Virtual Reality are not new in this respect. Mary Ann Doane describes the psychic uses of early cinematographic technologies in a way that

11

is strikingly similar: 'One could isolate two impulses in tension at the turn of the century – the impulse to rectify the discontinuity of modernity, its traumatic disruption, through the provision of an illusion of continuity (to resist modernity), and the impulse to embody (literally give body to) discontinuity as a fundamental human condition (to embrace modernity). The cinema, in effect, does both.'[36] The new virtual technologies now provide a space in which to resist or embrace postmodernity. It is a space in which the imperatives and impositions of the real world may be effaced or transcended. In the postmodern context, it might be seen in terms of the turn to an aesthetic justification for life: 'Morality is thus replaced by multiple games and possibilities of aesthetic attitudes.'[37] Lost in the funhouse. Through the constitution of a kind of magical reality and realism, in which normal human limits may be overcome and usual boundaries transgressed, the new technological medium promotes, and gratifies, (magical) phantasies of omnipotence and creative mastery.

The technological domain readily becomes a world of its own, dissociated from the complexity and gravity of the real world. Brenda Laurel thinks of it as a virtual theatre, in which we can satisfy 'the age-old desire to make our fantasies palpable'; it provides 'an experience where I can play make-believe, and where the world automagically pushes back.'[38] We might also see it in the context of what Joyce McDougall calls 'psychic theatre', involving the acting out of more basic and primitive instincts and desires.[39] The techno-environments of cyberspace and Virtual Reality are particularly receptive to the projection and acting out of unconscious phantasies. In certain cases, as I have already argued, this may involve receptiveness to narcissistic forms of regression. Narcissism may be seen as representing 'a retreat from reality into a phantasy world in which there are no boundaries; this can be symbolised by the early monad, in which the mother offers the new-born infant an extended period of self-absorption and limitless, omnipotent contentment'.[40] In this context, the virtual world may be seen as constituting a protective container within which all wishes are gratified (and ungratifying encounters with the frustrations of the real world 'auto-magically' deferred). In other cases, as I have again suggested, the created environment may respond to psychotic states of mind. Peter Weibel describes virtuality as 'psychotic space':

> This is the space of the psychotic that stage-manages reality in hallucinatory wish-fulfilment, uttering the battle-cry 'VR everywhere' ... Cyberspace is the name for such a psychotic environment, where the boundaries between wish and reality are blurred.[41]

7 WHICH IS NEEDED
7 FOR COMMUNITY

In this psychotic space, the reality of the real world is disavowed; the coherence of the self deconstructed into fragments; and the quality of experience reduced to sensation and intoxication. It is what is evoked in the fiction of cyberpunk, where 'the speed of thrill substitutes for affection, reflection and care,' and where, as 'hallucinations and reality collapse into each other, there is no space from which to reflect.'[42]

Marike Finlay argues that such narcissistic and psychotic defences are characteristic of postmodern subjectivity, representing strategies 'to overcome the ontological doubt about one's own status as a self by retreating to the original omnipotence of the child who creates the breast by hallucinating it.'[43] Virtual subjectivity – one crucial form through which the postmodern subject exists – may be understood in this light. The new technological environments of virtual reality and cyberspace confuse the boundaries between internal and external worlds, creating the illusion that internal and external realities are one and the same. Artificial reality is designed and ordered in conformity with the dictates of pleasure and desire. To interact with it entails suspension of the real and physical self, or its substitution by a disembodied, virtual surrogate or clone. Under these conditions of existence, it appears as if there are no limits to what can be imagined and acted out. Moreover, there are no others (no other bodies) to impose restrictions and inhibitions on what is imagined or done. The substantive presence of (external) others cannot be differentiated from the objects created by the projection of (internal) phantasies. Virtual empowerment is a solipsistic affair, encouraging a sense of self-containment and self-sufficiency, and involving denial of the need for external objects.

Such empowerment entails a refusal to recognise the substantive and independent reality of others and to be involved in relations of mutual dependency and responsibility. As Marike Finlay argues, 'Only in phantasy can one be omnipotent without loss or reparation.'[44] Such a reality and such a subjectivity can only be seen as asocial and, consequently, amoral. 'Floating identities,' Gérard Raulet observes, 'are in the realm of schizophrenia or neo-narcissism.'[45] The sense of unrestricted freedom and mastery belongs to disembodied identities. Such a phantasy, when it is socially institutionalised, must have its consequences for a real world of situated identities. As Michael Heim argues, the technological systems that convert primary bodily presence into tele-presence are also 'inroducing a remove between *re*presented presences.' They are changing the nature of interpersonal relationships. 'Without directly meeting others physically', says Heim, 'our ethics languishes.' Indeed, the machine interface 'may amplify an amoral indifference to human relationships ... [and] often eliminate the need to respond directly to what takes place between humans.'[46] We are reminded of the reality of our embodied and embedded existence in the real world, and of the ethical disposition necessary for co-existence to be possible in that world. It is the continuity of grounded identity that underpins and underwrites moral obligation and commitment.

It is not my intention to deny the imaginative possibilities inherent in the new technologies, but rather to consider what is the nature of the imagination that is being sustained. From this perspective, it is useful to look at experiences in and of cyberspace and virtual reality in the light of Winnicott's notion of potential space: the 'third area of human living', neither inside the individual nor outside in the world of shared reality, the space of creative playing and cultural experience.[47] In elaborating his ideas, Winnicott drew attention to the continuity between the potential space that supports infantile illusions of magical creative power, and that which is associated with mature aesthetic or spiritual creativity. In virtual environments, this link between infantile and imaginative illusion becomes particularly apparent, as I have already indicated, and it seems appropriate to think of them in terms of the technological institution of potential or intermediate space. This magical-aesthetic aspect of the technologies is clearly that which has gathered most interest.

But we cannot be concerned with creative illusion alone (which is precisely what the new romancers of cyberspace do). In his discussion of potential space, Winnicott also put great emphasis on the moment of disillusionment, which involves 'acknowledging a limitation of magical control and acknowledging dependence on the goodwill of people in the external world.'[48] As Thomas Ogden points out, the infant then 'develops the capacity to see beyond the world he has created through the projection of internal objects.' The individual thereby becomes

> capable of entering into relationships with actual objects in a manner that involves more than a simple transference projection of his internal object world ... mental representations acquire increasing autonomy from [their] origins and from the omnipotent thinking associated with relations between internal objects.[49]

Potential space is a transitional space. It is in this intermediate space, through the interaction of both internal and external realities, that moral sense is evolved. Transitional experience involves the differentiation of internal and external worlds – it is on this basis that aesthetic transgression becomes possible – and the acknowledgement of 'a world of utilisable objects, i.e. people with whom [one] can enter into a realm of shared experience-in-the-world outside of [oneself].'[50] This enables the development of capacities for concern, empathy and moral encounter. Potential space is, in this sense, transitive. We should hold on to this point in our discussions of the cultural aspects of

15

cyberspace and virtual reality technologies. When it seems as if the new technologies are responding to regressive and solipsistic desires, we should consider the consequences and implications for moral-political life in the real world.

Virtual Community and Collective Identity

This takes us to the question of collective identity and community in virtual space. Many of those who have considered these issues have made the (perverse) assumption that they are dealing with a self-contained and autonomous domain of technology. I shall argue, again, that the new technological developments must be situated in the broader context of social and political change and upheaval. The world is transforming itself. The maps are being broken apart and re-arranged. Through these turbulent and often conflictual processes of transformation, we are seeing the dislocation and re-location of senses of belonging and community. The experience of cultural encounter and confrontation is something that is increasingly characteristic of life in our cities. Virtual communities do not exist in a different world. They must be situated in the context of these new cultural and political geographies. How, then, are we to understand the significance of virtual communities and communitarianism in the contemporary world? What are their possibilities and what are their limitations?

Virtual Reality and cyberspace are commonly imagined in terms of reaction against, or opposition to, the real world. They are readily associated with a set of ideas about new and innovative forms of society and sociality. In certain cases, these are presented in terms of some kind of utopian project. Virtual Reality is imagined as a 'nowhere-somewhere' alternative to the difficult and dangerous conditions of contemporary social reality. We might consider this in the context of Krishan Kumar's observations about the recent displacement of utopia from time back to space. The postmodern utopia, he suggests, involves 'returning to the older, pre-eighteenth century, spatial

16

forms of utopia, the kind inaugurated by More.'[51] Virtual space, which is on a continuum with other hyperreal utopian spaces – from Disneyland to Biosphere 2 – is a space removed. As in utopian thinking more generally, there is the belief or hope that the mediated interaction that takes place in that other world will represent an ideal and universal form of human association and collectivity. Michael Benedikt sets it in the historical context of projects undertaken in pursuit of realising the dream of the Heavenly City:

> Consider: Where Eden (before the Fall) stands for our state of innocence, indeed ignorance, the Heavenly City stands for our state of wisdom, and knowledge; where Eden stands for our intimate contact with material nature, the Heavenly City stands for our transcendence of both materiality and nature; where Eden stands for the world of unsymbolised, asocial reality, the Heavenly City stands for the world of enlightened human interaction, form and information.[52]

The elsewhere of cyberspace is a place of salvation and transcendence. This vision of the new Jerusalem very clearly expresses the utopian aspirations in the Virtual Reality project.

Not all Virtual Realists are quite so unrealistic, however. There are others with a more pragmatic and political disposition who have more to contribute to our understanding of the relation between cyberspace and the real world. There is still the sense of Virtual Reality as an alternative reality in a world gone wrong. Techno-sociality is seen as the basis for developing new and compensatory forms of community and conviviality. Networks are understood to be 'social nodes for fostering those fluid and multiple elective affinities that everyday urban life seldom, in fact, supports,'[53] Virtual communities represent:

> flexible, lively, and practical adaptations to the real circumstances that confront persons seeking community ... They are part of a range of innovative solutions to the drive for sociality – a drive that can be frequently thwarted by the geographical and cultural realities of cities ... In this context, electronic virtual communities are complex and ingenious strategies for *survival*.[54]

17

But this involves a clear recognition that such communities exist in, and in relation to, everyday life in the real world: 'virtual communities of cyberspace live in the borderlands of both physical and virtual culture.'[55] Virtual interaction is about adjustment and adaptation to the increasingly difficult circumstances of the contemporary world. We may then ask how adequate or meaningful it is as a response to those circumstances.

The most sustained attempt to develop this approach and agenda is that of Howard Rheingold in his book, *The Virtual Community*. While there is something of the utopian in Rheingold (West-Coast style), there is also a clear concern with the social order. If we look at his arguments in a little detail, we can perhaps see some of the appeal of the pragmatic approach to virtual community, but also identify its limitations and weaknesses. Like other virtual communitarians, Rheingold starts out from what he sees as the damaged or decayed state of modern democratic and community life. The use of computer-mediated communications, he argues, is driven by 'the hunger for community that grows in the breasts of people around the world as more and more informal public spaces disappear from our real lives.'[56] Rheingold emphasises the social importance of the places in which we gather together for conviviality, 'the unacknowledged agorae of modern life'. 'When the automobile-centric, suburban, fast-food, shopping mall way of life eliminated many of these "third places" from traditional towns and cities around the world, the social fabric of existing communities started shredding.' His hope is that virtual technologies may be used to staunch such developments. Rheingold's belief is that cyberspace can become 'one of the informal public places where people can rebuild the aspects of community that were lost when the malt shop became the mall.'[57] In cyberspace, he maintains, we shall be able to recapture the sense of a 'social commons'.

The virtual community of the network is the focus for a grand project of social revitalisation and renewal. Under conditions of virtual existence, it seems possible to recover the values and ideals that have been lost to the real world. Through this new medium, it is claimed, we shall be able to construct new sorts of community, linked by commonality of interest and affinity rather than by accidents of location. Rheingold believes that we now have 'access to a tool that could bring conviviality and understanding into our lives and might help revitalise the public sphere': that, through the construction of an 'electronic agora', we shall be in a position to 'revitalise citizen-based democracy.'[58] It is envisaged that on-line communities will develop in ways that transcend national frontiers. Rheingold thinks of local networks as 'gateways to a wider realm, the worldwide Net-at-large.'[59] In the context of this 'integrated entity', he maintains, we will be in a position to build a 'global civil society' and a new kind of international culture.

Like many other advocates of virtual existence, Rheingold is a self-styled visionary. His ideas are projected as exercises in radical imagination. It is this preachy posture that seems to give cyberspace ideology its popular appeal. There is another aspect to Rheingold's discourse, however, and I think that this has been an even more significant factor in gaining approval for the project of virtual sociality. For all its futuristic pretensions, Rheingold's imagination is fundamentally conservative and nostalgic. He is essentially concerned with the restoration of a lost object: community:

> The fact that we need computer networks to recapture the sense of co-operative spirit that so many people seemed to lose when we gained all this technology is a painful irony. I'm not so sure myself anymore that tapping away on a keyboard and staring at a screen all day by necessity is 'progress' compared to chopping logs and raising beans all day by necessity. While we've been gaining new technologies, we've been losing our sense of community, in many places in the world, and in most cases the technologies have precipitated that loss. But this does not make an effective argument against the premise that people can use computers to cooperate in new ways.[60]

The Net is seen as re-kindling the sense of family – 'a family of invisible friends'. It recreates the ethos of the village pump and the town square. Rheingold can envisage 'not only community but true spiritual communion' in what he describes as 'communitarian places online.'[61] The electronic community is characterised by commonality of interests, by the sense of 'shared consciousness' and the experience of 'groupmind'.[62] The images are of maternal-familial containment. The ideas are of unity, unanimity and mutualism. Rheingold's image of virtual community turns out to be no more than an electronic variant of the 'Rousseauist dream' of a transparent society in which 'the ideal of community expresses a longing for harmony among persons, for consensus and mutual understanding.'[63] It is a social vision that is grounded in a primal sense of enclosure and wholeness.

The Virtual Community is a good condensation of the pragmatic case for association and collectivity in cyberspace. In a manner that contrasts with the otherworldliness of cyber-utopianism, Rheingold is intent on connecting virtual solutions to real-world problems. A sustained case is made for the possibilities of applying virtual and network technologies for the purposes of social and political amelioration (while, at the same time, there is an awareness of the dangers of 'misapplication'). There is a growing recognition that electronic media have changed the way that we live in the world. Joshua Meyrowitz has observed how much television has altered the logic of the social order by restructuring the relationship between physical place and social place, thereby 'liberating' community from spatial locality.[64] Anthony Giddens describes a process of 'reality inversion', which means that 'we live "in the world" in a different sense from previous eras of history':

> The transformations of place, and the intrusion of distance into local activities, combined with the centrality of mediated experience, radically change what 'the world' actually is. This is so both on the level of the 'phenomenal world' of the individual and the general universe of social activity within which collective social life is enacted. Although everyone lives a local life, phenomenal worlds for the most part are truly global.[65]

In the light of these very significant developments, virtual communitarianism assumes a clear resonance and appeal. It appears to have a philosophy of social action appropriate to the conditions of the new technological order.

Because virtual experiences and encounters are becoming increasingly prevalent in the contemporary world, I believe we must, indeed, take very seriously their significance and implications for society and sociality. What I would question, however, is the relevance of techno-communitarianism as a response to these developments. Let us consider what is at issue. That which is generally presented in terms of technological futures is much more a matter of social relations and representations of social life in the present. In a period of turbulent change, in part a consequence of technological innovations, the nature of our relation to others and to collectivities has become more difficult and uncertain. 'The old forms of solidarity were internalised within the extended family and the village community,' argues Edgar Morin, 'but now these internalised social bonds are disappearing.'[66] We must search for new senses and experiences of solidarity, he maintains, though these must now be at more expansive scales than in the past. And, of course, this is what virtual community seems to be all about. Solidarity in cyberspace seems to be a matter of extending the security of small-town *Gemeinschaft* to the transnational scale of the global village. There is, however, something deceptive in this sense of continuity and fulfilment. In considering another postmodern space, Disneyland, Michael Sorkin suggests that it 'invokes an urbanism without producing a city ... it produces a kind of aura-stripped hypercity, a city with billions of citizens ... but no residents.'[67] Jean Baudrillard says that it is 'an entire synthetic world which springs up, a maquette of our entire history in cryogenised form.'[68] We might see virtual and network association in the same light. There is the invocation of community, but not the production of a society. There is 'groupmind', but not social encounter. There is on-line communion, but there are no residents of hyperspace. This is another synthetic world, and here, too, history is frozen.

What we have is the preservation through simulation of the old forms of solidarity and community. In the end, not an alternative society, but an alternative to society.

We might go so far as to see a particular affinity between virtual technologies and this communitarian spirit. As Iris Marion Young argues, the idealisation of community involves denial of the difference, or basic assymetry, of subjects. Proponents of community:

> deny difference by positing fusion rather than separation as the social ideal. They conceive the social subject as a relation of unity or mutuality composed by identification and symmetry among individuals within a totality. Communitarianism represents an urge to see persons in unity with one another in a shared whole.[69]

Existence in cyberspace – a space in which real selves and situations are in suspension – encourages the sense of identification and symmetry among individuals. Dematerialised and de-localised, says Gérard Raulet, 'subjectivities are at once interchangeable and arbitrary ... The subject is reduced to pure functionality.'[70] The sense of unity and mutuality in a shared whole is 'artificially' created through the institution of technology.

The new technologies seem responsive to the dream of a transparent society. Communitarianism promotes the ideal of the immediate co-presence of subjects:

> Immediacy is better than mediation because immediate relations have the purity and security longed for in the Rousseauist dream: we are transparent to one another, purely copresent in the same time and space, close enough to touch, and nothing comes between us to obstruct our vision of one another.[71]

It is precisely this experience of immediacy that is central to the advocacy of virtual reality and relationships. According to Barrie Sherman and Phil Judkins, Virtual Reality 'can transmit a universal "language" ... It is a perfect medium through which to communicate in what will be difficult times ... Common symbols will emphasise common humanity, expose common difficulties and help with common solutions.'[72] Jaron Lanier puts particular emphasis on this quality of virtual encounter. He likes to talk of 'post-symbolic communication' and a 'post-symbolic world'. He believes that it will be possible 'to make up the world instead of talking about it', with people 'using virtual reality a lot and really getting good at making worlds to communicate with each other.' The frustrations of mediated communication will be transcended in an order where 'you can just synthesise experience.'[73] These virtual ideologies are perpetuating the age-old ideal of a communications utopia. Immediacy of communication is associated with the achievement of shared consciousness and mutual understanding. The illusion of transparency and consensus sustains the communitarian myth, now imagined at the scale of global electronic *Gemeinschaft*. It is an Edenic myth.

Techno-community is fundamentally an anti-political ideal. Serge Moscovici speaks of the dialectic of order and disorder in human societies. Order, he maintains, has no basis in reality; it is a 'regressive phantasy'. A social system is only viable if it can 'create a certain disorder, if it can admit a certain level of uncertainty, if it can tolerate a certain level of fear.'[74] Richard Sennett has put great emphasis on this need to provoke disorder in his discussion of urban environments. In arguing that 'disorder and painful dislocation are the central elements in civilising social life', Sennett makes the 'uses of disorder' the basis of an ethical approach to designing and living in cities.[75] He is in opposition to those planners – 'experts in *Gemeinschaft*' – who 'in the face of larger differences in the city ... tend to withdraw to the local, intimate, communal scale.'[76] Sennett believes that this denial of difference reflects 'a great fear which our civilisation has refused to admit, much less to reckon':

> The way cities look reflects a great, unreckoned fear of exposure ... What is characteristic of our city-building is to wall off the differences between people, assuming that these differences are more likely to be mutually threatening than mutually stimulating. What we have made in the urban realm are therefore bland, neutralising spaces, spaces which remove the threat of social contact ...[77]

What is created is the blandness of the 'neutralised city'. Disneyland is no more than the parodic extension of this principle. Here, too, 'the highly regulated, completely synthetic vision provides a simplified, sanitised experience that stands in for the more undisciplined complexities of the city.'[78] I have already noted the continuity between postmodern spaces like Disneyland and electronic virtual spaces. Virtual community similarly reflects the desire to control exposure and to create security and order. It also is driven by the compulsion to neutralise.

Cyberspace and virtual reality have generally been considered as a technological matter. They have seemed to offer some kind of technological fix for a world gone wrong, promising the restoration of a sense of community and communitarian order. It is all too easy to think of them as alternatives to the real world and its disorder. Containing spaces. I am arguing that we should approach these new technologies in a very different way. We must begin from the real world, which is the world in which virtual communities are now being imagined. And we must recognise that difference, asymmetry and conflict are constitutive features of that world. Not community. As Chantal Mouffe argues, the ideal of common substantive interests, of consensus and unanimity, is an illusion. We must recognise the constitutive role of antagonism in social life and acknowledge that 'a healthy democratic process calls for a vibrant clash of political positions and an open conflict of interests.'[79] For that is the key issue: a political framework that can accommodate difference and antagonism to sustain what Mouffe calls an 'agonistic pluralism'. This is so even in the matter of virtual association and collectivity.

The question of technology is not primarily a technological question. In considering the development of techno-communities, we must continue to be guided by social and political objectives. Against the wishful optimism of virtual communitarianism, I have chosen to emphasise those aspects of virtual culture that are inimical to democratic culture (in the sense of political thinkers like Young, Sennett and Mouffe). I have argued that virtual space is being created as a domain of order, refuge, withdrawal. Perhaps I have overstated my case. Maybe. The point has been to shift the discussion into the realm of social and political theory. Hopes for cyber-society have drawn their legitimacy from a metaphysics of technological progress – whatever comes next must be better than what went before. I am arguing for a different kind of justification, concerned with questions of pluralism and democracy now. We might then ask, for example, whether, or how, virtual technologies could be mobilised in pursuit of what Richard Sennett calls the 'art of exposure' (which I would consider to be the opposite of the science of withdrawal). Julia Kristeva considers the idea of a 'transitional' or 'transitive' space as important in thinking about national communities in more open ways.[80] We might consider what a transitional (as opposed to autistic) logic might mean in the context of imagining virtual communities. The point is to broaden and to politicise the debate on community and collectivity in cyberspace. Those who will, of course, continue to work for this new form of association should not be allowed to set the agenda on their own narrow, and often technocratic, terms.

The Worlds We Live In

We can all too easily think of cyberspace and Virtual Reality in terms of an alternative space and reality. As if it were possible to create a new reality which would no longer be open to objections like that which has been left behind. As if we could substitute a reality more in comformity with our desires for the unsatisfactory real one. The new technologies seem to offer possibilities for re-creating the world afresh. We can see virtual culture, then, in terms of utopia: as expressing the principle of hope and the belief in a better world. That is the most obvious response. It is the one that virtual marketing and promotion always peddles. But we can also see virtual culture from an opposite perspective: instead of hopes for a new world, we would then see dissatisfactions about, and rejection of, an old one. This would have the more apocalyptic sense of looking back on the end of the world; what would be more significant would be the sense of an ending. This is how I am inclined to see virtual culture. Because there is something banal and unpersuasive about its utopian ideal. Because what is more striking to me about it is its regressive (infantile, Edenic) mood and sentiments. This is what I have discussed in terms of omnipotence phantasies (at the individual level) and familial communitarianism (at the group and collective level). Regression as transcendence. Dieter Lenzen interprets contemporary society in terms of redemption through the totalisation of childhood. He sees a project of cultural regeneration through regression:

> A regression from adults to children could cause people to disappear completely in the end, opening the way to a renewal of the world. We can see from this that the phenomenon of expanding childhood observable on all sides can be interpreted as an apocalyptic process. Correspondingly, the disappearance of adults could be understood as the beginning of a cosmic regeneration process based on the destruction of history.[81]

We could see virtual discourse as drawing on this mythology (as well as the more familiar metaphysics of technological progress) when it imagines the possibility of new individuals and new communities.

The mythology of cyberspace is preferred over its sociology. I have argued that it is time to re-locate virtual culture in the real world (the real world that virtual culturalists, seduced by their own metaphors, pronounce dead or dying). Through the development of new technologies, we are, indeed, more and more open to experiences of de-realisation and de-localisation. But we continue to have physical and localised existences. We must consider our state of suspension between these conditions. We must de-mythologise virtual culture if we are to assess the serious implications it has for our personal and collective lives. Far from being some kind of solution for the world's problems –

could there ever be a 'solution'? – virtual inversion simply adds to its complexities. Paul Virilio imagines the co-existence of two societies:

> One is a society of 'cocoons' ... where people hide away at home, linked into communication networks, inert ... The other is a society of the ultra-crowded megalopolis and of urban nomadism ... Some people, those in the virtual community, will live in the real time of the world-city, but others will live in deferred time, in other words, in the actual city, in the streets.[82]

In the first society, you may be transported by the pleasure of 'fractal dreaming'. The other society will accumulate the reality that has been repressed. We know that what is repressed cannot be kept out of the dreams.

Notes

[1] Nicole Stenger, 'Mind is a leaking rainbow', in Michael Benedikt (ed), *Cyberspace: First Steps*, MIT Press, Cambridge, Massachusetts 1991, pp53, 58.
[2] Barrie Sherman and Phil Judkins, *Glimpses of Heaven, Visions of Hell: Virtual Reality and Its Implications*, Hodder and Stoughton, London 1992, pp126-127.
[3] *Ibid.*, p134.
[4] Krishan Kumar, *Utopianism*, Open University Press, Milton Keynes 1991, p28.
[5] Howard Rheingold, *The Virtual Community: Finding Connection in a Computerised World*, Secker and Warburg, London 1994, pp12, 14.
[6] *Ibid.*, p5.
[7] Krishan Kumar, *op.cit.*, p29.
[8] Larry McCaffery, 'Introduction: The Desert of the Real', in Larry McCaffery (ed), *Storming the Reality Studio*, Duke University Press, Durham 1991, p8.
[9] Cornelius Castoriadis, 'Le délabrement de l'occident', *Esprit*, December 1991.
[10] Myron W. Krueger, *Artificial Reality II*, Addison-Wesley, Reading, Massachusetts 1991, p256.

11 N. Katherine Hayles, 'Virtual bodies and flickering signifiers', *October*, 66, Fall 1993, p81.

12 *Ibid.*, p72.

13 Sherman and Judkins, *op.cit.*, p126.

14 David Sheff, 'The Virtual Realities of Timothy Leary' (interview), in Gottfried Hattinger *et al* (eds), *Arts Electronica 1990*, vol.2, *Virtuelle Welten*, Linz, Veritas-Verlag, 1990, p250.

15 Rheingold, *op.cit.*, p147.

16 *Ibid.*, p155.

17 Michael Benedikt, 'Introduction', in Michael Benedikt (ed), *op.cit.*, p6.

18 Jaron Lanier, 'Riding the Giant Worm to Saturn: Post-Symbolic Communication in Virtual Reality', in Goffried Hattinger, *op.cit.*, pp186-187.

19 *Ibid.*, p188.

20 Richard Kearney, *The Wake of Imagination*, Hutchinson, London 1988, p169.

21 David Tomas, 'The Technophilic Body: on Technicity in William Gibson's Cyborg Culture', *New Formations*, 8, Summer 1989, pp114–115.

22 *Ibid.*, pp124-125.

23 Nick Land, 'Machinic Desire', *Textual Practice*, 7(3), Winter 1993.

24 Donna Haraway, 'A Manifesto for Cyborgs: Science, Technology, and Socialist Feminism in the 1980s', *Socialist Review*, 80, 1985, pp66-67.

25 Claudia Springer, 'The Pleasure of the Interface', *Screen*, 32(3), Autumn 1991, p306.

26 Sadie Plant, 'Beyond the Screens: Film, Cyberpunk and Cyberfeminism', *Variant*, 14, 1993, p16.

27 *Ibid.*, p14.

28 Springer, *op.cit.*, p306.

29 Thomas H. Ogden, *The Matrix of the Mind: Object Relations and the Psychoanalytic Dialogue*, Jason Aronson, Northvale, New Jersey 1986, pp179-180.

30 See, *inter alia*, Stephen Frosh, *Identity Crisis: Modernity, Psychoanalysis and the Self*, Macmillan, London 1991; Anthony Giddens, *Modernity and Self-Identity: Self and Society in the Late Modern Age*, Polity Press, Cambridge 1991; Barry Richards (ed), *Crises of the Self*, Free Association Books, London 1989.

31 Frosh, *op.cit.*, pp57–58.

32 Carlo Mongardini, 'The Ideology of Postmodernity', *Theory, Culture and Society*, 9(2), May 1992, p62.

33 Christopher Lasch, *The Minimal Self: Psychic Survival in Troubled Times*, Pan, London 1985, p32.

34 Mongardini, *op.cit.*, p62.

35 *Ibid.*, pp56-57.

36 Mary Ann Doane, 'Technology's Body: Cinematic Vision in Modernity', *Differences: A Journal of Feminist Cultural Studies*, 5(2), 1993 pp13-14.

37 Mongardini, *op.cit.*, p61.

38 Brenda Laurel, 'On dramatic interaction', in G. Hattinger *et al* (eds), *op.cit.*, pp262-263.

39 Joyce McDougall, *Theatres of the Mind: Illusion and Truth on the Psychoanalytic Stage*, Free Association Books, London 1986.

40 Frosh, *op.cit.*, p93.

41 Peter Weibel, 'Virtual worlds: the emperor's new bodies', in G. Hattinger *et al* (eds), *op.cit.*, p29.

42 Istvan Csicsery-Ronay, Jr., 'Cyberpunk and Neuromanticism', in L. McCaffery (ed), *op.cit.*, pp192, 190.

43 Marike Finlay, 'Post-Modernising Psychoanalysis, Psychoanalysing Post-Modernity', *Free Associations*, 16, 1989, p59.

44 *Ibid.*

45 Gérard Raulet, 'The New Utopia: Communication Technologies', *Telos*, 87, Spring 1991, p51.

46 Michael Heim, 'The Erotic Ontology of Cyberspace', in Michael Benedikt (ed), *op.cit.*, pp75-76.

47 D.W. Winnicott, *Playing and Reality*, Tavistock, London 1971.

48 D.W. Winnicott, *Human Nature*, Free Association Books, London 1988, p107.

49 Ogden, *op.cit.*, pp193–194.

50 *Ibid.*, p196.

51 Krishan Kumar, 'The End of Socialism? The End of Utopia? The End of History?', in Krishan Kumar and Stephen Bann (eds), *Utopias and the Millenium*, Reaktion Books, London 1993, p76.

52 Benedikt, *op.cit.*, p15.

53 Heim, *op.cit.*, p73.

54 Allucquere Rosanne Stone, 'Will the Real Body Please Stand Up? Boundary Stories About Virtual Cultures', in Michael Benedikt (ed), *op.cit.*, p111.

55 *Ibid.*, p112.

56 Rheingold, *op.cit.*, p6.

57 *Ibid.*, pp25-26.

58 *Ibid.*, p14.

59 *Ibid.*, p10.

60 *Ibid.*, p110.

61 *Ibid.*, pp115, 56.

62 *Ibid.*, pp245, 110.

63 Iris Marion Young, *Justice and the Politics of Difference*, Princeton

University Press, Princeton 1990, p229.
[64] Joshua Meyrowitz, *No Sense of Place*, Oxford University Press, New York 1985; 'The Generalised Elsewhere', *Critical Studies in Mass Communication*, 6(3), September 1989.
[65] Giddens, *op.cit.*, p187.
[66] Edgar Morin, 'Les anti-peurs', *Communications*, 57, 1993, p138.
[67] Michael Sorkin, 'See You in Disneyland', in Michael Sorkin (ed), *Variations on a Theme Park*, Farrar, Straus and Giroux, New York 1992, p231.
[68] Jean Baudrillard, 'Hyperreal America', *Economy and Society*, 22(2), May 1993, p246.
[69] Young, *op.cit.*, p229.
[70] Raulet, *op.cit.*., pp50-51.
[71] Young, *op.cit.*, p233.
[72] Sherman and Judkins, *op.cit.*., p134.
[73] Timothy Druckrey, 'Revenge of the Nerds: An Interview with Jaron Lanier', *Afterimage*, May 1991, pp6-7.
[74] Serge Moscovici, 'La crainte du contact', *Communications*, 57, 1993, p41.
[75] Richard Sennett, *The Uses of Disorder: Personal Identity and City Life*, Penguin, Harmondsworth 1973, p109.
[76] Richard Sennett, *The Conscience of the Eye: The Design and Social Life of Cities*, Alfred A. Knopf, New York, 1990, p97.
[77] *Ibid.*, pxii.
[78] Sorkin, *op.cit.*, p208.
[79] Chantal Mouffe, *The Return of the Political*, Verso, London 1993, p6.
[80] Julia Kristeva, *Nations Without Nationalism*, Columbia University Press, New York 1993, pp40-43.
[81] Dieter Lenzen, 'Disappearing Adulthood: Childhood as Redemption', in Dieter Kamper and Christoph Wulf (eds), *Looking Back on the End of the World*, Semiotext(e), New York, 1989, p71.
[82] Paul Virilio, 'Marginal Groups', *Daidalos*, 50, December 1993, p75.

'It's life, Jim, but not as we know it': Rolling Backwards into the Future

Sean Cubitt

Past and Present

Some sixty-five years after the invention of the medium, the great French cinéaste René Clair wrote 'The cinema remains, and will no doubt remain for a long time, a medium of expression of immense but ephemeral power, an art dedicated solely to the present'.[1] The present, however, exists in three quite different ways: it is the moment of passing away of the past; of the endless extension of the instant; of the constant becoming of the future. Of these, in our time, the first two are predominant. We sing endlessly the praises of times gone, lamenting but unable to mourn the deaths of old verities (since to mourn would mean looking into the face of the unpardonable: the degradations on which such mythic times were founded). For lack of a future, we cannot sever the bonds of the past, and are condemned to regret, because we will not accuse, the European homeland of Dresden and Auschwitz. And so we cannot greet the present with an open heart, but must see it as an eternal repetition of old patterns, old oppressions, sheer extension of time but not its flow. *Blade Runner* (1982), *RoboCop* (1987) and the movies of the New Bad Future (Fred

31

Glass's phrase echoing Brecht's concern not for the good old days but for the bad new ones[2]) suggest the endless recurrence of everything that has so drained our world of life: racism, capitalist transnationals, patriarchy and colonialism. In the expensive cults of impressionism and abstract expressionism which now pass as the acme of the western culture, the utopia on offer is already in the past. No-one has understood this more wisely than Sam Peckinpah, whose elegiac westerns set the tone for so much of today's big-screen entertainment. The urgency proper to the present is always, for his characters, envisioned in the past, in the tragic vitality of Billy the Kid, not Pat Garrett's iron reason, and anchored not in the narrative clash of heroes and historical forces but in the mythopoeia of Dylan's mournful soundtrack. White Hollywood has only a mythologised past to support an unalterable and unconscionable present.

Despite their best efforts, artists from Pissarro to Brakhage who have attempted to renew the present, through the renewal of perception of the mythologised ideology of infantile innocence and untainted perception, are doomed to failure in a culture that cannot bear to understand the present as anything other than the graveyard of the past. For even the neo-Buddhist eternal present of the postmodern is no guarantee of immediate presence, for even the presence of the present is veiled in a mist of re-presentations. It is as if postmodernism has sacrificed history to the celebration of myth, only to find that its present has itself become ghostlike and insubstantial, leaving us to play amongst a faded mosaic of memories, nostalgic for events that never occurred and a past we never had. Millennial culture, plagued by its loss of history, has become a dead end, and against its furthest wall, dimly descried, are the shadows of events occurring to other people, in other places, at other times, returned at last to the simulacra of Plato's cave.

It is not so surprising then that the Hollywood turn to the postmodern in film-making has revolved so much around the figure of inauthenticity, of bogus experience, vicarious lives, false memories, masquerades, substitutions, voyeurism and virtuality. Nor, indeed, that so many films revolve around the figure of control and the lack of it. When Stallone discovers his aptitude for knitting in *Demolition Man* (1993), when HAL's double-bound madness is revealed in *2010* (1985), when the multi-layered paranoias of Philip K. Dick make it to the screen in *Blade Runner* (1982) and *Total Recall* (1989), over and again what is at stake in the narratives is the authenticity of the actions undertaken by the hero, the hero's self-knowledge and capacity to control his own actions. Motivation, a core of individuality, becomes questionable. Only action is definite. The audience gets both to identify with and assess the hero's struggles. There is something almost Brechtian about the coolness of the straight-to-video cyborg shoot-'em-ups of the early 1990s, but it is an alienation effect in the service of a games-playing or, more subtly, a managerial mentality. While those who control the minds of others are universally condemned in these films, as they are in other recent media productions like *Wild Palms* (1993) and a hundred pop songs, there is still an attraction in the cinema for an audience which can always presume that the narrative will deliver an assurance of truth in the final minutes. Even when, as in *Total Recall*, the truth is withheld, the effect is like that of a withheld punchline in a shaggy dog story: we still watch as if the truth will be delivered in the end, a narrative trick that's at least as old as *Citizen Kane*. We still, spectators and game-players, are put into the position of the uninvolved, administrative judges of the characters' success.

As in the cinema of Weimar Germany analysed by Siegfried Kracauer, when films like *The Cabinet of Dr Caligari* (1919) and *Dr Mabuse the Gambler* (1921) explored the social psychology of individuality in thrall to the mesmeric powers of the super-villain, our cinema is obsessed with the crumbling of individuality, this time in the throes of technologisation. But just as Weimar cinema shifted the blame for a social phenomenon onto malignant and inexplicable beings from beyond the boundaries of ordinary society, villains like *Nosferatu* (1921) and the evil inventor Rotwang of *Metropolis* (1926), so ours explores not the origins of the crisis, but the bogey of fancied technologies. Raising the spectre of a sociological crisis of identity, the films displace its playing-out onto clones, androids, robots, cyborgs, mutants and victims of the modern curse of radiation, the modern evil eye of the virus. If we are too cagey to accept Kracauer's style of argumentation by parallels, still there is something to learn from cinema about the societies that consume it and its multimedia spin-offs.

Oscars are won by films that centre on identity and roots, heartwarming tales that mobilise nostalgia for non-existent histories, encourage virtuoso 'depth' performances by actors and offer harmonious solutions to complex social issues: films like *Driving Miss Daisy* (1989), *Rain Man* (1988) and *A River Runs Through It* (1992). But the box office rewards the spectaculars and the effects movies, actioners and stunt comedies. Ironically, it is these films which, it seems to me, respond most acutely to the realities of contemporary life, while the Oscar movies articulate only a longing for something different: the sad utopias of a class whose only future lies in the past. For what is at stake in films like *Terminator 2* (1991) and *Lawnmower Man* (1992) is not just the present but the point at which it is experienced – the personal – and the question of whether or not action is possible in the present, the only moment in which action can ever be possible. So many films pitch their protagonists into conflict with predestination: most obviously the *Back To The Future* trilogy (1985-8). But even the destiny which awaits Luke Skywalker is premised on the lack of choices open to him. His future is already written for him. This fatalistic property of contemporary narratives is not simply a (post)modernist self-reflexive jape about the relation between characters and script, but a musing upon the nature of individuality as the capacity for action in an administered world. And it is about the terrifying realisation that, I believe, we are expected to take from such movies: that whatever we choose to do, it doesn't matter. The future is still only an extension of the past, and the present, as the field of action, is an empty category, even as it promises to be the only place in which the rewards of consumerism are to be had. They are awarded precisely for quiescence.

The constant return of our most successful films to nostalgic preyings upon mythologised pasts and baleful warnings about the terrors of the future should alert us to the emergence of a crisis in the present. On the one hand, it is the present which must extend forwards forever, an unchanging moment of consumption and reward, but at the same time it has to be constructed as empty time, in the sense that it is unalterable. What is at stake here in the figure of the present is not only the possibility of acting for the future, but the very central sociological category of individuality. For what is an individual if she is not able to act? Is not freedom the very essence of individuality? Yet everything we understand about society and about ourselves leads us to suspect that we are capable only of conformity to preordained actions, motivations, emotions and responses. At the same time, because individuality is, increasingly so, at the heart of the capitalist organisation of consumption as it is of production, there is no social route forward through the annihilation of individuality in favour, say, of a socialised humanity, like that envisaged by Marxist visionaries of the 1930s. We are stuck with a category of existence which is itself in crisis. The two crises match each other beautifully: crisis of the present as the endless extension of empty time; crisis of the individual condemned to exist but without that capacity for action which alone can prove to the individual that she exists. Perhaps no recent film gives a stronger impression of this nightmare of the imploding present than *Groundhog Day* (1993), even though that film rescues its protagonist with a solution to his endlessly repeated day every bit as inexplicable as the way he got into it in the first place.

Perhaps *Groundhog Day* does give us a sense of how the prison of individuality might be escaped: through a process of self-overcoming. But the film is as pure a fantasy as any of the nightmare social comedies of Frank Capra. As has been argued of *Gremlins* (1984), the ghost of Capra's *It's a Wonderful Life* (1946) haunts *Groundhog Day*. But where James Stewart's character has to unearth the reasons for his own existence in his past, Bill Murray's must discover his in the present. For each of them, the utopia that awaits successful completion of their supernatural experiences is the rediscovered joys of the ordinary, the individual resituated in a society that recognises their value as individuals, their capacity to act. But in each film, the schmaltz of the ending belies the power of the nightmare. For Hollywood, to get us in, has to offer us something which addresses our experience of life. But in doing so, it invariably opens up contradictions which the device of narrative closure is often incapable of restoring to ideological order. The reverberations of the primary situation last much longer than the memory of how the hero escapes from them.

As Margaret Thatcher notoriously announced, there is no such thing as society, only individuals. We remind ourselves with the repetitiveness of a dogma on the verge of truism, that no-one owes us a living. Everywhere we look in contempor- ary western culture, we are advised to let the dead bury their dead, to disassociate ourselves from the familial past, to lay the ghosts of childhood dependency, to denounce the sins of the fathers, to live for today and to assert and to look after our selves. The problem, though, is that the selves we have, the historically constructed social phenomenon of individuality, is, just like the family before it, not strong enough to bear the responsibilities which are laid upon it or the contradictions which they imply.

Perhaps the body cultures of the 1980s and 1990s indicate a sense of this crisis, and a reorientation of individuality around physical rather than social existence. But in the age of AIDS, the body is thrown into question. The visitations to which the individual is prone have shifted away from the linguistic dysfunctions of schizophrenia which dominated discussions of social disorder from R.D. Laing to Deleuze and Guattari, in which the individual misrecognises her place in the social organisation of language.[3] Instead, our fears of the dissolution of individuality are captured in the metaphor of infection, the violent irruption in the body of the physical traces of the Other. The viral regime has replaced the linguistic disorder as the core metaphor for the obverse of the social, a shift we can see repeated in the move from the image of the 'mad' computer

HAL in *2001* (1968) to the image of the computer 'virus'. The move to centring the individual as a body is an emotive one, one that invites both an empirical notion of individuality ('I am my body', 'you are what you eat', the centre of the 1980s craze for both food fads and health and fitness), and a plethora of metaphors of invasion, rape, incision and implantation: metaphors of the defence of individual integrity on the model of bodily integrity.

This apparently trivial shift marks a move from the centrality of language, by which we are bound to one another, to the centrality of the body, by which we feel ourselves marked as discrete from one another. No matter that the body can scarcely be said to end at the epidermis: the world, after all, touches us at the same moment that we touch it. Yet the ideological construction of the body as the model for individuality also persuades us, in despite of our own senses, that it is we who touch, and the world that is touched. An everyday experience is overlaid with socio-cultural meanings. The drift is towards an image of the unique and vulnerable body cased in a skin that divides it from the world, and which must be protected against the outside: the body as bastion. This model is part of a tendency towards yet another reorganisation of individuality within the social order, an adjustment which becomes necessary both as the older models of interactivity and bonding fail, and as the development of the market as the key interface between individuals demands a more hyperindividualised subjectivity than ever before.

One of the most remarkable handlings of this theme occurs in Bill Sienkiewicz's cult graphic novel *Stray Toasters*.[4] In a nightmare near-future, a small boy, modelled, I believe, on a case of autism recounted by Bruno Bettelheim, turns himself into a murderous machine made up of bits of domestic machinery. As in Sienkiewicz's previous project *Electra Assassin*,[5] identity is a constantly shifting quality, but the characteristic threat is of possession by another power, even if that power is, in *Stray Toasters*, derived from within. In both novels, the anti-hero's alcoholism forms a foil to themes of demonic possession, and in each the violation of the body is a core metaphor for loss of individuality. Intriguingly, however, what lies beyond the individual is not society but the void. A related but different handling of this theme occurs in the films of David Cronenberg, and notably in his biggest commercial success, *The Fly* (1986), in which masochistic identification with the mutating hero provides the horror, as with Sienkiewicz's graphic work, but in which the fly's side of things is clearly voiced as an alternative to rationality and order. Cronenberg's well-known interest in viral metaphors more frequently manifests itself in a vivid anti-humanism and an evolutionary take on the rights to life of this alien life form that's extremely rare in contemporary culture. Elsewhere we can begin to trace the evolution of a newer form of individualism premised on the integrity, coherence and distinctiveness of the body. Horror films and comics articulate the deepest cultural VR: fears of the dark, of evil spirits, of pain and death. But they articulate them with more contemporary fears, such as the terror associated with the inside of the body that is characteristic of a society which has professionalised healthcare and so alienated it from daily life. The inside-out figure of Freddy Kruger in the *Nightmare on Elm Street* series (1984-94) is typical of this mode of body horror: both carnivalesque confrontation with a world turned upside down, and bogie built out of the binary opposition between the integral body and the body with its wet parts on the outside. The complex relation of individual and society is worked through in all three of these examples on the model of bodily integrity, and the alternative to the hyper-individualisation of the integral body is shown as a world of disgust, formlessness, dirt and malice: the world of the abject.

On the one hand, then, hyper-individualisation on the model of the body is framed in terms of its alternative: regression to the pre-subjective moment of the abject, the early infantile state in which no sense of individuality has yet coalesced, but which the individual carries constantly with him/her as a fear of dissolution, of sinking back into the formlessness of infantile perception. Yet at the same time, the success of hyper-individualism is still marked in terms of the market: its reward to live in the perpetual present of consumption, a state which, in many ways, echoes all too clearly the infantile regressive state of abjection. The proximity of the perpetual present to both the consumerist paradise and the void of abject horror is again, I believe, experienced as a crisis, and one that is constantly reworked in two key forms. The negative might be called the Brundlefly-type, after Jeff Goldblum's mutating monster in *The Fly*. The second, however, takes the form of the perfect body with which the monster is always contrasted (again Cronenberg offers us exceptional purchase on this in the tortuous route to internal beauty taken by the twin gynaecologists of *Dead Ringers* [1989]). The constant harping on perfection in mass media product is, I think, different from the simple reminders of heterosexist patriarchy with which we have become familiar: an education constantly reiterated in what it is that we are supposed to desire. Nowadays, there is a minimal slippage towards a narcissistic identification with what was once the object of desire. The self is being reconstructed with itself as object of desire through the ritual production of fantasmatic performances in Hollywood, the comics, computer games and elsewhere.

The mechanisms of identification and desire which Hollywood, for example, institutionalises in continuity editing and camera positions are persuasively argued by recent feminist theorists[6] not to determine what the viewer thinks and feels, but to establish a field of fantasy in which the viewer can enjoy moving between and even simultaneously entertaining several roles in the fantasy scenario of the unfolding plot. On the one hand, I would argue that this emerges as a mode of narcissism (by which I understand a kind of nostalgia for infancy), a self-involvement characteristic, for example, of the pleasures of console games. But on the other it opens us up to the problem of how to comprehend, individually, the experience that we all share that we are not discrete entities, but that we owe our being and even our most intimate daydreams to the social world that has made us what we are. Realising that subjectivity is porous, that it absorbs indiscriminately from experience, we are driven to a contradiction between self and the oceanic communicative world that forms us. Under similar strains, the schizophrenic diagnosis asks that the self let go of coherence and subject itself to wider currents. This was the sense of the anti-psychiatry movement of the 1970s, which tied the experience of mental illness to a politics of free development and the opening out of the individual to experience. The viral metaphor closes the door on such a utopian prognosis, and offers us only the binary choice between closed individuality or death.

Individuality is a social construct which is prone to crisis. Freud's was neither the first nor the last investigation of this ongoing crisis, but it gives us a better language than most for understanding it. What we have to take from Freud, however, is not his models but his methods, since his work is in any case the product of a specific moment in the history of individuality. The constant renegotiation of the status and nature of individuality depends on a set of regressions, individual and social, towards earlier forms of organisation. In our time and our societies, this regression is not only towards the mythologised, idyllic past, whether Victorian England or Eisenhower's USA. Nor is it simply to the moment of the child's first awakening intimations of separation from the rest of the world, suggested by Mulvey as the core of cinematic identification.[7] The characteristics of the eternal present in contemporary culture suggest that today the crisis has deepened to the extent that our regressions are to a moment prior to the mirror phase to which she refers us. The crisis of history is also the crisis of hyper-individuality: forced yet further from sociality by the intensification of market relations in late capitalism, the self regresses more and more towards the pre-subjective moment of primary narcissism.

Having the ideological role of eternal and universal value, the present itself implodes under the demands made of it. Individuality must bear the burden of the end of history as change, of culture as common memory, even of validating beliefs that would make its own position supportable. Individuality is a result, today, not of consensus but of a crisis of hegemony, enforcing the new individualistic social order through the threat of infection. Hence the turn of popular Hollywood to the body as itself an alien, the body of Cronenberg movies like *Videodrome* (1983) and *Dead Ringers*. Within the boundaries of the individual body, however, the impossibly contradictory demands of social life have to be mediated culturally. The world of the perpetual present is both external and internal. Externally, it must mediate the contradiction between the present as endless consumption and as empty time in which no action can be meaningful. Internally, it must mediate the contradiction between the self-absorbed satisfactions of narcissism and the dissolution of the self in abjection. It is a profoundly unstable state of affairs, and one in which the micro-history of the subtle changes in subjectivity has as great a significance as the shifting balances of society at large.

The analysis of cultural forms such as the console game suggests that they depend upon the discourse of mastery and success that power the managerial ideology of contemporary finance-led capitalism. But they do so by matching the pursuit of success with the dynamics of narcissism, the endlessly self-centred search for a stabilised, coherent, integral and ultimately impossible self-mastery. Like so many facets of the perpetual present, the many levels of the game exist contemporaneously in machine memory. To move between them, to master each, is experienced as a process of mastery that mirrors the infant's struggles to control its own body and its environment. Thus the very early stages of infancy are recalled in the vain pursuit of a workable identity. But we will have to travel through this regressive process, and employ the very instability of the system itself, if we are to rebuild a sense of the future in the face of the millennium.

The Machine

The 1956 film *Forbidden Planet*, rather like the early songs of Chuck Berry, explores the interface between human and technological in a way that prefigures our own concerns. The

41

now-extinct Krell have attempted to leave their bodies behind in order to dwell in their machines, but have succumbed to the 'monster from the Id', a crudely Freudian construct of their communally atavistic unconscious. Reawakened by the Prospero-like Dr Morbius, the ancient magic unleashes his unconscious (and incestuous) jealousy in the form of a monster attacking the heroic visitors from space. As in so many episodes of *Star Trek*, we are reminded of the sacrosanctity of the individual, the heroism of self-sacrifice, and the humanness of emotion. Defining the difference between human and machine has become a major cultural activity at the end of the century. But in this process of differentiation, the qualities of machines have themselves been in question, and ironically, a key element in their redefinition has been the use of metaphors taken directly from biological life. The Krell computer is a variant on this theme. We have to understand that to be human is other than to be machine. But at the same time, the film invites us to reflect upon how a machine can take on the characteristics of its creators: how a machine can be like a human.

Some have argued quite convincingly for the predominance of technological metaphors in the description of both human and cosmic affairs, citing the centrality, in different epochs, of the potter's or spinner's wheel, the clock, the heat engine and now the self-governing cybernetic system.[8] It seems characteristic of our time that managerial terminology has ousted metaphors formed by analogy with less authoritarian technologies. It could be, of course, that the computer and management share very similar architectures, and that computers are designed primarily both to meet the needs of administrative rationality and on the presumption that this is the best or only way to organise information and decision-making. It is all the more frightening, then, to find that the computer is now being taken up as a model for both social and intrapsychic formations. The limitations of computer design in the service of instrumental and managerial purposes are, however, further limited by the complications that arise in the application of the metaphor to human beings. For now we want to see the two as both distinct and yet similar. But if the human individual is the same as a computer, is a computer sufficiently like a human individual to catch germs? As machine communication became possible, or at least thinkable, our first fear was that language would become autonomous in the computer, just as it appeared to have done in the schizophrenic: the mad computer of *2001*. Now our fears are of the invasive: the hacker (surely not without its surgical subtext) and the virus.

Ross puts the case that hacking becomes a social evil by analogy with viruses: that the socialisation of knowledge becomes a site, not of sharing and common growth, but of the invasion of corporate integrity, and can therefore legitimately be described as a dangerous, even a proscribed, activity.[9] There are certainly those within the hacker culture who understand computer viruses conspiratorially, as devices generated by power groups (usually the Pentagon or selected transnational corporations) in the computer network to close down the openness of computer network sharing. One factor in particular makes me feel more strongly the power of the biological metaphor here, from my own experience and that of colleagues and acquaintances. The loss of computer files, and even more so of programmes, is experienced as a computer 'death'. Though relatively trivial, the loss of treasured files and programmes is experienced as enormity not necessarily because of the real damage, which may be serious enough, nor because of the sense of having been trespassed upon, but because it means that you have to disconnect the machine from its communications; makes you suspicious of interlinking with other network users, and enforces a closure of 'individual' systems against the flux of the social world of digital dialogues.

On the other hand, and again Ross argues this case, there are hackers for whom certain kinds of virus can be read as mutations spontaneously generated within the system, a system which is, from this perspective, in the process of achieving its autonomy from its users and from human purposes. The analogy then is no longer between individual machines and individual humans, but between the network and the (human) ecology, a variant on the Gaia model, in which the ecosphere as a whole is understood as a single organism, within which particular species function more or less as enzymes do within the human metabolism, as functional but ultimately replaceable elements of a system whose whole is far greater than the sum of its parts. This theological claim must be taken seriously, if only because it can be interpreted as an expression of the complex cultural formation which is developing in the computer culture, a culture in which it is so closely entwined with the apparently contradictory conspiracy theorem.

In this realm, we can understand culture in two ways: as a way of life, whole but complex, in Taylor's classic anthropological definition, but also as a Petrie dish of growing spores, in which spontaneous mutation can only with difficulty and uncertainty be distinguished from the products of environmental impurities introduced from without. The life science model seems to be an amazingly fruitful one for the understanding of the utopian possibilities of cultural life in the late twentieth century. But first it is necessary to quiz a shared weakness of these two models as they begin to interact. Both the anthropological and the life-science model, each in their own ways, derive from nineteenth-century models based in the notion of the closed system, whether the isolated tribe or the isolated laboratory experiment. Both thereby open themselves to a tendency in nineteenth-century scientific and cultural endeavour towards pessimism, a tendency most clearly expressed in the Second Law of Thermodynamics, from which we derive the concept of the universe as a closed system tending towards entropy, and culminating in the human sciences in Spengler's sombre presentiments of *The Decline of the West*. The theory of entropy, with its glum prediction of eventual dissolution and dispersal, suited the curious impasse of European bourgeois culture in the mid to late nineteenth century. The Second Law universalises the process of decline to which the late Romantics in particular gave voice.

We need look no further than the elements of Darwin's theories left undeveloped in his own century to see where one critique of entropic thought might arise: the principle of genetic diversification. Darwin, Marx and Freud, among others, argue that the processes of life move in quite the opposite direction to the physical 'law' argued for by nineteenth-century physics, in which the conservation of energy was confounded with the 'running down' of the universe. More recently, the mathematics of the 'lumpy' universe begin to provide substantial evidence that the supposedly universal and absolute tendency towards stasis, while it may be true of closed systems, is untrue of systems which are open, the characteristic state of naturally-occuring ecologies and, as astronomy increasingly seems to demonstrate, of the cosmos as a whole. (The observation here is that, for example, there are vast tracts of more-or-less empty space, and then very dense local aggregations of matter that cannot be explained by the Second Law; more familiarly, we might ask why our local corner of the universe seems to have gathered up so much of the carbon, and even more so, structured it into relatively minute living creatures.)

A spate of radical reworkings of the life, social and human sciences (parallelled in physics and mathematics as well as the arts) in the 1920s have become increasingly important to contemporary understandings of individuality and the social. The foundations of ecological thought demanded a new understanding of organisms not as bound by their external surfaces but as internally structured according to the relationships they have, systemically, with their environs, both immediate and more distant in both time and space. Freud's later work on the necessity of intersubjective relationships in the formation of individuality, Poincaré's first contributions to what would become the mathematics of chaos, Bakhtin and Volosinov's socialised and historicised reformulations of structural linguistics, and Heidegger's reworking of German Idealism as hermeneutic are moments of 1920s vanguards that have become central to the intellectual life of the late twentieth century. What they share is a sense of the complex interweaving of subjectivity, language and environment, of complexity as itself a source of new developments and new diversity, of the interpenetration of the elements of any system, whether mathematical, biological or cultural. For many of us, these images of the dependence and openness of the form of life otherwise restricted by the label of 'individual' promise a utopian exit from the crises which beset contemporary subjectivity.[10]

But for all the apparent delight with which it is possible to contemplate the open system as an alternative to the alienation and breakdown of individuality, there are those forces in society for whom the dissolution of this fundamental unit of the market economy is potentially disastrous, and from whose point of view the openness of individuals and their mutual dependency is equivalent to the physiology of a virus which, lacking the means to reproduce as a species, requires the support of a cell of another genus, whose nucleotides it replaces with its own, reproducing itself but destroying the host cell. Here the virus's lack of independence is seen as the source of destruction, rather than the creativity of a species which, like our own, relies utterly upon the graces of a host environment in order to reproduce.

Perhaps because it is fundamental to a virus that it interacts with other cells, a virus has the capacity for extremely rapid mutation, a feature which again we share ('The plague is life', wrote Camus). But to take it as a metaphor of contagion is at once to presume the integrity of the cell with which it interacts (even the terminology of 'host' is loaded) and to legitimate a counter-attack based on maintaining that integrity and limiting, if not destroying, the virus's ability to mutate. Taken as a metaphor in the new media of communication, what this seems to me to reveal is a sense in which ideological formations drawn from the management of crisis in an administered society have been drawn up against the openness of a system in which diversity might be generated as a function of the system's ability to provide the grounds for mutation. If some of these mutations are less functional than others, and some even dangerous, then that is the price one has to be ready to pay if one wishes to move from a managerial model of efficiency to an ecological and utopian model of democracy.

Utopia

No more do silver pencils of the United Planets battle against evil emperors in some distant galaxy. For us, the future has become claustrophobic, ugly and aimless. The collapse of the 'grand narratives' has affected our science fiction. Where once we dreamt of democracies without limits, we now have cyberpunk futures dominated by the same transnational corporations, tower-blocks and warring gangs as the Los Angeles, or the Silicon Glen, of the contemporary West. This is the landscape of Lyotard's 'postmodern condition', a time without the reassuring vision of future enlightenment, rationality and wealth that inspired the architects of modernity.

When Engels turned the scalpel of his criticism on the utopian socialists of the nineteenth century, he was doing something very similar to Lyotard. He locates the utopian socialism of Saint-Simon, of Fourier and of Robert Owen in the triumph of bourgeois reason in the Enlightenment, arguing that the claims of equality, justice and the rights of man were but the idealised expression of the new legality, the new property rights and the new political formations typical of capitalism. For Engels, the failure of utopianism lies in its devotion to the principles of reason rather than to the material circumstances of life. Material life, then, formed the basis for the critique of the enlightenment, a critique in turn dedicated to creating the conditions for the end of 'pre-history' and the commencement of the socialist future. While Lyotard is on safe ground in criticising the mechanical systems of thought that promise a teleological end of history, he makes the error, amplified into dogma by less able minds, of mistaking the end of goal-oriented histories for the end of history itself. It is not a mistake that emerges from the Marxist classics, for whom the purpose of critique was to aid in creating the terms under which the future might become possible, despite the foregone conclusions of the utopian socialists, but more specifically despite the predations of a material world established and run in the interests of those most firmly opposed to change of any kind.

What emerges from this aspect of the Marxist tradition is a resistant hope in *a* future, even if faith in *the* future is denied us. The utopian strain in twentieth century Marxism is perhaps best associated with the work of the German philosopher and sociologist Theodor Adorno, who presents a negative conception of utopia. Adorno's thought was shaped by the rise of Nazism, by the failure of any simple belief in the German proletariat as the agents that would bring about the socialist millennium, and by the experience of Auschwitz, after which, he said, there could be no more lyric poetry. Convinced, especially by the apparent power of Goebbels' propaganda machine and by the alien culture of California and New York in which he spent a decade of exile, that the mass media of the mid-century had no positive aspects at all, he devoted an important part of his working life to supporting some of the more inaccessible reaches of the twentieth century's avant-gardes, notably the music of Arnold Schönberg, of whom he was a pupil. In an extraordinarily rich body of work, which certainly cannot be summed up, as it often is in communications courses, as 'Teddy hates Jazz', it is a fundamental contention that the business of an avant-garde is to negate the world in which it finds itself. Historical processes have removed art from the daily world of human affairs, to the detriment of both, and yet this new found autonomy has produced a situation in which the sheer abstraction of art from the demands of the entertainment, propaganda and culture industries, has placed it in a unique position to create autonomous islands of meaning and order which, since they are apart from the world, can give the lie to the ideologies that state that the world is only as it is, necessarily and permanently so.

Adorno's negative utopia exists side by side with the quotidian hurlyburly. But by its very existence, it demonstrates the limits of the ordinary world. It exists, however, quite materially, in the 'wishful thinking' which we have learned to disparage, and whose political significance we have encouraged ourselves to deny, even as we persist in our pipe dreams. At the same time, it is a hard won voice, the voice, as he puts it in the extraordinary essay on Schönberg in *Prisms*, whose structure is so interwoven that it is only possible to quote the last line, of 'the protest of mankind against myth'.[11] Thus the kind of utopia suggested by the exploration of the autonomy of art is negative and critical. It is not recognisable by a 'positive' utopian *content*, by pious sentiments and devout harmonies. On the contrary: yearnings for completion, wholeness and integrity are powered by the opposite of utopia, by nostalgia, and by the regressive impulses of narcissistic hyperindividualism.

In an interview between Adorno and the East German thinker Ernst Bloch first published in 1975, the contradictory outlines of the purpose of the utopian conception in contemporary life become clear.[12] Both men agree that there is 'nothing like a single, fixable utopian content' (p7) and that 'there is no *single* category by which utopia allows itself to be named' (p8), not freedom, not even happiness. Indeed, 'there is no such thing as utopia without multiple goals' (p12), while at the same time, 'one may not cast a picture of utopia in a positive manner' (p10). The discussion at one point revolves around the image of the elimination of death, a topic clearly close to Bloch's Christianity. While both agree that identification with death actually sides the one who so identifies with the existing social conditions to which they are subjected, and that therefore the overcoming of death is a central element of the possibility of utopia, still Adorno argues that 'where the threshold of death is not at the same time considered, there can actually be no utopia' (p10). Bloch's concurrence is signalled in an elegant, if harsh conclusion: 'Hope is not confidence. If it could not be disappointed, it would not be hope ... Hope is surrounded by dangers, and it is the consciousness of danger and at the same time the determined negation of that which continually makes the opposite of the hoped-for object possible' (pp16-17).

It is the quality of most computer utopias, a category rarely found in science fiction but common in the hacker culture and in popular journalism about new media, to present just such a 'positive' (or nostalgic) utopian content, just such a confidence, as Adorno and Bloch decry. Indeed, Adorno in the same discussion rewrites a saying of Spinoza's to read *Falsum index sui et veri*: the false is the sign of itself and of the true, which he glosses as 'insofar as we do not know what the correct thing would be, we know exactly, to be sure, what the false thing is' (p12). In this context at least (and without wishing to disparage the rather different terms under which feminist utopian literature functions, as knowingly and therefore negatively and critically fictional), we might legitimately argue that the utopian visions of the wired society, from MacLuhan's global village to the wilder enthusiasts of the hacker and New Age fanzines, are false because contentful, confident and positive.

The Long Term

There is then a rationalist and systematic notion of the future into which the new media might be said to propel us, but that has been undercut by the arguments of Lyotard concerning the nature of the postmodern and the failure of the master narratives of the enlightenment. There are the more intuitive but still content-laden imaginations of utopia that fill the bulletin boards and station bookshops, which have at least the virtue of being generated by enthusiasts. These are characterised by the way in which they imagine utopia as just around the corner, despite the experience of elements of previous utopias – flight, spare-part surgery, television, for example – already being with us, although they have made us neither happy, nor free, nor wealthy. And they share a diffuse sense of 'we' and 'they': 'they' can already do such and such; soon 'we' will be able to do the same: this despite the obvious fact that our existing utopian achievements have not created a 'we' for all people, while 'they' still control the world's wealth and millions starve.

And then there is the rather gloomy and forbidding notion of utopia espoused above. For me, the core of this is Adorno and Bloch's recognition of the incompatibility of the idea of individuality and the imagination of utopia. As utopia moves, historically, from being in another place to being in another time, its relationship with the individual begins to separate: it is no longer a space which *I* can arrive at, and that surely is a mark of this kind of utopia: it is a place in which egoism, individualism, individuality itself, has no place. To demand a place for oneself, or for any self, in the utopian future would be to ascribe a content to it, and therefore to destroy the possibility, which is the very purpose of utopian thought, of keeping the future open to all possibilities.

Adorno's bleak utopianism rests on the thesis that the only home of negativity is in the avant-garde. Yet it seems necessary to argue that, despite his genius, Adorno fails to remark upon the other great source of negativity in contemporary culture, a source deep within the productions of the mass media industries. The Hollywood film, the computer game, the multimedia product launch itself, has to address us where we live: it has to speak to us of things that concern us. But in doing so, it has to open up the contradictions which capital has produced in our experience of life, contradictions far more radical than can be resolved with a cute ending. The Hollywood cinema and the rest of the entertainment industries, when they are at their most successful, are also taking the greatest risks, for they have to reach out to our deepest fears, our most intimate longings, and the truths of both social and personal life.

Among these contradictions, we have singled out the problems of the eternal present and hyperindividualism. The quality of both of these factors that I want to draw out is that their instability means that they cannot be sustained in equilibrium, nor can they be expected to sink gently towards some entropic state of rest. The internal state of contradiction means that these are unbalanced systems, radically incomplete. This contradiction is apparent right across the cultural field. The Complete Novels of Dickens includes the incomplete one: *The Mystery of Edwin Drood*. No 'Schubert' is complete without the *Unfinished Symphony*. The recutting of films from *The Birth of a Nation* (1914) to *The Abyss* (1989) points in the same direction: art works are rarely completed, least of all under the pressures of production for the market. At a certain point, they are merely abandoned. Knowledge too is interesting because of what we don't know. What makes the past so fascinating is what cannot be recovered from it. The future engrosses us because it is the very incompleteness of our present. The instability of the eternal present, and the dialectics of stasis and regression in the narcissistic individual, point us ineluctably towards future resolutions, future vicissitudes, of our experience of time and of ourselves.

Pace Adorno, the forms of popular culture can perform the tasks of negative thinking too. We are not restricted to the appreciation of avant-garde reworkings of the impasse of modernism in order to uncover the radical otherness of the future. A second path is opened up in the exploration of the voicing of capitalism's internal contradictions in mass media forms. The future can be understood both in the sense of its complete difference from what we have now, but also in the form of the instability and incompleteness of the contemporary. Admittedly, all texts, and especially the richer texts of popular culture, are polysemic, and are most frequently charged with carrying the preferred readings of a hegemonic culture. But the very complexity and instability of the cultural codes we use – codes of lighting, performance and editing, of production design and narration – is a source of excesses of meaning, responses that outstrip the ability of producers to control and channel them. The craze in the last decade for crane shots and deep-focus, for example, is because they are intended to confirm the completeness of the fictional worlds presented as the backdrop for stories in films. But they are also in Bazin's sense, pledges of an unfulfilled and perhaps unfulfillable dream of a complete picture of such worlds.[13] The constant overload of detail, the constant swirling and swooping of cameras, indicates an uncertainty about the positions from which such worlds can be seen; deep focus suggests that the actions of individuals, on which the Hollywood narrative is so firmly based, are incomprehensible outside of a social world. At the same time, the high-gloss rendition of new colour film stocks and the prevalence of widescreen formats, despite the economic lure of TV sales, tends towards a presentation of fictional worlds as precisely those regressive paradises of perpetual consumption which we both long for and dread. The gorgeous, ecstatic unification of the world in sequences such as the opening of *The Pelican Brief* (1994), with its National Geographic style of nature photography, can then only be belied by the return of the same footage later, film as part of a TV documentary, and contrasted both with its commodification on TV and with the paranoid, conspiratorial world of the fictional narrative. The search for aesthetic unification, along the lines of the Romantic organic unity of the art-work, has all the hallmarks of the infantile yearning for reunification with the maternal body, the regression so characteristic of consumerism. But at the same time, to have a film at all, that unity has to be disrupted for there to be a narrative. Hollywood is condemned to show us a paradise it has dreamed of for us, a paradise precisely identified with the sweet organicism of consumption, but at the same time, always to show us that enclosed system in turmoil, in crisis and incapable of interesting us. In its own way, by showing us the impossibility of its own dream, it offers us a negative glimpse of the future that it would deny us.

Some inkling of this post-individualist utopia might be discernible in some new ways in which machines are conceived. Hackers show an emergent understanding that machines may be able to gain their own autonomy, and take upon themselves activities which are not immediately congruent with the goals which we set for them. But this conception rests upon a prior one: that the ability of computers to interrelate is central to what they are and are capable of. Most machines are still treated as discrete: we don't, in general, consider the transport system when buying a car. But computers are selected on the basis of their capacity to network. At present, however, the relationships between the machines are subordinated to relationships between people, a fine principle, were not those relationships themselves governed by a complex and contradictory construction of individuals as both discrete entities and, at the same time, mutually dependent in hierarchies defined, ultimately, economically.

So our systems, though as systems they bear the possibility of a computer democracy, are designed in the image of a social order formed on the priority of protecting the discretion of each machine. Any intrusion into the discrete workings of the machine is a risk, and we deploy all sorts of virus detectors and security devices to protect our machines as we protect our selves. But as we close down on the risks, we also close down on the opportunities for diversification, whether through communication itself, or through the proliferation of undesigned or unmanaged programmes. If our offices are still, by and large, run on lines that would have been familiar to Bob Cratchett and Mr Scrooge, our experience of them has changed a little, if only because the computer nets have provided the possibility for a little personal bravado, a little office samizdat, small acts of sabotage. The recent managerial practice of consultations with staff, a pale shadow of industrial democracy, rebounds upon us: failures are now due not to the system, but to the individuals within it. The power to act has been abrogated by those who do not wish to use it. Our systems reflect this authoritarianism.

But they also reflect the necessity, inherent in capital, of using all the creativity of workers in order to develop. The office 'democracies' of firms like IBM and Volvo are designed to maximise our involvement and identification with our own oppression, but at the same time, they must do so by promising to recognise our individuality, our difference from the firm. The contradiction would be nearly unmanageable, if the protocols of office hierarchies were not built in to the means of communication. The sad point is that this is itself a contradictory and unstable state of affairs. Computers communicate: without communication, they are merely dumb terminals, glorified typewriters and adding machines. But without the openness of common access and common control, there is no likelihood that computer communications will come up with the kinds of novel thinking which capitalism requires if it is to survive its cycle of crises. Somehow, the net must be managed in such a way as to be both open and closed. Openness, from the point of view of the administrator, is a recipe for anarchy, for chaos, for breakdown, for abjection. Yet closure means that no benefits can accrue.

One way of coping with this state of affairs is to deploy the law of intellectual property. Today it is not only entertainment and inventions that are copyright: knowledge itself, both as information in databases and as research in universities, is subject to legal control and ownership. The absurdity of this system is all too apparent. It is not, for example, the 'immorality' of patenting elements of the human genome in the current international Big Science project that is so shameful, but the interference of this demand for profit with the working of the project itself. The demand for profit interferes not just with knowledge but with the very processes of extracting profit, which in frontier industries like bio-engineering, depend heavily on the free flow of information. At the same time, the list of people with a legitimate claim to royalties from a successful film runs into the thousands: the recent case of Art Buchwald vs. Paramount revealed some of the shady casuistry involved in apportioning receipts. The claim to authorship is damaged profoundly by the intensely cooperative and corporate nature of production in the vast multimedia productions associated with products like Superman and the Ninja Turtles.

The arguments of Barthes and Foucault provide further critiques of the foundations of copyright.[14] An author, for Foucault, is a polite fiction we invent as a way of classifying otherwise disparate texts, a fiction of limited usefulness compared to questions of the origination, organisation, distribution and power of discourse. For Barthes, language is at work in texts, and the author is an effect of that textual practice, not its origin. Language, after all, is profoundly social, and not only spoken and written but visual and aural languages too belong to whole cultures, not to individuals. The amassing and deployment of skills in culture industries to produce products is then certainly conceivable as an act of origination and authorship, but that is neither the only nor the best way of considering them.

Yet authorship, despite its inability to ask or explain anything very interesting about cultural products, is vital to the construction of ownership and hence of profit in the media. In any capitalist economy, it would be unfair to ask workers in the media industries to forego their wages because they are not authors. The fragility of the concept of authorship is visible in the way that the ownership of creative product can be transferred from hand to hand (Michael Jackson owns the publishing rights to Northern Songs, the Beatles' publisher, while Paul McCartney owns the rights to the Buddy Holly songbook), while copyright in thousands of films, photographs, songs and stories belongs not to individuals but to companies. So the right of intellectual property covers a more banal system of corporate ownership and simple wage-labour, though the rewards are bigger than in factories producing less glamourous artefacts.

At present, copyright acts as another block upon the free flow of communication. Culturally, the image of Elvis Presley or Marilyn Monroe is an element of a vocabulary shared by vast numbers of the world's population. But legally, you could be sued for reproducing their images, or simply not allowed to. The enormous extent of copyright theft on a global scale, and the constant rewriting of antiquated laws, forged in the first furor of the printing press and now endlessly, hastily and messily rewritten for each new copying and distributive medium, are evidence of the crisis of this system of ownership. The technology has outstripped the ability of the economic system to manage it.

But though the internal contradictions of popular culture, both as aesthetic system and as industry, can reveal the instability of the present, and are forced, despite their own interests, to act out the incompleteness, dissatisfaction and anguish of modernity, there is still a powerful argument for Adorno's belief in the pure negativity of vanguard arts. Nowhere is this more important than in the emergent electronic media. While much media art is enjoyable and even articulates something of the dialectics of the present, too much of it is locked into the regressive pursuit of wholeness and aesthetic autonomy. But in the work of some artists, and the names Bill Viola and Mona Hatoum spring to mind here, an inkling of what the potentials of these forms are comes into play, a sense of a world utterly different from that which we have learnt to inhabit. Both intimate and global in their address, both artists create a sense of the limits of contemporary understanding and feeling, of the destructiveness of our world, and of the act of refusing to accept it which lies at the heart of negative utopianism.

We cannot afford to give up the struggle on either field, of the arts or of popular culture. If, in line with a trend stretching back to Courbet and before, high and low cultures are constantly in dialectical interaction, so much the better. But if the grounds on which hope for any kind of future are to be kept open, then we will need all the help we can get, from every quarter and against the grain of the dominant cultural distribution networks as well as within them. We cannot tell, and should not wish to, the shape the future will take. But we will have to sacrifice a piece of the present if we are to have any future at all.

Notes

[1] René Clair, 'How Films are Made' [1953], trans Vera Traill, in Daniel Talbot (ed), *Film: An Anthology*, University of California Press, Berkeley 1959.
[2] Fred Glass, 'The "New Bad Future": *RoboCop* and 1980s sci-fi films', *Science as Culture* 5, 1989.
[3] R.D. Laing, *The Divided Self*, Penguin, Harmondsworth, 1960; Gilles Deleuze et Félix Guattari, *Capitalism and Schizophrenia*, trans Robert Hurley, Mark Seem and Helen Lane, University of Minnesota Press, Minneapolis 1983; and *A Thousand Plateaus: Capitalism and Schizophrenia*, trans Brian Massumi, University of Minnesota Press, Minneapolis 1987.
[4] Bill Sienkiewicz, *Stray Toasters* (4 parts) Epic, New York 1988.
[5] Frank Miller and Bill Sienkiewicz, *Electra Assassin*, Epic, New York 1986.
[6] See for example Mary Ann Doane, *Femmes Fatales: Feminism, Film Theory, Psychoanalysis*; Routledge, London 1991; Constance Penley,

The Future of an Illusion: Film, Feminism and Psychoanalysis, Routledge, London 1989; Kaja Silverman, *The Acoustic Mirror: The Female Voice in Psychoanalysis and Cinema*, Indiana University Press, Bloomington 1988.

[7] Laura Mulvey, 'Visual Pleasure and Narrative Cinema', *Screen*, vol.16 no.2, 1975.

[8] Cf. J. David Bolter, *Turing's Man: Western Culture in the Computer Age*, Penguin, Harmondsworth 1984.

[9] Andrew Ross, *Strange Weather*, Verso, London 1991.

[10] Though for a negative view of these characteristic formulations of the 1920s, see Peter Wollen's work on Gramsci in the essay 'Le cinéma, l'américanisme et le robot' in *Communications* 48, Seuil, Paris 1988.

[11] Theodor W. Adorno, 'Arnold Schoenberg, 1874–1951' in *Prisms*, ed and trans Samuel and Shierry Weber, MIT Press, Cambridge, Massachusetts, p172.

[12] 'Something's Missing: A Discussion between Ernst Bloch and Theodor W. Adorno on the Contradictions of Utopian Longing' in Ernst Bloch, *The Utopian Function of Art and Literature: Selected Essays*, trans Jack Zipes and Frank Mecklenburg, MIT Press, Cambridge, Massachusetts 1988.

[13] André Bazin, 'The Myth of Total Cinema' and 'The Evolution of the Language of Cinema' in *What Is Cinema?*, Volume One, edited and trans Hugh Gray, University of California Press, Berkeley 1967.

[14] Roland Barthes, 'The Death of the Author' in *Image-Music-Text*, edited and trans Stephen Heath, Fontana, London 1977; Michel Foucault, 'What is an Author?' trans Donald F Bouchard, in *Screen*, Spring 1979.

Interacting With the
Divine Comedy

Nickianne Moody

Introduction

> From now on television isn't just something you watch, it's
> something you do.
>
> Philips' television advertising campaign for
> the CD-I System 1994

Interactive personal media is a new instalment to the mythology
of the information society. Unlike the personal computer,
interactive media is perceived as wholly user friendly and
inherently virtuous. The popular imagination has already fused
the hardware for interactive compact disc (CD) systems to its
signifieds: excitement, high technology, the currency of
information, possession of 'the edge', investment, advancement,
control and overall a sense of limitless accessibility. 'Interactivity' is a consumer durable which is understood through its
representation rather than its actuality. An antidote to
powerlessness in a culture of rapid social change. In theory
interactivity suggests a continuous and equal exchange of
information between user and communications system. Philips
defines its product as a combination of creative concepts, book
design, audio and visual effects alongside animated graphics. As
the text is already authored and committed when the disc is
produced its use remains tied to the multiple options of
narrative. CD especially is read only; the graphics and texts are
rendered; there is no room as yet for the user to leave any
original marks. They can only follow quite varied, but
nonetheless anticipated routeways.

The battleground for these advertising campaigns seems not necessarily to be the future but the imagination. The recognition of this power has a precedent in the culture of the middle ages. The medieval church feared the power of the visual image because of the way it appeared to licence the imagination and the consideration of alternatives. Obversely, contemporary cultural critics fear that the abandonment of the written word in favour of graphics is stifling critical and creative powers. In both cases the experience of social and cultural change necessitating new work skills is interlinked with metaphors of memory.

At the heart of the interactive myth is a desire to produce information which will counterfeit knowledge. The glorification of possessing and presenting information is counterproductive to the acquisition of knowledge. Knowledge implies familiarity, the personal and experiential gathering of observation, fact and figure that is committed to memory. The data bank, whatever its electronic form, may store a large amount of information but only mimics human memory. Until the disc becomes interactive, a personal repository of information rather than a commercial one, it is only capable of artificial memory storage and display rather than connection and understanding.

Medieval Forest Allegory

At the beginning of the 1980s publishers and booksellers experimented with marketing fantasy alongside science fiction. The previous distinction between the two genres, and the unhappy marriage of science fantasy in the previous decade, was gradually effaced. By the end of the decade fantasy emerged as the victor, although outclassed in the sales and popularity gained by the detective novel. Here one can point to a particular subgenre which had extraordinary success – the medieval whodunnit. Even the cyberpunk future, which characterised the science fiction diegesis, exhibited a definite tendency to draw upon medieval metaphors in its Marlowesque hard-boiled style. Such imagery was used to express the value placed on communication, work and social life a postmodern dark future, where power lies not just in information but a hierarchy based on access to it.

Much fantasy fiction shares a clearly defined quasi-medieval diegesis. One which fits snugly into Umberto Eco's categorisation of the 'new middle ages'. One aspect of the re-appearance of the medieval is the 'middle ages as a barbaric age, a land of elementary and outlaw feelings'.[1] He further describes it as 'a shaggy medievalism, profoundly ideological in its superficial naivety.' For Eco it would be entirely logical that the 'high tech' personal computer is used to play dark and labyrinthian games with a medieval diegesis.

If we are returning to a visual society instead of a literary one then we should fully consider the implication. Allegory was the dominant form in medieval writing and created a particularly visual imagery. C.S. Lewis described allegory as a mode of expression adopted 'to represent what is immaterial in picturable terms'.[2] Aers (1986) qualifies allegory's expressive potential, by identifying it as a practice designed to stimulate and contain imaginative writing within the ideological framework maintained by the medieval Catholic church.[3] Gay Clifford also sees allegory as having the visual power to debate the abstract in fiction.[4] She refers to legible images which require visual imagination and creativity to convey abstract and moral meaning. She finds that the narrative action in allegory places an emphasis on change and movement as a metaphor to express a process of learning, both for the protagonist and the reader.

Allegory requires narrative which takes specific forms, a journey, battle/conflict, a quest, pursuit, search or transformation; the same general syntagmatic structure as computer or interactive games. The similarity is striking if we consider the seminal interactive computer game *Adventure*.[5] The game begins with a specific orientation:

YOU ARE STANDING AT THE END OF A FOREST BEFORE A SMALL BRICK BUILDING. AROUND YOU IS A FOREST. A SMALL STREAM FLOWS OUT OF THE BUILDING AND DOWN A GULLEY.[6]

The player is directed to visualise a scene which is indigenous to medieval allegory. Moreover in a similar way the interactive nature of the game assumes the participation of the reader in decision making. There is an apparent dialogue between the communication system and the user. At present interactive media appears limited because of its inability to deal with abstractions but there is potential to negotiate their forms in icons. Medieval allegory did not just expect the reader to spot clues but to engage with the text in an imaginative exercise. Examining the text does not necessarily tell us how it was used. In allegory the writer could assume a constant interplay between the work and the audience who had to be prepared to undertake an energetic and demanding form of reading.

The connection between medieval allegory and the imperative speech of the computer game is not theoretical but actual. Some game designers have spoken about their attempts to capture or imitate the interactivity of role-playing games (RPG) in their programming. I have encountered groups of RPG players either navigating or preparing their way through Hell, Purgatory and Paradise. RPGs simulate the quasi-medieval world with a greater frequency than any other fictional universe open to them. The activity for their players is a true pattern of interactivity, continuous information exchange. Similar to the computer game their shared fantasy follows a template but one from which it is possible to deviate. They can effect the attractions of the interactive system, i.e. slow down, make seamless jumps, even engage in 'true real-time branching down alternative paths'.[7] The player can watch the scenario from different angles, focus on particular points of the action going on around them and moreover stop, save and edit.

The opening to Inferno in Dante's *Divine Comedy* situates the reader in exactly the same location as the early interactive game. Michael Sexson[8] has pointed out that Dante is in the same position as the game player:

> Half way along the road we have to go
> I found myself in a great forest

Bewildered, and I knew I had lost the way.

Dante faces repeated encounters in the form of dialogue, combat or imprisonment.

The beginning of Langland's *Piers Plowman* is also reminiscent of a RPG scenario:

> I was in a wilderness, wist I not where,
> And eastwards I looked against the sun.
> I saw a Tower on a hill, fairly fashioned.
> Beneath it a Dell, and in the Dell a dungeon.
> With deep ditches and dark and dreadful to see.
> And Death and wicked spirits dwelt therein
> And all between, between the Hill and Dungeon
> A fair field full of folk.[9]

Clifford describes allegory as confronting the reader with a strange world which remains elusive through its very familiarity. The strangeness is intensified because the images are neutral rather than exotic. The visual forms are so archetypal that their indefiniteness lends itself to making them important and worthy of contemplation.

> The worlds of allegory are on half-familiar and they are rarely safe. Neither protagonist nor reader can predict with any security what phenomena they will encounter or precisely what the phenomena will signify. We have to immerse ourselves in the world of each allegory until we discover its peculiar and persuasive internal logic.[10]

The feeling of many computer game players.

It is significant that the computer game *Adventure* chooses the forest for the start of its quest. Medieval allegory uses certain distinct landscapes and the forest is one of them. Moreover allegory, with its roots in Prudentis' (348-c 410) *Psychomachia*, is often a narrative space that is taken up by a particular battle, the bellum intertinum, the holy war, a battle of virtues and vices which is clearly associated with the psychological. Piehler has argued in *The Visionary Landscape* that medieval allegory effects the outward journey in order to explore inner life and the forest affords a precise situation for that discussion.

But outside the city lie forest and ocean, not merely symbols of the vast powers of the unconscious, but in early periods at least, the very place of their operation.[11]

Piehler traces an interesting double meaning of the Greek word *hyle* which means literally forest, but is used by Plato to denote the chaos antecedent in the creation of matter. Latin poets used *silva* as the term for the chaotic mass of elements out of which all things are created, a word that still pertains to forest. Silva has been understood, and medieval allegorists were aware, as the original chaos and abode of darker instincts which were manifest in the forest's stylised and unpredictable animal inhabitants. The meaning of the wood in allegory is an example of chaos which can be resolved by taxonomy, the process of ordering and naming what one finds en route.

Forests are also associated with the underworld, a dark forest of bewilderment and hopelessness. Dante encounters two, the selva oscura which he succeeds in passing, negotiating his way through its inhabitants before entering hell. Later he encounters the un-natural wood of the suicides in the seventh circle of the Inferno. In the first wood he is aware that he has lost his way, but in the infernal wood there is an absence of way. He is brought to a standstill in front of trees that bleed while they imprison tormented souls. The symphysis of man and tree is grotesque and expresses the ultimate condition of loss of identity overwhelmed by the forest, the *selva se'vaggia*.

Despite the instability of the form it is well to remember that allegory adhered to a particular cosmic or political system which was both hierarchical and conservative. Allegory built in a certain level of interactivity into its moral instruction but nonetheless established a hierarchy of value. The heroes of allegory learn by trial and error but they discover which ideals are worth pursuing and which are merely hindrances to be abandoned along the way.

Artificial Memory

The visuality of allegory has an association with traditional mnemonic techniques. Visual images fix themselves more readily in the memory and are used in allegory to suggest thematic associations between ideas and abstractions. The striking detail of allegory has a mnemonic function. Dante cannot remember how he got to the forest. In order to seek salvation he has to enter the forest and question those he meets. In the Philips CD-I game catalogue other scenarios operate on the same premise, the loss of memory and the recovery of understanding. Through graphics, audio and visual effects or the presentation of narrative, the software aims to create a memory theatre for the player. A vast network of innumerable locations is stored where the player will seek, enquire and retrieve information which then acts as a key; knowledge (i.e. experience of the game rather than signposts) takes them further into deeper and more complex levels of the game. Commercial interactive games require not only the sophistication and speed of graphics now found in the new generation of video games but greater amounts of memory on the part of both the hardware and the player. The exercise of the game begins to require mental interactivity, rather than the physical dexterity of hand/eye co-ordination.

Artificial memory means either the surrogate storage of information and experience outside the brain or in the medieval usage a system of internal ordering, arranging and structuring of memory. The intense visuality of medieval allegory and the development of metaphor disobeyed the old testament prohibition placed on images in Deuteronomy 4 and therefore needed to justify itself. The training of artificial memory allowed the layman to contemplate the salvation of the soul by recalling the paths to heaven and hell and the guises of the virtues and the vices. The classical pagan art of memory became a devotional exercise for Christian mediation.

Simple and spiritual intentions slip easily from the memory

unless joined to corporeal similitudes.[12]

As well as spiritual survival memory was a strategy for economic success in the new mercantile world order.

Frances Yates provides a definitive account of the history of memory before the popular advent of the computer reshaped the imagery associated with the term.[13] She traces a European tradition of artificial memory through its pagan and Christian practice and philosophy. In the current age of data processing some of the metaphors and explanations of the working of memory, which Yates explores, are especially resonant. Classical artificial memory was constructed on the principle of loci and imagines, the ordering of places and things, a technique still used by the current World Memory Champion, and to train those with amnesia or severe memory loss.[14]

> In order to form a series of places in memory, he [Quintilian c.35-100] says, a building is to be remembered, as spacious and varied a one as possible, the forecourt, the living room, bedrooms, and parlours, not omitting statues and other ornaments with which the rooms are decorated ... We have to think of the ancient orator as moving in imagination through his memory building whilst he is making his speech, drawing from the memorized places the images he has placed on them.[15]

The practitioners of artificial memory creates in their mind's eye a building or place within which they store images or simulacra of what it is they wish to remember. In this way the memory could be trained to recall accurately and promptly speeches, sermons, law suits, memoranda, genealogies and philosophical or devotional treatises. In contemporary metaphor they would be using icons to create, edit and then locate files which store information.

Yates sees Dante's *Inferno* as a memory system. Its sophistication and scope demonstrate the scale of work and ambition which were undertaken by medieval and renaissance memory theorists. They envisaged the possibility of encompassing and impressing universal knowledge upon the human mind.

The Divine Comedy would thus become the supreme example of the conversion of an abstract summa into a summa of similitudes and examples, with memory as the converting power, the bridge between the abstract and the image.[16]

Allegory granted medieval thought the use of imagination in order to help the memory recall and contemplate the ways to salvation. In the Renaissance, with the abeyance of monastic power, Yates is able to identify less visual and more schematic methods for artificial memory. Methods which resemble the tree diagram rationale of computer programming. She points specifically to the static algebraic notions of Ramon Lull. Lull, a Spaniard (1235-1316), who spent his youth as a courtier and troubadour outside the monastic tradition, embarked on a different approach to memory. He developed a system which aimed not just to help the individual to recall but acted as a database. The system realigned and made connections between separate items stored in the memory. Lull saw the memory as a process of logical investigation through information which had already been deposited. The image of the forest is used by Lull in a new configuration: the *Arbor Scientiae*, an entire encyclopaedia of knowledge interconnected by its roots. Knowledge through the activity of memory is no longer dramatic and visual (even magical) but increasingly mechanical, manoeuvering its data into new combinations on the revolving wheels of Lull's diagrams.

The fluid memory of oral culture and the interplay of the corporeal similitude does not have pride of place in a mechanised society. The art of memory becomes mnemo-technics, the science of memory. The human memory is no longer seen as infinite, but as Steven Rose in *The Making of Memory* outlines, it is seen as inferior to computer memory.[17] Artificial memory as a term takes on new significance. It refers to the interaction of technology with biology. Its implications are no longer the effective storage of abstract knowledge but the fragility of personal memory in the technical age.

New technologies change the nature of the memorial processes
... they do more than just reinforce memory: they freeze it, and
in imposing a fixed, linear sequence upon it, they simultaneously
preserve it and prevent it from evolving and transforming
itself ...[18]

The simulacra becomes less of an aide-memoire and more its
replacement. Memory and its artificial manipulation or
instalment becomes a major motif in postmodern science fiction
narrative. In *Blade Runner* artificial life, in the form of android
slaves, is supplied with artificial memories. Such memory is not
the computations of a machine, but the simulation of personal
memory, internal records of their own pseudo-exeriences. *Total
Recall* (1992), based on another P.K. Dick short story, the far
more evocatively titled 'We can remember it for you wholesale',
is centred around a scene where a documentary of artificial
experience is inserted directly into the hero's memory. Rather
than the Renaissance vision of power over the universe,
psychology identifies memory as giving power over the self.
Memory, its loss and substitution becomes the prevailing motif
of identity in postmodern narrative.

An ontological concern for memory, its fallibility, fragmentation and frailty is evident within cyberpunk writing. Although
popular experience of 'cyberpunk' is not just limited to print
fiction, criticism inside and outside science fiction treats
Gibson's *Neuromancer* (1984) as a definitive text. The prefix
cyber references the writing's association with cybernetics
which seeks:

The common element in the functioning of automatic machines
and the human nervous system, and to develop a theory that will
cover the entire field of control and communication in machines
and living organisms.[19]

Punk defines the perspective from which the fiction is
generated. Characteristically cyberpunk fiction is situated in a
decaying urban environment subject to a technocracy which has
normalised anarchy in a corporate controlled 'late capitalist'
city. Narrative action is at street level, juxtaposed by the high

fashion of the corporate boardroom. It pursues the past as much as the future and common to earlier *fin de siècle* fiction balances technology with a spiritual philosophy. Gibson's most successful neologism is cyberspace which refers to the mind/machine interfacing that grants access to an artificial memory. Cyberspace takes the form of a simulated parallel world of data transference. The cyberspace user 'jacks' into a console which can project their 'disembodied consciousness into the consensual hallucination that was the matrix'.[20] The simulated reality or work environment, virtual reality, is constructed by iconic computer representations of data that form a navigable architecture. The space and depth created and envisaged makes architecture, like memory, a key metaphor in the popular discussion of software. Michael Sexson compares Gibson's description of cyberspace:

> Disk beginning to rotate, fast, becoming a sphere of paler gray. Expanding – And flowered, flowered for him, fluid origami trick, the unfolding of his distanceless home, his country, transparent 3D chessboard extending to infinity. Inner eye opening to the stepped scarlet pyramid of the Eastern Seaboard Fission Authority burning beyond the green cubes of Mitsubishi Bank of America and high and very far away he saw the spiral arms of military systems, forever beyond his reach.[21]

with Yates's citing of St. Augustine's discussion of memory:

> I came to the fields and spacious palaces of memory, where are the treasures of innumerable images ... Behold in the plains, and caves, and caverns of my memory, innumerably full of innumerable kinds of things ... over all these do I run, I fly; I dive on this side and that, as far as I can, and there is no end.[22]

Artificial memory is prosthetic, existing outside the body, accessible at will but existing simultaneously and open to others. The implications resulting from this understanding of artificial memory-power begin to redefine the meaning of memory itself. Instead of a private resource refined for public speech it becomes visualised as a public utility occasionally reappropriated for private contemplation. Memory is a facility for a different set of survival skills required and necessitated by the popular fictional discourse of the information society.

Hyperreality

Hyperreality is a term used by various contemporary cultural critics. It refers to the excess of simulation, the endless recycling of form, content and style, most remarked upon in fashion, pop video and advertising. Imitation has superseded representation. The perfect copy has been reified by the service industries of the last quarter of the twentieth century. Memory has different objectives, one of which is the recording of trivia for the pop quiz. The contemporary memory has to emulate the machine, quick to absorb, perfect recall and always ready to update reclassify and delete.

In *Simulations* Baudrillard regards hyperreality as the predominating form of simulation. One of his main concerns with its ascendancy is the loss of imagination hyperreality engenders. Hyperreality is the external construction of similitude. The cultural product of the information society is tangible rather than mental simulation, that is the simulacrum which negates the realising power of imagination.

> ... So goes creativity.
> This also means the collapse of reality into hyperrealism, in the minute duplication of the real, preferably on the basis of another reproduced medium – advertisement, photograph etc. From medium to medium the real is volatilized; it becomes an allegory of death, but it is reinforced by its very destruction; it becomes the real for the real, fetish of the last object – no longer object of representation, but ecstasy of degeneration of its own ritual extermination; the hyperreality.[23]

As a simulation the simulacrum is actually untenable because it is void of meaning. As pure simulation rather than representation it exists without particular reference to the real. This existence neither reflects presence nor masks absence. Both Eco[24] and Baudrillard hold Disneyland as their perfect model of the simulacrum.

> Disneyland is presented as imaginary in order to make us believe that the rest is real, when in fact all of Los Angeles and the America surrounding it are no longer real, but of the orders of the hyperreal and of simulation. It is no longer a question of false representation of reality (ideology), but of concealing the fact that the real is no longer real and the means of saving the reality principle.[25]

The simulacrum negates the energy Yates describes in her account of the agency of memory. Instead the action is completed externally to the individual mind and designated for mass consumption. Nevertheless the experience of Disneyland is a real commodity, it is a work as well as a leisure environment. Employees take money from real people who have made a conscious decision to consume.

In the material world of late capitalist consumer society the distinction between the real and the imaginary is less sustainable and begins to be effaced; as Eco phrases it, in his earlier discussion of hyperreality, 'absolute unreality is offered as real presence'.[26] The reasons for this are ontological. In his examination of hyperreality in American culture, Eco speaks of the demand made by the American imagination for real things; to supply this need, the cultural industry generates the fabrication of the absolute fake. Unreality, dream, fantasy or hallucination are no longer private experiences but public and collective. Baudrillard's metaphor for the experience of postmodern culture is schizophrenia, or hysteria surrounding the subjugating transvaluation of hyperreality. The simulacrum has become more authentic than the original.

Lack of imagination is a symptom of lived experience in the 'perpetual present'. The total instanteity of things overwhelms the human agent until they are prepared to take up a role of passivity. For Baudrillard, the supremacy of simulation occurs through the non-distinction of active and passive, an implosion of meaning.[27] He identifies the lack of any referent allowing postmodern culture to operate in the mode of referendum. Such passivity is very specific, it is the difference between user and read only access. The consumer is permitted a semblance of interrogation – they are allowed to select upon a yes/no basis.[28] The exercise of belief is outweighed by the expression of opinion. Eco sees hyperreality coming to prominence because it is controllable. The chaos that it simulates is, with the help of a tourist guide, negotiable, 'An allegory of the consumer society, a place of absolute iconism, Disneyland is also a place of total passivity.'[29]

The atrophy of memory is a key to survival in fictional late capitalist society. Johnny Mnemonic, a character in one of Gibson's short stories, rents out his memory as a storage facility, 'I'm not cheap to begin with, but my overtime on storage is astronomical'.[30] The crucial difference in the discussion and description of hyperreality and cyberspace is that the former is a leisure construct or cultural policy and the latter is a work environment. The presentation of hyperreality in the context of leisure prevents us from engaging with these issues, hyperreality's domain of popular cultural does not appear of strategic importance. The role of popular culture is often seen as that of consensus and harmony, not protest.

The constant reference to 'the edge' in cyberpunk writing acknowledges the necessity of survival strategies in the hostile world of corporate capital. In the cyberpunk diegesis the worker (or employed, unemployed, self employed) must outrun the obsolescence of their skills, personal technology or basic corporal integrity in order to remain competitive. As Gibson's narrative technique implies, the characters are alienated from each other and sequentially dislocated from the environment that they inhabit.

And we're all making good money, better money than I made before, because Jones's Squid can read the traces of anything that anyone ever stored in me, and he gives it to me on the display unit in languages I can understand. So we're learning a lot about all my former clients. And one day I'll have a surgeon dig all the silicon out of my amygdalae, and I'll live with my own memories and nobody else's, the way other people do. But not for a while.

Artificial memory is useful because the material stored can be readily erased. The expectation of longevity and rejuvenation in cyberpunk fiction means that memory becomes a liability rather than asset. Memory is cumbersome and interferes with the smooth running of personality and often in these narratives it has to be edited. The routine memory wipe is common place. Memory however, is not just a capacity, but an active faculty for the continuity of personality. Sanity is necessary for the efficient functioning of the cyborg. This functionality may necessarily be augmented through circuitry or chemicals. In fiction the cyberpunk character has no need of knowledge as they can chip in franchised skills at will or indeed franchised personalities.

Eco's point of departure for his expedition among the artefacts of the American hyperreal is holography. Here Eco locates an initial depthlessness and passivity in its formation and appreciation which characterises hyperreality. A hologram is a virtual object. It exists in effect though not in fact. Oliver Stone has the same problem with his science fantasy television mini-series *Wild Palms* (1993), which has done much to substantiate the myth of interactive media. Stone has difficulty in portraying interactivity. The holosynth sitcom visualised in the programme is really three dimensional television. The audience cannot interact with the show, but due to the intensification of the medium it apparently can interact with them. The myth of hyperreality is one of acquisition, attaining the sublime without personal involvement. Information does not have meaning, it has exchange value to be produced as a trump card on the business negotiating table. Topic webs are used to navigate vast recesses of information and locate singular items, trivia, rather than encompass the broader pattern. It may actually be harmful to retain any organising schema in the mind or make connections which may hamper effective presentation.

73

Conclusion

> Computerized information is as evanescent as the quantum vacuum, with virtual truths and falsehood endlessly popping in and out of existence. Deceptions of any magnitude are possible, on a short enough time scale; laws only apply to data that sits still long enough to be caught out.[32]

Control and public order in the late twentieth century rest upon surveillance and record, new versions of which are offered through information technology to an extent never before experienced. The implications of this are central to any debate on memory power and simulation. Personal computing comprises many applications of artificial memory. Memory power is more than just an anthropomorphic term and reminds us that memory can be impressed, manipulated and erased as much as it can be read. Personal computing follows three basic functions, storage, copying and the interplay of modification between these two. Internal software architecture allows interconnection between rooms and the moving of imagines or agents from place to place. The culture and practice of personal computing asks the participants to understand, to gain skills, communicate, criticise and devise their own programmes. Gradually it begins to incorporate a fourth basic area that of modelling, extrapolation and speculation. Extrapolation is a major exercise in an attempt to understand the significance of hyperreality. Cyberpunk proposes a counter-simulator, the computer hacker who belies the authoritarian passivity of excess simulation and screen leisure.

Putting information on screen and replacing paper is not in itself interactive although it may soon be cost effective. Interactivity is foreseen in hypermedia, 'open architecture television' permanently fuses the computer and television screen. The home computer in the corner can then access all digital information. Software will be developed to allow the human mind to order and make sense of the morass. The principles of hypertext mean that texts and information structures are no longer fixed. The reader is expected to form a text of their own, refusing a single authority. A simulation of communication perhaps, but a model of active consumption.

However, assuming that the simulacrum is passive is an assumption made from elitist pretexts. Virtual Reality has afforded a technical discourse through which to exclaim the dangers of oblivion in artificial playgrounds. The real issue is the virtual work environment. However, such widespread contention over similitude in the late twentieth century tells us much about the present cultural climate and suggests parallels with the late medieval period of infrastructural change. Rather than a model of domination, 'the end of creativity', similitude marks the site of cultural struggle during a period of social transition. Open memory and the meaningless sign are ripe for reappropriation and spark off interactivity. If Disneyland appears more real than the rest of America it is because it is stable unlike the same use of hypermedia forms which refute it. The simulacrum is waiting to be filled by individual and collective memory to become a point of visible contradiction. Even the perfect copy is subject to graffiti.

Reality, however, exists through interaction. Concern for the loss of reality, expressed through the criticism of popular culture, is one that acknowledges the anxiety of cultural and social change. Prosthetic memory systems are a symptom of the necessity for new survival strategies in the social environment.

Science fiction performs modifications on the brain or the psyche, so that the worker can reach optimum efficiency and emulate the machine. In theory medieval allegory concentrated the mind upon spiritual salvation and not material reward; in practice it is part of the process which enabled secular scientific thought. A modified worker who can ignore hunger, pain and distraction is being given the skills for work which allow her to engage with the complexities of cyberspace. However, the pleasures of simulation, which are the reward for such employment, will be denied to a vast number of the unemployed created by such a system. A future where all have equal access to new technology is utopian or equally dystopian but nonetheless ideal.

Dante's fiction is interrogative, requiring sustained contemplation, the route for which is composed of social and political comment. Interactive CD has already been launched twice on the public market. The graphics and storage capacity are superior to other systems but their capabilities do not fit in with public requirements. Eurodisney also appears to have failed although, undeterred, Disney plans to launch the Disney America theme park in Washington. The mythology of interactive media is not all encompassing. At best its polysemy is governed by comedy and not tragedy, where there are still as yet unnegotiated opportunities for the human agent to dispute the adversity of simulation.

Notes

[1] Umberto Eco, *Faith in Fakes*, Secker and Warburg, London, 1986, p69.
[2] C.S. Lewis, *The Allegory of Love*, Oxford Universirty Press, London, 1946, p44.
[3] David Aers, 'Reflections on the "Allegory of the Theologians' Ideology" and *Piers Plowman*' in David Aers (ed), *Medieval Literature: Criticism, Ideology and History*, Harvester Wheatsheaf, Brighton, 1986.
[4] Gay Clifford, *The Transformation of Allegory*, Routledge Kegan Paul, London, 1974.
[5] Developed at Stanford Artificial Intelligence Laboratory (SAIL) in the 1960s.
[6] Erick Davies quoted in Michael Sexson 'Miranda's Attendants: Memory, Medievalism, Cyberspace and the Sail', unpublished paper given at the International Medievalism Conference, University of Leeds, 1993.
[7] Philips Consumer Electronics publicity for CD-I Full Motion Video, authoring tools geared for presentation and promotion.
[8] Sexson, *op.cit.*
[9] William Langland, *Piers Plowman*, trans. A. Burrell [1912] World's Classics, Oxford, 1978, p1.
[10] Clifford, *op.cit.*, p2.
[11] Pami Piehler, *The Visionary Landscape*, Arnold, London, 1971, p73.
[12] Frances A. Yates, *The Art of Memory*, Routledge Kegan Paul,

London, 1986, p93.

[13] *Ibid.*

[14] Interview on *How Do They Do That?*, ITV, 8 February 1994.

[15] Yates, *op.cit.*, p18.

[16] *Ibid.*, p104.

[17] Steven Rose, *The Making of Memory*, Bantam Press, London, 1992, p80.

[18] *Ibid.*, p61.

[19] Norbert Wiener, *Cybernetics, or Control and Communication in the Animal and the Machine*, MIT Press, Cambridge, Massachusetts, 1948.

[20] William Gibson, *Neuromancer*, Grafton Books, London, 1984, p92.

[21] *Ibid.*, pp68-69.

[22] St. Augustine's *Confessions*, Book X, Chapter 8, quoted in Yates, 1986, pp60-61.

[23] Jean Baudrillard, *Simulations*, Semiotext(e), New York, 1983, p141.

[24] Umberto Eco, *Travels in Hyperreality*, Picador, London, 1975.

[25] Baudrillard, *op.cit.*, p25.

[26] Eco, *op.cit.*, p48.

[27] Baudrillard, *op.cit* p57.

[28] Baudrillard, *op.cit* pp115-121.

[29] Eco, *op.cit.*, p48.

[30] William Gibson, *Burning Chrome*, Grafton Books, London, 1986, p15.

[31] *Ibid.*, p36.

[32] Greg Egan, *Quarantine*, Legend, London, 1992, p33.

Cyberpunks in the White House

Fred Johnson

Sometime in the fall of 1993 a surge in public awareness of telecommunications and new media took place in the United States. An ensemble of events began to unfold before the public's eyes that seemed orchestral in their timing and scope. The newly elected government announced its plans to rationalise national communications policy. A wave of restructuring, mergers and intended mergers was announced between the telephone, cable and entertainment industries, setting off endless speculation on the future form of telecommunications. Representations of an all digital network, cyberspace, an information highway, burst into popular culture.

The news of these events was accompanied by the appearance of an overwhelming array of new digital media, information hardware and software. The personal computer reached the mass market take-off point with over 30 per cent of the population owning or using PCs. The new PCs came with CD-ROM multimedia players and enormous increases in computing power. There has been a palpable, media-induced quickening of interest and movement as the use of new media have speeded up changes in everyone's workspace, transforming nearly every process associated with creating, distributing and storing images, data and sound. Speculation on the artistic implications of digital media have been frenzied.

It is no accident that this cluster of events took place simultaneously; they are all parts of a larger whole. At the core of the development of digital media is the need of the economy to manipulate and transport information simply and rapidly; image, sound and text are given digital form for this reason, and digital or new media arise from this need. All the new media technology can be understood as being a part of the telecommunication network. They code and decode information for transmission, they display information received from the network, they are designed to interconnect on the network in order to work in more than one place simultaneously, their operations are augmented with data from the network and they store information for eventual use on the network. These are not separate technical developments, they are not isolated moments of artistic innovation – nor are they merely technological change.

New Media are the representational adjunct to a profound restructuring of everyday life, and the patterns of connection they create through the network are compelling images not easily separated from the very definitions and metaphors we use to understand our social relationships. In the past it was common to imagine the shape of society or the workings of mind and body as machinery and engines; but surely by now no one has avoided some form of 'networking', or thinking of social or personal relationships in terms of networking.[1] New Media are part of a cluster of social changes – New Media come with new space and time, new economies, new organisational structures, new industries, new management attitudes, new skills at all levels, new occupational and industrial classification, new labour relations, new design, new training, new kinds of money, new kinds of ownership.

In the US this kind of restructuring is driving the most significant changes to take place in US communications policy since 1934. The hands-off, *laissez-faire* years of Reagan and Bush have been replaced with the Clinton administration's dreams of 'cybernetic capitalism', a new phase of capital accumulation in which microelectronics/information technology are deployed in a complete, corporate reorganisation of society.[2] At the centre of this new world is an information infrastructure, a privately owned, global network to be created through government subsidies and tax abatements to the megacorporations who dominate communications. Vice President Al Gore unveiled a new US communications policy initiative in early 1994, 'The National Information Infrastructure: Agenda For Action', (NII). It reads like a blissed out cyberculture fantasy of the future:

> NII, the National Information Infrastructure, a seamless web of communications networks, computers, databases, and consumer electronics that will put vast amounts of information at user's fingertips...

> Development of the NII can help unleash an information revolution that will change forever the way people live, work, and interact with each other.

In the language of an AT&T television spot the Clinton administration asks us to

> imagine ... you had a device that combined a telephone, a TV, a camcorder, and a personal computer. No matter where you went or what time it was, your child could see you and talk to you, you could watch a replay of your team's last game, you could browse the latest additions to the library, or you could find the best prices in town on groceries, furniture, clothes – whatever you needed.[3]

This is the language of techno-utopian futurism, 'all information, in all places at all times, at no cost', another spasm of the technological euphoria that periodically accompanies US social and technological shifts. The Government's NII policy statements are mute or very vague regarding the critical social issues that arise from changes of the magnitude and type proposed. Will the current developments embody long-standing traditions of public space, common property held for the common good? Will the global communications infrastructure widen the gap between the rich and poor nations or will it work to encourage democratic development? How can our traditions of civic life find expression in the spaces for representation being created by the market-driven development of cyberspace?

Increasing numbers of people around the world have come to recognise the potential of the new media to create social and political benefits. It is also recognised that this potential will not be realised in the absence of clear social policies and none are present in the NII. The government's policy proposals have not addressed the fact that the communication and information industries have become central in establishing the direction of social and political change globally. Nor does it acknowledge that the domination of this sector by corporate and military interests threatens democracy, the evolution of civil society and bio-diversity. Instead we are given simple techno-romanticism while huge numbers of the world are living in shantytowns and an urban sprawl that appears set to explode in a nightmare of diminishing resources, 'road-warrior culture' and environmental catastrophe.[4]

This is technocratic ideology infused with blind faith in deregulated markets. The language and images used in the US to imagine the future of telecommunications have a structure of their own, predictable patterns that recycle and play a recurring role culturally. The NII, along with concepts like the 'information revolution', and the 'information society', are central themes in the tradition of technocratic thinking. They always promise to distribute power and wealth through decentralisation; and, the proposed technical changes are always presented as the solution to social problems, never an embodiment of those problems.[5]

They perform perfectly as ideology by focusing on the technical potential of the technology rather than the social relations that will ultimately determine the form in which those potentialities are realised.[6] Technocratic ideology also consistently denies history, exaggerating the novelty of each technology being introduced. Everything is presented as new, new media, unprecedented communications potential, new societies, new times, new space.

Policy *Déjà Vu*

Of course none of this is new. Indeed, as already noted, ideas of new media and the information society seem to get recycled periodically during times of social and technological phase shifts. It is critical to see these patterns historically in order to understand that this is not an unprecedented moment. Indeed fascination with 'information highways', integrated networks, with 'single, unified systems of electronic communications' is one of the central themes and recurring utopian images of US communications policy, a kind of network monotheism.[7] The 1994 'National Information Infrastructure, Agenda for Action' is no exception. It stands in a long line of futurist proclamations. In the late 1960s the Johnson administration initiated the 'Wired Cities' programme which was part of the so-called 'Great Society', a multifaceted attempt to address urban social problems during a time of unprecedented urban unrest and violent uprising. This led to the formation of a federally convened panel of the National Academy of Engineers, chaired by Peter Goldmark, who was at that time the reigning communications scientist for CBS. The panel came forward with a plan for a national communications infrastructure which combined cable television, telephones, institutional and community owned networks.[8]

Popularised by Ralph Lee Smith as 'The Wired Nation' and an 'information highway', the concept of the 'Wired City' initially featured significant components that were dedicated to social uses, and owned or controlled by the public sector. There was much discussion of electronic democracy, voting, education and publicly supported interactive information services; policy-makers saw telecommunications as a vehicle for social and political reform.

Hopeful plans indeed, but historically the implementation of those plans has left much to be desired. The regulation in behalf of reform has given way to deregulation in behalf of international trade and economic development, to monopoly cable companies marketing the most simplistic video entertain-

82

ment and home shopping channels. Of course no one should have been surprised by the paltry social outcomes in comparison to the projections. Very similar projections of social change through technology came with the introduction of broadcast television and before that radio, with similar disappointing results.

Now we begin again. Even more than the 'Wired City' projections, the 1994 'National Information Infrastructure' uses the language of social promises and development in behalf of the common good; and, even more than the 'Wired City', it is alarmingly deficient when it comes to giving one a clue how any of that might come about. The NII takes a classic neo-liberal position by assuring us that all will be provided by competition and the market. There is absolutely no evidence that would support such a notion.

The Neo-Liberal Lie

Along with all the technology of global communications restructuring comes the big economic lie that market-based media and information systems are more democratic, more culturally diverse, less centralised and more capable of delivering quality. In fact, in the absence of regulation and public control, market-based systems tend to create barriers to market entry, monopoly and restrictions on choice, while shifting the definition of 'information from that of a common good to a private commodity.'[9] While the introduction of competition into some moribund state-owned information systems can in fact be in the public interest, that must not be confused with the simple 'free market' and deregulatory positions now prevailing. Such ideology is simply a justification for empowering investors over citizens.

The tendency of information industries to become centralised in ownership and control is based on the high costs associated with the initial building of communications networks, and the nature of information as a commodity. Most of the costs associated with making information go into producing the first copy. After that making more copies is extremely inexpensive and the more copies you make the cheaper each copy is. That means those companies that distribute most widely and grow the largest make more profit on each copy. It costs almost as much to make one music recording or software package as it does to make millions. This is reinforced by the fact that it is impossible in media to know which products are going to sell. For example only one in ten films makes a profit but since it is difficult to predict which one, a company must make all ten. This rewards big, centralised, capital-intensive corporations and punishes small ones.

The capital requirement for success in communications is enormous, for both content producers as well as network owners. The results of all this can be seen in the tendency of the media and communications corporations to grow larger and larger while becoming increasingly concentrated in terms of control and ownership. It is important not to confuse their geographic decentralisation with ownership. They may be dispersed around the world but many predict there will only be five or six telecommunications corporations globally by the end of the century. The social implications of such an outcome are staggering.

Policy Tech Noir

At the core of the ideas of the 'information society' is systems analysis, the study of electronic feedback systems, frequently referred to as cybernetics. Cybernetics is derived from the Greek word *cyber* meaning steersman, or helmsman. Cybernetics was coined by MIT mathematics genius Norbet Weiner to refer to the study and science of communications and control systems. From there it has gone on to the big pop culture show as cyberspace, cyberpunk, cyberculture, cyberwear ... it is difficult to keep in mind that it all goes back to control, or that communications and control are two virtually inseparable social processes; we separate them 'by denying history and exaggerating the novelty of the process.'[10]

In *The Control Revolution*, an exploration into the technological and economic origins of the information society, James R. Beniger suggests that the social processes involving the increasing use of communications technology are about an on-going process of control. Beniger points out that a wave of communications technology was introduced in the nineteenth century in order to re-establish the social control that was lost and fragmented with the infusion of speed and power that came with the introduction of fossil fuels: photography and telegraphy (1830s), rotary power printing (1840s), the typewriter (1860s), trans-Atlantic cable (1866), telephone (1876), motion pictures (1894), wireless telegraphy (1895), magnetic tape recording (1899), radio (1906), and television (1923).[11]

Technocratic thinking neglects that information processing (transmission and storage of image, voice, data and text) is deployed not as separate technology but as part of a repertoire of control techniques such as bureaucratic forms of organisation, the modern corporation, the plan, forecasting, the abstraction of information into statistics, case studies, models and the replacement of judgment with decision-making rules. It is not surprising that much of the development of control technology stems from military and police applications – for example, automated weapons systems, electronic crowd control, missile guidance systems, computerised on-line credit checks and an enormous elaboration of surveillance technology of astonishing power. Indeed the same technology that makes possible a shiny camcorder or the new personal computer also monitors the activities of your friendly airline ticket agent, the telephone operators who assist us with long-distance, and most customer service workers we come in contact with daily. Sophisticated surveillance technology now represents virtually a new form of spatial organisation as it oversees our activities while shopping, working or visiting the public spaces of the world.[12]

Discussion of control tends to both over and understate the

dangers of communication control technology. Often overstated are the dire warnings of the totally managed society of the panopticon. Such portrayals frequently represent control as a simplistic image of cameras watching us in a confined space, and tend to be very dark and pessimistic in their projections concerning hopes for human liberation. They can in fact reinforce the strength of surveillance, by neglecting to explain that frequently the systems do not work, that it is a physical impossibility to watch everything. The surveillance system would eclipse the network. Many times there is simply no one watching.

Conversely, what is often understated is the extent to which modern media and advertising control by managing desire and consumer notions of everyday life, or the extent to which media control the framework or agenda for political debate. The tracking of personal data by law enforcement, insurance companies and corporate credit agencies is becoming web-like and omnipresent. Likewise, the extent to which the language of science now functions as a control on production is rarely mentioned.[13] Finally it is rarely clear that much of the modern infrastructure is industrial control technology, handling tasks like transportation coordination, weather forecasting and market integration. The list is enormous and the industrial world would crash without it, a point technocrats are quick to make.

However one conceives of control it is important to understand that Cyberspace, or the developing 'information highway' is the nervous system of this control matrix; it will integrate, augment and amplify the technology of communication and social control. Communication technology is meaningful in many ways and can be understood from a number of different perspectives but one perspective rarely mentioned is that it is a key component in a process that threatens our privacy, our autonomy and our very definitions of public space.[14] In that light, or dark, the White House pronouncements on the National Information Infrastructure take on new meaning; the seamless web could become an enclosure whose power and scope would have been unimaginable to previous generations:

NII, the National Information Infrastructure, a seamless web of communications networks, computers, databases, and consumer electronics that will put vast amounts of information at user's fingertips...

Development of the NII can help unleash an information revolution that will change forever the way people live, work, and interact with each other...[15]

Global Development: A Little Totalising Never Hurt Anyone

The New Media and the networks are developed, that is selected for investment and developed to address the social and economic needs of power. It is important not to make the mistake of defining these changes as yet another technological innovation or pure discovery. They represent fundamental change in the structures in which society is organised, and the effects of the converging use of computers, communications technology and global transport systems are rippling through every sector of society.

Since the oil crisis of 1973 there has been an acceleration of the pay-off and implementation phase for research in communication and electronics undertaken since World War Two. The response of corporate and government decision-makers to the contradictions of dwindling energy resources, overburdened eco-systems, increasingly better organised citizens and a world market glutted with cars and home gadgets has been massive long-term investment in global communications and transportation systems. This, coupled with huge subsidies from US war and space research, has set the arena for economic development throughout the world.[16]

Long standing time and space relationships are being crushed, the relative value of labour, capital and energy has shifted once again; global and local economies interpenetrate in a rapidly expanding global financial system that by-passes national levels of regulation and control. Corporate organisations are being physically moved to all parts of the globe in search of cheap labour, while ownership and control of those corporations becomes more and more concentrated and laced together with telecommunications. Selling electronic images, sounds and information appliances is one of the few avenues of expansion in a world economy glutted with home goods and cars. Compare the time it takes to consume a movie to the time it takes to consume a car; the consumption time is decreased to the 'twinkling of an eye' and the circulation of money is speeded up. This is the New Media's social context. Home television is being redesigned to concentrate recreation and cultural consumption within the home, thus lodging within private space the means to manipulate public opinion and taste for a corporate sector with an increasing need to sell images and information. Global television, linked by satellite and fibre, makes it possible to experience a rush of images, sound and data from nearly anywhere on the planet. In such an information environment all the spaces of the world are collapsed into the home television.[17]

These kinds of shifts alter our notions of space and time; they reformulate and reorder our perceptions and sensibilities; they alter the maps of the world and shift the conceptual and physical relationships of regions, cities and nations. In such times there is a near crisis need to find new media tools and new means of artistic expression and representation. Cultural production becomes the site of active struggle for explanation, for control of images that can resolve the reordering of our perceptions.

Cyberspace vs the 'Information Highway': What's a Meta(phor)?

It is interesting to think in geographer's terms of space and place when considering the US government's decision to frame the telecommunications policy discussion in the US with the idea of an 'information highway' rather than 'cyberspace', or any space for that matter. Space is socially constructed to create specific places that are always inscribed with relations of race, class, gender and regional difference.[18] There is a long-standing tendency in the US to use social movement and travel to avoid confronting the politics of place. Vice-President Gore gives us a clue with his remarks that it is satisfying to be following in his father's footsteps, to be creating the highway into the information age just as his father, Senator Gore, helped create the interstate auto-system that propelled the US into post-war dominance.

Foregrounding ideas of transportation rather than space functions to suppress the point of view most useful to understanding the class and justice implications of this new technology. Our attention is diverted from the points of scarcity in the network and directed to points of near unlimited capacity, fibre optic transmission lines. Consider what happens when the information gets where it is going, the cyberplaces: the commercial computer communication services, the space on the gopher servers and the data bases, all of which are becoming effectively the programming interfaces of the network. These communication forms and software shape the rush of information in order to make it more manageable, in other words to be 'selected' to be 'packaged', to be 'compiled', to be 'condensed', to be 'spatialised' in a way that can be used. This is programme creation. This is where the economics of scarcity creep back into the discussion. All the old information economics go into effect just as always. Mystifying fibre optics, and its massive frequency capacity, continues the illusion that the technology is limitless and that issues of access and control of culture are no longer relevant.

All the programming interface systems are and will continue to be in need of talent and resources, creativity, time and money in order to attract users, i.e. an audience. Further, the databases that now continue to codify, store and commodify the social knowledge and wisdom of the planet into privatised 'bases' are not about transportation or bandwidth; these are enormous 'information spaces' that can best be understood in terms of the enclosure movement and the seizure of commonly held resources. When the global restructuring further asserts itself the economics of culture and money power is poised to reproduce its social relations in a new digital space. It won't be any surprise who is locked out; the information poor and the poor are the same people. Caution requires that we understand this as a system predisposed to behave much like commercial television, except that it will be much easier to charge admission to these systems.

There are parts of cyberspace where people actually connect with the network. Where's that space? William Gibson has described cyberspace as 'the place where a long distance call happens'. For our purposes it is important to locate cyberspace as extending beyond the enormously expanded spaces for representation, beyond hundreds of channels and the electronic network's capacity for real-time connectivity, beyond the databases and electronic archives. Cyberspace should be looked at not as virtual space, but as a massive reorganisation of all space.

The new media and telecommunications are infrastructure that allow the global economy to develop interconnected spaces in distant cities so that the corporate centres in one city exist intimately side by side, and much closer than their respective suburban peripheries and sprawls. Cyberspace allows planning elites to code the urban grid and design around whole neighbourhoods blinking them into invisibility and out of the flow.

Perhaps the most significant cyberspace is the city centre corporate enclaves. 'Nested complexes' of corporate offices and interconnected hotel and recreation areas designed with their backs to the street, under constant surveillance, these are the command centres of the global economy. They house the management, financial, media and legal support firms that monitor the multi-nationals throughout the world. As much as 30 per cent of the costs of such citadels represents the electronics and 'intelligent' systems built into their designs. Cyberspace is far more than the space where a long-distance telephone conversation happens.[19]

Policy in Cyberspace

> Good Morning. The Public Interest Summit is today.
> Here's how to plug in. There are a number of ways to plug in.
> Here's what's Happening. Plug and play![20]

Public policy discussion in America happens in hotels, in completely dislocated environments. The Public Interest Summit on 29 March 1994, on communications policy and infrastructure, sponsored by the Benton Foundation, is in Washington DC. It is raining and grey in DC but no-one really notices the weather – 'it's just not an issue' – everybody is contained in some part of cyberspace. Those present in body arrive in cars gliding in off the DC streets, closing conversations on cellular phones, packing their laptops. Quickly hopping across a small zone of outdoor air and into the vast, terrarium-like lobby of Capital Hill's Hyatt Regency. The Hyatt is global. Inside it could be and nearly is anywhere. Everything is washed in a soft combination of artificial light and muted daylight from the multi-storeyed glass enclosure, there are lots of plants and somewhere the pleasant gurgling of water. Already our movements are being monitored although the cameras are very well hidden here, not so many of those dumb-looking smoked glass half-bubbles attached to the ceiling. Wherever they are you can be sure someone is watching; there are plenty of private security people around patched into a central bank of monitors, somewhere. That's just standard operating procedure and this is no standard security day. Vice-President Al Gore is speaking to the conference.

This was the first time either the VP or the President deigned to address an audience of non-corporate communications policy people since Ronald Reagan came to power in 1980. I do not think anyone knew exactly how to play this one. Most of the people present here have never worked in a policy environment where the Executive Office was willing to even give lip-service to the public interest, let alone come and speak to a hotel full of them. Indeed many at this conference had not begun their professional lives when Reagan's first appointment to chair the Federal Communication Commission rang in the 1980s with the declaration that television did not need regulation, it was just another home appliance, 'a toaster with pictures'. Of course that was merely the thudding completion of a long slide into deregulation that started with the Carter administration in the 1970s.

Now for another descent. Down a series of switched-back escalators into the deepest basement conferencing facilities of the hotel. The escalators give a floating motion that propels us through a mirrored lobby where our attention is focused and organised by a series of wide doors, around a corner and into a huge vault-like room. There are no windows, this is buried two storeys into the ground; everything is muted, the lighting and grey and burgundy colours dampening everything down so that the huge, stage-to-ceiling video projection screens at the front of the room glow prominently. The screens are where the action is. They flank a stage with seating for five or six panellists and a podium at stage-right. The video screens are flickering bluish light, one has Internet text scrolling up, the other a video image of the stage being fed from the video recording systems wired throughout the room. Policy space, cyberspace.

Who's here? The 600 or more people biologically present will take their seats alongside a broadcast audience of radio stations in all the major markets fed through the National Federation of Community Broadcasters; C-Span, the cable's policy network, will feed the majority of the Conference to every cable system in the US. On-line on the Internet and its interlinking networks are thousands world-wide. There are Singapore network managers, Canadian Free-Nets, local, regional and state telecommunications policy initiatives, community communications centres, media arts centres, rural educators and librarians in many countries, citizens' advisory groups, cable access centres and university policy and technical participants.

The Summit affords an opportunity to assess who in the 1990s is concerned for the public's common interest in communication. This is best understood as handful of types of groups, but numerically their membership would be in the millions. There are the liberal, reform-minded public interest groups like the Summit's sponsor, the Benton Foundation, or the Consumer Federation of America. Also present are the non-profit groups with a large stake in securing some kind of protected access to telecommunications. Finally there are the radical practitioners, the alternative media, cable access centres and the community computing and networking groups. The most obvious change one would notice in contrasting the make-up of this group to a pre-Reagan event would be the presence of large numbers involved in cable access and community computing networks.

Easily the most significant aspect of this gathering is its on-line, mediated presence expanding through cyberspace, not simply a passive audience but an interactive body engaged in discussion. The Center for Civic Networking facilitated the design of the agenda and the creation of questions for the panel in a publicly open process, on-line on the Internet. This was done as part of the planning and run-up to the conference in the weeks preceding the event. This kind of public discourse and discussion had been taking place within networked groups for some time, but this is the first time it went 'public' in that it engaged with and stimulated a national debate among the uninitiated. The interaction was further extended via 800 numbers that allowed the broadcast and cable audience to call in questions to the conference participants throughout the day in real time.

Using communication technology in this way to create public participation represents a small qualitative change in how public policy gets discussed. Despite the fact that it was the largest public gathering in over a decade to bring together the non-profit sector and telecommunications public interest advocates, the conference was not really different from other political spectacle and awareness raising schemes, with that one exception. There may have been a glimmer of a way for people to start using telecommunications to organise and actively participate as citizens in public policy. Perhaps one little utopian seed that could represent a significant shift.

While we may indeed have had a significant shift of form, the content at the gathering was pretty much the plodding rhetoric of the loyal opposition. A series of panel discussions with questions from an audience far too large for meaningful discussion. The focus shifted between specific issues and current legislative initiatives, or wandering discussion with the words democracy, diversity and open architecture liberally sprinkled throughout. There was very little openly stated that would help people understand the overall issues of restructuring and I am sure it was confusing to the uninitiated. The popular and regulatory language of telecommunications has been scrambled to such an extent by the changes brought on by digitalisation that many are fumbling to find some frame of reference from which to analyse and stake out clear positions. This all in a time when the corporate media is saturating our symbolic environment with the most outrageous and confusing constructions equating freedom with consumption and unregulated markets with democracy. Little wonder the confusion.

Confusion finds many well-meaning expressions. I am sure I was not the only one who noted with some amusement an Internet message scrolling up the big screens encouraging people to participate in the Policy Summit. It was a reminder, 'Remember: the public doesn't get a chance to design a new infrastructure very often.'

In the 1970s many thought cable television would be the new infrastructure. It was even called an 'information highway' in those days. We thought we would design it, or thought we were designing it, by fighting for democratic local policies and undertaking countless demonstration projects in local cable throughout the US and Canada. Those times have the feel of these times, another massive infusion of capital and communications technology. There were policy gatherings throughout the late 1970s and early 1980s, full of the same high-pitched rhetoric of 'democracy and interactivity'. Of course it turned out that we were not designing a new infrastructure at all. We were small-time political actors who had stumbled into the midst of an enormous communications land grab and we preceded to place ourselves in the public right-of-way just as

94

one corporate juggernaut after another, full of big money and lawyers, hit town. Any illusions about designing infrastructure were quickly wiped clean. This was a brawl and many who thought they were in the middle of some genteel 'communications experiment' never knew what hit them.

Cable was the first cut at the post-war technical and regulatory structure of mass media. It embodies a few features of a telephone system, many features of broadcasting and a few that are completely new. One of those new features turned out to be local channels whose communications dynamics did not behave at all like broadcasting. These channels were more like electronic meeting halls that had the ability to bring together a bit of each viewer's living room to construct an entirely unanticipated community communications space. Add cheap US local telephones as a feedback loop and you have an 'interactive' system, and a very nifty organising tool. Something worth fighting for.

The cable access groups and organisations that survived did so by adopting a pragmatic organising style that wisely eschewed the rhetoric of 'high-radicalism' and 'post-political' scientism that permeated much of the alternative media movement of those times.[21] If there was any consistent rhetorical style it would probably best be described as invoking deep American traditions of community cooperation, civic discourse and free speech. Now, twenty to fifteen years later, cable access television centres are successful institutions that have become part of community life, in many cases at the centre of community life. They have become a qualitatively different kind of media practice; that is, publicly provided production equipment and channels with First Amendment protection allowing anyone (with the time) to produce in the dominant medium of the times for little or no costs.

The 1990s equivalent of the 1970s and 1980s struggle for public control of the local cable channels is clearly the community computing and civic networking movement. The struggle to secure a portion of cyberspace, or Vice-President Gore's 'information highway', is taking on a tone and rhetoric that is similar to that used by cable access advocates from the last two decades. They may also be making similar mistakes. Many cable access advocates thought that small format video and an abundance of local cable channels would be inherently democratic. There was the sense that the problems of television were technical: insufficient frequency space, 'not enough channels'. Of course the notion that social diversity in media could be achieved by providing more channels failed to understand that the diversity of media content is determined by information economics. The absence of diverse people and ideas in US media is a structural feature of commercial media and the market. It is not a technical problem, it is a social problem.

Many in the civic networking movement are enthralled with a similar idea. They believe in the inherent openness of computer networks. This is a notion that has captivated many thinkers in the recent past. This idea of openness views network structures as 'a natural repository of co-operation, equality and harmony. They are seen as systems of exchange and integration rather than violence and coercion.' It is not uncommon to encounter folks in the community computing movement who think that networks decentralise and dissolve the traditional pyramid structure of the bureaucracy and corporation, naturally. This ignores the distinction between 'technical openness in communication and widespread access to the competencies needed to communicate effectively'. It also ignores history. The same claims are consistently made for most new technology as it is introduced. Electricity was going to decentralise society. The rifle was going to make tyranny obsolete by giving each person a powerful weapon and ending the state's monopoly on violence; and the railroads were figured to end war by uniting people rather than speeding people to the front.[22]

Issues

Telecommunications and new media systems are the critical infrastructure of the times. Because that infrastructure is the technical core of economic restructuring it has become central to the direction of social and political change globally. That development is currently being driven by corporate and military interests. While new media and telecommunications offer considerable potential to empower and enhance the lives of the people of the world, the current mode of development (monopolisation and commercial control of information) represents a dire threat to democracy, biological diversity and the growth of any notions of democratic, civil society.

From this perspective there are two overriding issues. First, how can people locally, regionally, nationally and globally find a way to participate democratically in communication development. Keeping in mind that this question has very different answers depending on whether you live in a developed country or an unevenly developed country, it is possible to identify one common issue. That is that market driven development and commercial media systems by themselves are incapable of fostering democratic communication systems or assuring universal access to telecommunications for diverse people and ideas.

The second issue is defining universal access. Universal access must be defined socially not technically. This is particularly true as telecommunications networks become only the interlinking component in services that include metered use fees, and smart and expensive end-use software and hardware connecting to the edges of the network, all requiring enormously expanded user education and competence. That means universal access must be defined as the capability to construct significant, local, national and international audiences. This will be true for global computer networks as well as global television. It may be a different audience, assembled in a different time frame, for example, but the issue will remain access to both the system and an audience. You can have access to the technology and still fail to have an impact without a significant audience. This is the lesson of alternative media.

Alternative media is just that, something besides the mainstream media. That is not to say that the alternative media's work in creating media literacy, new forms of programming or a culture of media participation is not incredibly important work. It is to say that media dominance is a function of economic power, not truth, artistry or free expression. The ability to daily massage mass consciousness, to set the framework for public debate and delimit the universe of popular concerns means having the raw power to construct and maintain a large or significant audience. These are times when the US can move a half million troops and support around the world, invade a country or two and leave an occupation force in place, all in a couple of months. Popular support gets created by packaging the whole thing in the mass media as a sports event, complete with high-end graphics, computer simulations and live feeds from the 'front', giving the audience video images from cameras installed in the nose cones of descending missiles. Grassroots organising and local alternative media do not address this situation.

Cultural Resistance

Exploitation and tyranny have historically been accomplished through sanctioned violence and legal coercion, and there is surely no decrease in such methods in this calamitous century. But the information economy requires a whole new set of options. With our homes, public space, work places and our bodies, as well as our national communication policy, being penetrated by yet another round of media and electronic networks, exploitation and tyranny are increasingly accomplished through the complex manipulation of our symbolic environment.[23] Resistance to manipulation of the symbolic space tends to blur the lines between art and activism, and strategically it tends to make all sites of representation – art, advertising and media, for example – intensified places of struggle.

In popular culture this shows up as 'cyberculture' or 'cyberia'. This is the face of white, middle-class bohemia in the

1990s, and it is captivated by cyberspace and technology, by images of power and information, such as the advertising images melding souped-up engine parts with speedy, sleekly designed personal computers. In fact cyberpunk science fiction writer Bruce Sterling defines cyberpunk as 'bohemians with computers'. Cyberculture represents a heady mix of techno-shamanism, chaos theory, psychedelic and designer drugs, personal computer network wizardry, industrial music, video and audio experiment, house music and the standard varieties of anarchism, out of which has boiled up a series of images of resistance that were quickly seized by the media: cyberpunks, hackers, crackers, cyperpunks, phone phreaks and any number of mixtures of previously commercialised images of 1960s-style hippies and the more grim cyberpunks, fashioned after the style of the science fiction genre with the same name.

Much of cyberculture is the cutting edge of the emerging consumer culture of the digital age. This is a data storm of commercialism not unlike the one that played a significant role in burning the 1960s bohemia to the ground. A quick glance at any of its leading publications, such as *Mondo* or *Wired* magazines, reveals a host of advertisers hawking an enormous array of computer hardware and software, digital information appliances, new electronic mail and data base services, video games, CD-ROMs of every imaginable subject, music, videos, books and 'cyborg and techno-fashions', all pulling stylistic references out of the cultural impact of information technology on the body, mind and society. All of this is packaged for the digital 90s with recycled rhetoric from the 1960s utopian counterculture. A recent issue of *Mondo 2000* depicts a resurrected Dr Tim Leary making all the claims for Virtual Reality that he made for LSD in the 1960s. When *Wired* decided to use science fiction writer and cyberpunk genre guru William Gibson on their cover they instructed the photographers to 'make him look like a rock star'.

This is serious business, not resistance, and it is tempting to write it off as a complete loss. A critical look at expression emerging from this sector reveals an incredible blend of individualism, old avant-gardism dressed up in techno-fashion, rampant deconstruction and the worst kind of nihilism, signifiers and signifieds slipping and sliding into a heap of unspeakableness – poised to go crashing off into one reactionary debacle after another. But it's not that simple. It is important to keep in mind that this has been pretty much the nature of bohemia since the beginning of the industrial age and that it tends to be a vantage point from which both reactionary and progressive critique and art find their way into much wider circulation. Amongst the nihilism and commercialism you find people mounting real resistance to cybernetic capitalism as often, or at the same time, as you find them wearing advertising's symbols equating computers and communication with power, sex and money.

Cyberculture is also a place where you will find networks of people learning how to sabotage the modern information-based office or techniques of rewiring corporate surveillance systems to monitor management's monitoring systems. This a significant context for social, artistic and political experimentation, a zone of unpredictability and shelter for people fleeing or avoiding the repressive world of corporate space.

As more and more information is collapsed into each locale, more people are able to be in touch with other regions and cultures, and our economic and social relationships become more complex and contradictory; the sheer quantity of information builds, and social control and domination are increasingly involved with the manipulation of the symbolic environment. It is not surprising that a major kind of resistance to these shifts takes the form of fragmenting narratives, dismantling and deconstructing the information flowing on the networks and media. All sites of representation logically become more significant as sites of struggle in an information economy. It shows up culturally in many places, in fashion, gender-bending, musical styles, using drugs to fragment structured ways of mind; and in the use of new media to come up with new styles of representation that combine, copy and raid other media and art which is now readily available through the data networks directly, or indirectly through video and audio recordings or text and photos. Much of this work has done its part in identifying and confronting the structures of language, thought and representation implicated in oppression through race, gender, sexual orientation, class and regional difference.

In the context of an information-based economy, it's not so clear where real resistance will come from, or that critics will recognise it when it arrives. Cyberpunk science fiction was a case in point. It was frequently mis-recognised and implied to be nihilistic, or 'anti-humanistic', by critics; and, of course, science fiction is not considered a source of serious political critique, and for good reason in most cases. But listen to Bruce Sterling commenting on cyberpunk's passing into commercialism and non-distinction:

> In cyberpunk analysis, FRANKENSTEIN is 'Humanist' science fiction. FRANKENSTEIN promotes the romantic dictum that there are Some Things Man Was Not Meant To Know ... Dr Frankenstein commits a spine-chilling transgression, an affront against the human soul, and with memorable poetic justice, he is punished by his own creation, the Monster.
>
> Now imagine a cyberpunk version of Frankenstein. In this imaginary work, the Monster would likely be the well funded R&D team-project of some global corporation. The Monster might well wreak bloody havoc, most likely on random passers-by. But having done so, he would never have been allowed to wander to the North Pole, uttering Byronic profundities. The Monsters of cyberpunk never vanish so conveniently. They are already loose on the streets. They are next to us. Quite likely WE are them. The Monster would have been copyrighted through the new genetics laws, and manufactured world-wide in many thousands. Soon the Monsters would all have lousy night jobs mopping up at fast-food restaurants... This 'anti-humanist' conviction in cyberpunk is not some literary stunt to outrage the bourgeoisie; this is an objective fact about culture in the late twentieth century. Cyberpunk didn't invent this situation; it just reflects it... Jump-starting Mary Shelley's corpses is the least of our problems; something much along that line happens in intensive-care wards every day.[24]

This thinking arises from an extremely commercial genre, sci-fi, acting or being used to provide an important critique of the times. In spite of its domination by men writing for boys, much of it could serve as at least one of the guide books needed for late capitalism. That is in all likelihood the basis of its popularity. Even in its most commercial forms, cyberculture gives people some ways of constructing identities that are rooted in traditions of resistance and opposition to the consolidation of corporate control. While not perfect, this is surely a distinction worthy of consideration.

Of course cyberpunk's style and tone have passed into a general cultural sensibility by now. The transitioning image of hacker culture is instructive in that context. Originally 'hackers' were imagined to be bright, innovative, mostly young men, with entrepreneurial but unconventional, anti-authoritarian spirits – brilliant nerds, but basically good guys. This hacker culture, the mythology now goes, invented the Apple and Macintosh computers, and thus freed the masses by giving us affordable computing power with brilliantly designed control screens that were easily understood, almost intuitive. The early hackers started Apple Computers Inc. and hacker Bill Gates is on his way to being the 'Rockerfeller of the Information Age' through his near software monopoly at Microsoft Inc.

The hackers coming after the early development phase of the digital era have been represented very differently. Appropriating the imagery of cyberpunk sci-fi, the media have used it to tag a whole generation of computer hackers, who have been demonised and hunted down by federal authorities. In fact about all that remains of much of cyberpunk are the media's simplistic and romanticised notions of 'Data Criminals', 'Outlaw Console Cowboys', 'Cyberposers' and consumer driven role modelling, whose sole reason for existence seems to be to provide a legitimate reason for the existence of the beefed-up computer crime divisions of the FBI, or to provide yet another round of fashion for the mall kids.

Bruce Sterling's account of attending 'CyberView 91', a summer convention of the hacker underground, reads like an updated version of Sam Peckinpah's film *Pat Garret and Billy The Kid*.[25] In Peckinpah's telling of Billy The Kid, the frontier is being closed and the lawless anarchy of early development in New Mexico is being cleaned up and brought under the control of the cattle corporations, with the help of their puppets in the new state government. Of course the cowboy-outlaw culture is being forced to choose between their old way of life and joining the 'regulators'. Old friends are being split up, and Pat Garret and Billy eventually confront each other as icons of the conflict. At 'CyberView 91', Sterling reports a replay of the same scenario with many of the 'heavy hackers' looking at going to prison, under indictment or adjusting to their new life as ex-convicts. All for hacking their way into a few corporate computers and manipulating the telephone system. It was never clear that significant damage or theft had occurred from any of these stunts, in fact there is good indication that there was little to none. What is clear is that cyberspace's frontier days are closing and the cattle, uh, telecommunications corporations are doing mop-up. Predictably, many of the 'heavy' hackers are following Pat Garret's example and opening up businesses consulting in computer security and video game design. And once again we see that none of this is really new.

It is important not to minimise the significance of pop resistance in the information age, but it is equally important to see its weaknesses, or perhaps blind spots. Much of what gets portrayed as resistance is really nothing but extreme versions of the culture of privatisation. In the diversity of expression represented in cyberculture there seems to be consistently the same things missing. That is any kind of notion of commonwealth, or collective action, nor, with the exception of some science fiction, any critique of the information-economy, global capitalism or the power of telecommunications as a means of social control. Pop cyberculture's pretensions as a vanguard or edge culture is based on its willingness to take existing commercial cultural tendencies to their farthest extension. We see extreme commercialism discussed as a 'media virus', as a kind of organising tool. Cyberpunk heroes are typical American male literary constructions: psychologically isolated, lonely, painfully individualised characters who have been expanded, collapsed, fragmented, penetrated and simulated by technology.

One way to read cyberculture's fascination with the romantic notion of teenagers as data criminals or innovative venture capitalists, or the media's fascination with cyberpunk's isolated, street smart 'console jocks' and smugglers, is to read it as a kind of accelerated development project, a way of unleashing the most aggressive forms of individualist, entrepreneurial energy. After all what are software pirates, data thieves and designer drug dealers if not the cutting edge of digital consumer culture? This is not to suggest the existence of some vast conspiracy, rather it suggests that this cultural tendency fulfills a convergence of needs. For example, what better way to do research and development for the 'heavy' corporate players than to let some easily managed but nevertheless real 'fringe' group spin out something against which to test themselves? You do not have to decide to do that, you just have to need the conditions out of which it arises.

Chaos theory is interesting in this context as a metaphor for such an overarching capitalist development agenda. Based on the mathematical theories of Benoit Mandelbrot, chaos theory puts forth the notion that chaos has an order to it, that there is no real chaos in nature. Behind the incredible diversity of nature are patterns of regularity. Likewise capitalism is a process 'capable of generating a seemingly infinite range of outcomes out of the slightest variation in initial conditions or of human activity and imagination ... Behind all the ferment of modernity and post-modernity, we can discern some simple generative principles that shape an immense diversity of outcomes.'[26] It is worth considering for a moment that pop cyberculture seems to be fascinated with chaos theory because it feels like what should go in the silent, gaping, hole left by the absence of any understanding or critique of capitalist development. Something to mark a place in a radical utopian discourse so it hangs somewhat together?

Conclusion

Finally it should be noted that its pretty much cyberpunks all around. Andrew Ross has written that one way to understand cyberculture is to see it as suburban fantasy. A technocratic, mostly male, white middle-class conception of life in the inner city, where its audience of young urban dwellers grapple with their dark perceptions of urban life and the minorities and poor who live there.[27] This is a site where the worlds of policy and pop culture intersect. The Clinton administration constructs policy from the same point of view of the white middle-class suburbs. The Administration has been unable or unwilling to articulate an urban policy, consistently making political choices that protect the middle class at the expense of the minorities and poor. They have failed to confront the economic and social issues that would allow them to build any social or political bridges and common ground between the middle class, minorities and the poor.

The Clinton government and cyberculture have defaulted to a strand of technological utopianism and free market ideology in American culture. It is not surprising that the administration's attempts at policy and cyberculture's attempts at resistance to 'cybernetic capitalism' confusingly draw from the same ideological well. For now both have abandoned our traditions of community and civic culture, public space and values of commonwealth managed for the common good. Once separated from those values and traditions development options are extremely limited. It may be that their absence explains how early cyberpunk sci-fi's radical critique of capitalism devolves to the digital consumerism now being peddled in *Wired*, a magazine started by former Whole Earth Catalogue writers and now owned by a major publisher. The absence of a commitment to those values may also explain how the promising Clinton campaign with its rhetoric of social investment has been redefined as the Clinton administration's commitment to deficit reduction and 'redesigning government.'

It certainly explains how the Administration's communication policy proposals failed to be adopted by Congress. There was no popular understanding or support for the National Information Infrastructure proposal. Its rhetoric of democratic development to be delivered via the market fooled no one. Least of all the megacorporations driving development. They stalled congress while continuing to pursue their long-term interests. They have dropped any pretence of democratic development and continue to merge and globalise. The 1994 congressional elections brought in a Republican majority which is even more receptive to private development and market-driven information and media than the Democrats. The largest shift of US communications policy since 1934 is still underway but it's going even further right than most believed possible.

In times such as these it is important to hold in mind the notion that the power to control development, to structure time and space, which is what the new media and telecommunications are about, does not mean that the objectives of the powerful always win out. Contradictions arise.[28] The reason restructuring is occurring is to solve problems that have arisen for the powerful, problems they do not have complete flexibility in solving. For example, information systems are being introduced to give corporations the freedom to move and control the flow of capital, people and materials. But to make information more fluid opens up new means of expression and resistance.

New opportunities for resistance arise with the introduction of every control technology. Communications and control systems introduce new levels of speed and complexity that take decision beyond human control; they create new perceptions, new skills are required. More not less education is needed to work in an information-based work place, even one that has hard-wired two centuries of skilled labour into their robotics. While communications technology has replaced millions of workers it is not unthinkingly utopian to expect that similar technology could be used to create many jobs. It may even prove true that more cooperative, participatory and democratic work environments are more productive in the information economy. It is almost certain that if they are not they are at least more easily and non-violently disrupted.

Notes

[1] G.J. Mulgan, *Communication and Control: Networks and the New Economics of Communications*, Guilford, New York and London 1991, pp22-23.

[2] Kevin Robins, with Frank Webster, 'Cybernetic Capitalism: Information, Technology, Everyday Life', in *The Political Economy of Information*, Vincent Mosco and Janet Wasco (eds), University of Wisconsin Press, Madison 1989, pp46-52.

[3] Information Infrastructure Task Force, 'The National Information Infrastructure: Agenda for Action', Department of Commerce, 1993 pp3-5.

[4] Robert D. Kaplan, 'The Coming Anarchy', *The Atlantic Monthly*, February 1994, p59.

[5] Thomas Streeter, 'The Cable Fable Revisited: Discourse, Policy, and the Making of Cable Television', *Critical Studies in Mass Communication*, SCA 1987, pp180-181.

[6] Nicholas Garnham, *Capitalism and Communication: Global Culture and the Economics of Information*, Sage, London 1990, p121; Raymond Williams, *The Year 2000*, Pantheon, New York 1983, pp129-132.

[7] Streeter, *op.cit.*

[8] William H. Dutton, Jay G. Blumler, and Kenneth L. Kraemer, 'Continuity and Change in Conceptions of the Wired City', in Dutton, Blumler and Kraemer, (eds), *Wired Cities: Shaping The Future of Communications*, G.K. Hall, Boston, Massachusetts 1987, pp5-10.

[9] John Keane, ' "Liberty of the Press", in the Nineties', *New Formations*, 8, Routledge 1989, pp41-46.

[10] Garnham, *op.cit.*

[11] James R. Beniger, *The Control Revolution: Technological and Economic Origins of the Information Society*, Harvard University Press, Cambridge, Massachusetts 1986, pp6-13.

[12] Oscar H. Gandy, *The Panoptic Sort: A Political Economy of Personal Information*, Westview Press, Boulder, San Francisco 1993, pp35-52.

[13] Mark Poster, *The Mode of Information: Poststructuralism and Social Context*, Polity Press, Cambridge 1990, p75.

[14] John Pickles, 'Geography, G.I.S. and the Surveillant Society', *Papers*

and Proceedings, J.W. Frazier, B.T. Epstein, F.A. Schoolmaster, H.E. Moon, (eds), Applied Geography Conferences, 1991, pp82-83.

[15] Information Infrastructure Task Force, 'The National Information Infrastructure', *op.cit.*

[16] Garnham, *op.cit.*, p117.

[17] David Harvey, *The Condition of Postmodernity*, Basil Blackwell, Oxford 1989, p293.

[18] Doreen Massey, *Space, Place and Gender*, University of Minnesota Press, Minneapolis 1994, pp233-238.

[19] Michael P. Smith and Joe R. Feagin (eds), *The Capitalist City*, Basil Blackwell, Oxford 1987, pp14-16.

[20] Richard Civille, 'The Public Interest Summit is Today', Internet message, 29 March 1994. Text from the Internet calling a sprawling global network of telecommunications and network activists to attention in preparation for an interactive session with the first public interest policy conference staged in the US since the Democrats took office.

[21] William Boddy, 'Alternative television in the United States', *Screen*, Spring 1990, pp92-93.

[22] Mulgan, *op.cit.*

[23] Poster, *op.cit.*

[24] Bruce Sterling, 'Cyberpunk In The Nineties', *Well Gopher* (bruces@well.sf.c.us), 1991, p3.

[25] Bruce Sterling, 'CyberView 91', *Well Gopher* (bruces@well.sf.c.us), 1991, pp3-4.

[26] Harvey, *op.cit.*, pp343-344.

[27] Andrew Ross, *Strange Weather: Culture, Science and Technology in the Age of Limits*, Verso, London 1991, pp145-146.

[28] Harvey, *op.cit.*, pp179-184.

The Revelation of Unguessed Worlds

Jon Dovey

Video in New Media Utopias

> We have then to try and clarify, first, the new technology and, second, the effects this may have on institutions, policies and the uses of television. But we have to do this while remembering that the technology will not determine the effects. On the contrary, the new technology is itself a product of a particular social system, and will be developed as an apparently autonomous process of innovation only to the extent that we fail to identify and challenge its real agencies.
>
> Raymond Williams.[1]

In this chapter I want to locate video within the developing digital New Media. In particular I want to use the history of video technologies as a paradigm for thinking about how digital New Media will develop. My considerations of video are therefore part of the wider concerns of the book as a whole, especially in its attempt to re-historicise the current wave of 'New' (i.e. without history) Media technologies. Or, to use Raymond Williams' terms 'identify and challenge' the 'real agencies' of innovation. This work derives wholly from my biography – I have been working with video since the late 1970s, producing work within a tradition of counter propaganda that had its roots in what Martha Rosler has called 'the utopian moment of video':

> Not only a systemic but also a utopian critique was implicit in video's early use, for the effort was not to enter the system but to

109

transform every aspect of it and – legacy of the revolutionary
avant garde project – to redefine the system out of existence by
merging art with social life and making audience and producer
interchangeable.[2]

Those of us working with video have had the closest experience,
historically and technologically, to that generation currently
being inducted to computer-generated communications techniques. It is this experience that I wish to bring to bear as we
attempt to navigate the new territories emerging within the
digitally mediated world map.

A good deal of the writing about video in the 1970s and 1980s
concerned itself with what video was – what were its essential
characteristics as a medium? This tradition of work comes to a
merciful full stop with Fredric Jameson's conclusion that video
is the perfect, empty post-modern form:

> There remains to us only this pure and arbitrary play of signifiers
> which we call post modernism ... the logic of post modernism
> which I have tried to portray in its strongest, most original, and
> most authentic form in the youthful art of experimental video.[3]

I want rather to insist on and accept video's hybridity, the
difference which it reflects and replicates.

> Video media can only be understood as the product, the site and
> source of multiple contradictions, lived out in multiple practices,
> caught up in multiple struggles.[4]

Within this multiform practice I will also be looking at that
blighted, yet distinctive, flowering of video culture which is
represented through the widespread use of camcorders. I will
argue that camcorder cultures are making a significant
contribution to a radical reformulation of televisual and
cinematic realism. What interests me is the contrast between this
mass impact as I experience it as a subject and the utopian
predictions for low gauge video which greeted its birth.

Archaeologies of Utopia

Invention, innovation and the associated chimera of technologically mediated utopias have characterised the industrial and modernist age. Nowhere has this been more apparent than in the enthusiastic reception given to each new wave of media technology. Frances Frith in 1859, referring to photography's '*essential* truthfulness' writes

> we find it difficult to express how fully, and for how many different reasons, we appreciate this attribute of photography. We can scarcely avoid moralising in connection with this subject; since truth is a divine quality, at the very foundation of everything that is lovely in earth and heaven; and it is, we argue, quite impossible that this quality can so obviously and largely pervade a popular art, without exercising the happiest and most important influence, both upon the tastes and morals of the people.[5]

The very 'essence' of the technology, will, it is claimed, exercise a benevolent influence upon 'the people', technology itself equated with social change.

Here is the early American portraitist Albert Sands Southworth addressing the National Photographic Association of the US in 1870. His address culminates in passionate advice for the fulfillment of the promise of photography:

> Observation is the locomotive to be attached to the train of thought and engineered under your own conductorship; the power which turns the revolving wheels must be created by fuel from your own stores. Your freight is to be truth, and knowledge and wisdom, in all their purity, from the overflowing treasuries of the creator of nature. For your harvesting he has sown with a lavishing hand.

He goes on to insist that the photographic destiny is the delivery of truth:

> The question, 'What is truth?', began to be asked more than eighteen hundred years ago, and will continue to be asked as long as human nature exists.[6]

111

Here is the full force of the realist project in all its youthful, imperialist vigour.

Such texts also illustrate the importance of social context to the construction of the significance of media technologies – for Sands Southworth the new medium is a train, just like the iron leviathans that created America during his lifetime. Just like the metaphors for the colonisation of cyberspace which characterise discussion of the digital 'information superhighway'. The rhythm of the triumphalist hegemony of scientific rationalism sounds throughout early writings about photography – a medium which for the Victorian mind perfectly synthesised the virtues of Mechanics (Science), Nature (Truth), and Art (Man). The technology provides a sounding board against which the utopian aspirations of the age ring out.

Similar processes are at work in the reception of cinema at the end of the century. The promise of realism is further inflated:

> The cinema may not give a complete history, but what it gives is incontestably and absolutely true. Ordinary photographs can be retouched to the point of transformation. But just try to retouch, in a uniform way for each figure, those thousands of microscopic negatives.[7]

For the early cinematographer W.K.L. Dickson, the potential for cinema was even more wide ranging; leaders would be revealed 'intact with all the glowing personalities which characterised them', gone would be 'the dry and misleading accounts tinged with the exaggerations of the chroniclers minds.' Film would assist in the 'promotion of business interests, the advancement of science, in the revelation of unguessed worlds, in its educational and recreative powers, and in its ability to immortalise our fleeting but beloved associations.'[8]

Dickson's claims advanced for the technology extend much further into the realm of the social, transforming business, science, education and entertainment. In the phrase, 'the revelation of unguessed worlds' we hear that powerful note of visionary speculation which has continued to echo through writing about technology for the past hundred years, from the 'going boldly where none have gone before' techno-imperialism of *Star Trek* to the promise of transcendence in cyberspace. It is the visionary appropriation of media technologies as the engine of social transformation; innovation used to reinforce and amplify the interests of emergent groups in the culture, interests represented by their positive and utopian social aspirations.

This theme of visionary aspiration has not declined with successive waves of media technological innovation. Indeed, through radio and television, it seems to have intensified as the exponential curve of technological change has accelerated until we find ourselves awash in the neo-McLuhanite speculations inspired by digital New Media which are detailed in my introduction to this book. A brief summary will suffice here. The tired rhetoric of the old revolutionary avant garde is pressed into service again, this time in support of the inexorable march of multinational capital – art is finally over, dissolving into everyday life as consumers become producers. A New Renaissance of knowledge and creativity is promised; Euclid, Newton and Descartes are finally dragged across to the digital wastebasket of history as all difference is transcended in the highly publicised virtual worlds of the not too distant (but never to be present) future.

Even my brief examples of claims made for nineteenth-century media innovations should encourage us to start to recontextualise such grandiose claims, to examine their origins and the interests which they represent. Obviously it is beyond the scope of this piece to trace the subsequent histories of photo-mechanical media, to compare their social realities with what was originally envisaged for them. What I want to do now is to move on to consider some video histories. To compare the utopian moment of video with the utopian moment of digital new media which we are currently living through. As I've already hinted, the debates around video and television that took place in the late 1960s and early 1970s seem to me to suggest some of the nearest analogous enthusiasms and engagements to the current, early 1990s, wave of digital discourse.

Mongrel Media

Video does not have a single history – either as technology or form. We could, for instance, consider the impact of video within the feature film industry, from its influence at the point of production through the widespread use of 'video assist' on cine cameras, to applications in post-production where video is employed to create special effects, through to the revolution in distribution and reception created by VHS domestic markets. Or we could trace its impact on television, where tape made live television the exception rather than the rule, and the entire look of the medium has been transformed over the last decade by the use of video graphics. News and documentary television rely almost exclusively on video-based methods of production and transmission. Or we could choose to trace the impact of video within the educational and training sector, which has exploded on the back of video technology. Or the misnamed 'pop video', which although usually generated on film, has utilised every video post-production effect possible above and beyond the point of utter redundancy.

These are multiform, mongrel histories. Video moving into cultural spaces that already existed, changing them, inflecting them, hastening particular patterns of development. Effects which are comfortably absorbed within the existing cultural landscape. There is another history here too, video's own creation myth that functions alongside Louis Daguerre's unveiling of photography in 1839 or the Lumière Brothers first film show in 1895. This is the myth that takes us back to the New York Café Au Go Go in 1965, to Nam June Paik's first portapak playback show, and to his apocryphal soundbite 'TV has been attacking us all our lives, now we can attack it back'. This is a history that returns us not to a definitive explanation of the significance of video, not to some mythic canon of identity, but to an understanding of its own utopian moment. I want to look in a bit more detail at the kind of claims made for video technologies in the first decade of low gauge portable systems (1965–75) and to trace the connections and echoes between such

114

claims and the construction of the digitally determined future.

Paik's first remark about TV attacking us all our lives is worth noting, not for the spirit of guerilla TV which it has come to symbolise, but for the more obvious reason that Paik's *was* the first generation to have been brought up with television, the original forms of TV at that. The first decade of non-broadcast video coincides with a period in which the effects of TV in mass media culture were first beginning to be assessed by writers like Lewis Mumford, Raymond Williams, and Ralph Lee Smith, who wrote *The Wired Nation* in 1971, predicting 'the most total revolution that the human race has witnessed since the industrial revolution.'[9]

The most widely influential and popular writer in the field was Marshall McLuhan, whose infuriating tautologies and aphorisms created a popular discourse on the impact of electronic mass media which caught the imagination of the period. Transcendent, de-politicised and optimistic, his work stands in a similar relation as Baudrillard's to our own period, powerfully resonant without being the least use to anyone actually producing in the field. His work emphasised an infinite potential for electronic media that was later inflected by early video users.

> Ours is a brand new world of all at onceness. 'Time' has ceased, 'space' has vanished. We now live in a global village ... a simultaneous happening. We are back in acoustic space. We have begun to structure the primordial feeling, the tribal emotions from which a few centuries of literacy have divorced us.[10]

Observations such as these explain why McLuhanism is enjoying a revival amongst the enthusiastic explorers of cyberspace. Combining the idea that the human sensorium can be extended to encompass the whole world in an interactive relationship with the pre-literate global village concept more or less sums up the rave culture/cyberpunk interface.

Further in the same text we find McLuhan coming up with the kind of copy we now find encouraging us to hook up to the Internet:

> We have now become aware of the possibility of arranging the entire human environment as a work of art, as a teaching machine designed to maximise perception and to make everyday learning a process of discovery.[11]

Such a statement could also be taken as describing the potential of multimedia with its enormous educational data storage, conjuring up the revolutionary's dream of dissolution of the consumer/producer difference.

McLuhanism is here providing a kind of metadiscourse, a background primary colour scheme for those artists and activists involved in exploiting the new video technologies. Here is the first editorial of the magazine *Radical Software*, published in 1970 and entitled 'The Alternative Television Movement.'

> Power is no longer measured in land, labour or capital, but by access to information and the means to disseminate it. As long as the most powerful tools (not weapons) are in the hands of those who would hoard them, no alternative cultural vision can succeed. Unless we design and implement alternative information structures which transcend and reconfigure the existing ones, other alternative life styles and systems will be no more than productions of the existing process.[12]

Low gauge video is here seen as key to developing such 'alternate information structures'. Again much of the rhetoric translates to the 1990s; we could argue an equally forceful case for developing alternative uses of digital new media, for public service and democratic inroads to be made into the hegemony of the consumer market. This raises the possibility that not only the development of technologies, but also this 'techno libertarianism' is actually part of a continuous development that started at this time. 'When any two points on the earth's surface can be linked in a single second, there will be a steady decentralization of human affairs'.[13]

Certainly mass media were seen as having *intrinsic* democratic potential:

> The technologies of mass media communications (satellite, broadcast, cable, and closed circuit) make opportune a people's tool for access and input by the many into the decision making function of whatever social system prevails at any given moment. Here exists the arsenal of weaponry by which to *confront* the imperialization of the human intellect ... (my italics)[14]

There are particular qualities of video as a medium which suggested themselves as the perfect tools for promoting this slippery notion of 'access':

> Half-inch video tape is a new medium. No one really has a grasp of its full potential. But through our involvement with video tape for the last year or two things have become rapidly apparent. The first is that the medium is no longer the sole dominion of 'experts'. The technology is such that anyone with minimum training can have access to the medium. The audience no longer has to consist of large groups and the tapes do not have to appeal to mass interest.[15]

The fact that the moving image could be played back immediately was also seen as inherently democratic, offering subjects and participants a far greater measure of control over their representation. Indeed the National Film Board of Canada Challenge For Change workers were required to offer immediate playback and editorial veto to their subjects. Such notions of interactive feedback, accessibility, democratic working practices and resistance to dominant systems of representation combined into an often intoxicating brew:

> I have this utopian dream, wherein as the pollution and the smog slowly lift and the fires in the ghettoes die down, fish jump in the streams once more, greenery is renewed, people sing in the streets, one catches glimpses everywhere of a cable–VTR crew, composed of three people: Johnny Appleseed, Cesar Chavez, and a little old lady in running shoes.[16]

So, to summarise this utopian moment, video was seen as inherently democratic and challenging. Inevitably positive. It was seen as challenging of prevailing orders of media in the same way as many of the political movements of the period sought to challenge dominant power relations. The excitements offered by all new media forms are here seen representing the utopian aspirations not of the dominant class, but of the liberal oppositional movements of the West in the late 1960s. Concepts of access, interactive feedback and decentralised media were central to the way in which the technology was constructed. Unfortunately, and inevitably, neither the work nor the organisational abilities of the countercultural video movement proved able to deliver the promise which had created such excitements. The work was for the most part unwatchable beyond the immediate closed circuit audience of the producers. The institutions of mass media remained apparently unshaken. This massive dichotomy between the work and claims of the rhetoric is characteristic of the utopian moments of media technologies. It is hard to see how, on the basis of the actual work, the artist de la Roche forecast the death of painting in 1839 after seeing Dageurre's fifteen minute smudgy exposures, or indeed how David Hockney forecast 'the end of chemical photography' in 1990 after witnessing the wonders of photoshop. Again anyone viewing computer art, or trying to penetrate the mysteries of the Internet, will be familiar with the dichotomy between the sales pitch and the frustrating reality.

Camcorder Culture

I want now to consider some aspects of contemporary video culture. I have neither the space nor the inclination to attempt a review of the intervening history of video practices. I am concerned not with definitive histories but with an exploration of the practice of prediction with reference to technological media. I can only inflict some intellectual grievous bodily harm on history by noting how the video as fine art project has established itself as a central part of gallery practice, especially in its installation form, and in so doing has become very much part of the modernist canon which it sought to challenge. The democratic media, video access project has all but disappeared in its original form. Right up to the mid-1980s there were more than a hundred groups involved in this kind of practice in the UK; however these numbers have declined steeply as a result of ever decreasing funding and dwindling ideological capital.

Meanwhile, back in the multinational market place, far away from the white lofts of the gallery elite or the leaflet encrusted bunkers of the media activists, the hardware producers, Sony, JVC and National Panasonic had been steadily pursuing their original mission, the miniaturisation of consumer electronics. The first VHS, combined camera and recorder units become available in the mid-1980s. Size has been steadily reduced with the introduction of C format VHS, and Video-8 formats, quickly refined to include both the S-VHS and H-8 broadcast quality formats.

Around twenty years after the original visionary predictions, finally, those who could afford it could lay their hands on a very simple, very high quality system that allowed them to progress a little further along the arc of TV literacy, to start to write TV as well as to read it. Recent estimates are 40 million camcorders worldwide with 14 million in the US. Again, to pick up on a point made by Martha Rosler, it may be in the markets of the mass consumer that the more facile aspects of the utopian dream are recognised; that art and every day life finally merge, not in the galleries or manifesto-laden committee rooms but in the shopping malls. While the avant-garde becomes the academy, popular culture becomes mass media.

The camcorder has become a ubiquitous symbol of being, of having control, of presence. It has replaced the ghettoblaster on the streets of the US as the sign of being there, of patrolling, controlling your space. It is the physical manifestation for intervention in social systems mediated through looking. Camcorder practice is compelling, pleasurably, reassuringly self-defining.

The quality of the camcorder image has flooded our TV screens in the public sphere; however it is worth stressing that the pleasures of the camcorder begin with the private, domestic, the intimate, the subjective: the 'closed circuit'. They are used mainly as part of the home movie domestic photography cultural domain. Again, we see video in the shape of the camcorder inhabiting pre-existing cultural forms, that of the domestic photograph and the home movie. (Though it is worth noting that Super 8, the home movie film stock, appeared on the market in 1965, the same year as the first Sony Portapak.) Camcorders have however radically expanded and reshaped the home movie experience so that it now defines itself as a uniquely video based process. Super 8 movies from the 1970s now feel as distant and curious as black and white Pathe newsreels. The relative ease of use of the camcorder has seen it establish itself rapidly as an essential part of our family histories, documenting, prompting, and authenticating our domestic lives. (There is a parallel here between video and photography. It was not until 1888 that Kodak introduced the first domestic camera with the slogan 'You push the button, we do the rest', nearly fifty years after the original 'invention'. Yet it is the expansion into this domestic, consumerist sphere, that in someway completes and identifies the form for the mass of the audience.)

The instant playback quality so valorized by early video users here becomes a crucial part of the domestic context, process becomes part of the product. No sooner has the door closed behind the last child with its goody bag in its sticky hand than Mum, or Dad, and the rest of the 'inner family' flop down in front of the TV and re-run the whole of the kids' party on the VCR. The video is both an authenticating part of the whole process and an entertainment in its own right. It's important to hold for a moment or two in the pleasures of the domestic camcorder culture. For these pleasures, these audience responses, inform and determine our perception of camcorder material when it appears in other guises. In the domestic context we enjoy the shock, horror and delight of self recognition, we love the socially sanctioned opportunity to laugh out loud at our nearest and dearest, endlessly re-running the pratfalls and pitfalls of the video actors. The pleasures of domestic camcorder culture are all about defining our own individual family identities around a TV screen that usually pumps out bland, homogenised otherness; representations of other lives and other families that could never match the specific delights afforded by your own personalised, intimate, closed circuit production. (Even if your own life lacks the narrative coherence offered by the mass media versions.) What is on offer here is first person rather than third person, 'us-ness' rather than 'otherness', 'me' as opposed to 'them'. These are pleasures measured in hundreds of pounds, from around £500 for the cheapest camcorders to £2000 for a broadcast quality machine.

The important quality here is subjectivity. The camera is actually an accepted part of the event itself, neither outside, controlling and structuring, nor inside lost in the flow, but mediating for us between these positions. Anecdotal evidence also suggests that this flexibility is reflected in who uses the camera. It is no longer the invisible patriarch structuring the family album from behind the camera, its more than likely that all members of the family or group can 'have a go'. Intimacy, engagement and subjectivity replace structured poses in which meaning is precisely accrued through absence rather than inclusion. With these domestic pleasures in mind we can move on to consider some of the effects of camcorder culture beyond the immediately domestic sphere, in the wider moving image culture on TV.

First of all I want to highlight some of the overtly political uses of camcorder technology – uses which seem to me to echo directly some of the early predictions for video tape. Predictions in which the technology was seen as implicitly democratic when used in the particular cultural context that was concerned to challenge dominant power relations. These are examples of camcorder practice which use the technology for counter-propaganda or counter surveillance.

We could cite in this context the use of camcorder footage during protests against the Suchinda government in Thailand in 1989. Events in Bangkok were not being reported on government-controlled national TV. Camcorder footage shot on the streets recorded government troops attacking protesters with extreme brutality. The resulting footage was widely distributed in a number of contexts which are particular to the market conditions of South-east Asia. The rampant free market competition between video vendors on the street led to claims that each stallholder's edited compilations were more violent than the next. This competition is also based on an almost complete disregard for copyright law – footage recorded on the street was broadcast back into the country on international satellite, recorded off air on VCR then pushed back out onto the streets. The success of the camcorder subversion of the state propaganda machine was based on a commercial as well as political proposition. The combination of camcorder, VHS distribution and the satellite created a situation where the State could not control the flow of information.[17]

There are numerous other examples of camcorder use which both resists local power relations as well as attacking the hegemony of the North in global information production. These uses of the camcorder, echoing its domestic domain, seek to reassert the local over the global, to articulate the regional, the tribal and the individual over the multinational. The Kayope Indians of the Amazon basin are no longer content for visiting anthropologists to record their lifestyles, they now make their own programmes on tape. In the Bolivian Andes video is being used to document the lives of people by the people. In Ahmadabad, India a women's video collective records the struggle of the street vendors to get official licences; in the occupied territories of the West Bank and Gaza the Palestinians have deployed the camcorder to subvert Israeli media.[18] Australian Aboriginal people use video as a means of preserving and disseminating their cultures.[19] These are all examples of video again used as counterpropaganda, used as a way of speaking of difference, of the particular, rather than the endless replication of homogeneous *Dallas*-culture or 'first world' objective realism.

Then again we can find examples of camcorder culture as countersurveillance. As a means to collect evidence of oppression. This is a use of the technology that can be traced back to the earliest uses of the portapak to record the eviction of squatters from alternative communities in London's Camden. Today countersurveillance begins to operate on a global scale. Peter Gabriel and the Reebok Foundation have teamed up together to create 'The Witness Project': groups who are subject to human rights abuses worldwide are to be issued with Hi 8 cameras and fax machines in order to document their plight and collect evidence.[20] We have already seen how camcorders have been used in the US to document police brutality, most famously with George Holliday's tape of the Rodney King beating. However, this seemingly chance recording comes in a context where black groups such as the LA-based 'Coalition Against Police Abuse' have organised camcorders to surveille the police. Here, crucially, we move into the area of camcorder as evidence, as people's evidence used against the State. (This evidential status itself rests upon a whole set of assumptions about realism to which we will return.)

So there would appear to be a number of outcomes to the slow development of video represented by camcorder culture that bear out the predictions of the early video pioneers and visionaries. Video here appears to challenge the homogenous centralised power of capital to replicate itself through mass media. However it is important to note that these outcomes have developed from very different institutional bases from those envisaged during the late 1960s. Indeed, these outcomes are centrally related to the fragmentation of the entire political culture, a fragmentation in which mass media has progressed from structuring a homogenous consensual model of culture to the manufacture and replication of difference itself as niche market and cultural model. Video technologies have played a part in refracting this fragmentation; however it has been driven by far wider cultural and economic forces. What is notable about video in this context is the way that its insistence upon the particular and the specific is reflected in wider cultural developments, especially in the spread of 'identity politics' as a progressive discourse. It is also clear that notions of the evidential status of the moving image which derive from the age

123

of mechanical reproduction are here being given a further electronic lease of life.

Despite these apparent 'successes' for the 'techno libertarian' video project, there have been other, less foreseen though entirely predictable uses of camcorder techniques. Uses which are determined by the context of mass media culture, in particular in relation to economics, audience and notions of realism.

Accidents Waiting to Happen

Through the early years of the 1990s the whole presentation of realism has been transformed by the impact of camcorder techniques. Major programmes like *You've Been Framed, Video Diaries, Undercover Britain, Emergency 999, Private Investigations, Horizon, Video Nation, Living With The Enemy, Caught on Camera* have all been based on the use of low gauge camcorders or even smaller fibre optic-based minicams. Nor have the effects of the technology been confined to major TV projects; camcorder footage has infiltrated itself into every corner of television. *This Morning*'s Richard and Judy invite us to send in home videos of our ghastly domestic interiors for ritual humiliation and decor advice; kids' shows like *Live and Kicking* or *As Seen on TV* invite children to submit home made tapes. General Accident and Radion spend thousands on reproducing camcorder style for use in their advertising campaigns. Suddenly camcorder footage is everywhere.

Its embrace by the mainstream has been simultaneous with the development of the TV style known as 'Reality TV'. The two developments interpenetrate. 'Reality TV' is the vogue term for factual programming which uses camcorder footage, reconstructions, and narrative dramatic techniques to construct a raw, high energy and sensational form for factual TV programming. It has also been called 'Tabloid TV'. Camcorder footage is not a prerequisite for the style; however it is more likely to be present than not. The developments are related, and overlapping, through not causal in any simplistic sense. 'Reality TV' is driven more by the increasing competition for ratings within TV networks. The increasing dominance of the market squeezes the public service tradition of factual programming into more popular, more immediate, forms. 'Reality TV' offers its audiences the most sensational, tabloid, voyeuristic pleasures which it justifies by proclaiming them socially responsible, challenging, engaged or even access television. Within this broader mass media market framework the camcorder comes as a godsend to the mediocracy, the hard pressed TV executive can programme in camcorder footage knowing it will pull an audience and knowing that it's cheap. No crews to pay with their tiresome union agreements, no expensive equipment. You may even be able to get away with just some really cheap royalty payments if all you're doing is buying in homemade footage.

I would argue that it is the applications of the camcorder within the regime of 'Reality TV' that characterise the dominant face of its culture. These mainstream applications relegate the kind of radical interventions that I've discussed above to a continuing marginal position. I want to discuss these mainstream effects of the camcorder apparatus, with reference to the concepts of surveillance and voyeurism, concentrating upon the particular pleasures and power of camcorder footage for the viewing subject.

It is a commonplace of media studies that all new media increase the potential for Bentham's panopticon to be realised on a grand scale. It is clear that the increasing miniaturisation and sophistication of video technologies have made video surveillance a pervasive feature of our everyday lives. Contemporary security operations depend overwhelmingly on the electronic image, fuzzy date-coded frames from jewellers' stores, banks and shopping malls make increasingly frequent appearances on our TV screens and indeed constitute the main stories in shows like *Crimewatch UK*.

However, there is another aspect of surveillance that relates more directly to camcorder use. It concerns the way camcorders are now used to surveil one another. And here we have to radically reconfigure Bentham's panopticon. Here the process of state surveillance is delegated to any unauthorised deputy with a palmcorder in his or her hand. Police in the San Fernando valley California have equipped the local neighbourhood watch with camcorders;[21] a network news show in the US, *A Current Affair*, issues camcorders to a group of residents trying to clear prostitutes off the streets and broadcasts the results.[22] Parents surveil their kids for drug abuse, and vice versa.[23] Here's a panopticon where the warders in the all-seeing tower can go home, safe in the knowledge that the inmates are all busy trying to record each others' misdemeanours on videotape. In a particularly striking inversion of the public and private, a couple from Tampa, Florida, recently found themselves the victim of an 'invasion of privacy' court case brought by a neighbour. The neighbour alleged that his privacy had been invaded by the couple having sex in their bathroom; as evidence he used camcorder footage of the couple *in flagrante*. His case depended upon the fact that he could see *them* through the bathroom window from his backyard, and record what he saw on video.[24]

This use of the camcorder for a kind of lateral, intrasocial surveillance aptly demonstrates how the kinds of cultural form arising from a particular technology will reflect the social context. Here we have camcorder users assuming the evidential status of 'home' video in order to protect themselves (or the space which they regard as theirs within the domain of looking, within the public space). The camcorder is being used as a means to collect evidence which can be deployed to prosecute your own individual rights, your particular space. This may take the form of video as evidence against police or state oppression, or to control your neighbours, or the 'deviants' in your neighbourhood. These uses of the camcorder reflect precisely a sense of powerlessness in the user – a sense that the mechanisms of control have broken down. There is here a heavy investment in the idea that your own personal visual evidence is a defence against a world that is unjust, threatening and chaotic. A world where you know you'll be lucky if the cops even answer your call let alone do anything to solve your problem. The video vigilante is here recolonising the domain of sight in an attempt to impose his or her local and particular sense of order upon it.

These individual acts of surveillance reflect and support some of the uses of camcorder material within the 'Reality TV' regime; the sense of powerlessness is a constant dynamic of the 'Reality TV' narrative strategy. In the US, network programmes like *Newshound* or *I Witness Video* are based on non-professional camcorder news stories, which tend towards the disaster, the multiple pile-up, jumping from the burning building, and so on. In the UK Michael Aspel presents *Caught on Camera*, a similar compilation of gruesomely compelling 'happenstance' recordings. At the same time the massively successful *Emergency 999* is adapted from the US *911*, bringing us camcorder disasters and documentary reconstructions in which the essential narrative element of eventual safety is guaranteed. The emergency services are foregrounded, the new heroes who are there to protect us from all that is dangerous in the wild wood. Seemingly endless documentary and fictional series devoted to police, ambulance workers, firefighters, lifeboatmen, customs officers, and hospital casualty units testify to our deep longing for the agents of state promoted safety to keep the wolves of chaos at bay. So, whilst individuals deploy the camcorder to protect themselves, 'Reality TV' adapts the same techniques, trading in the same fears of powerlessness and disaster, creating new heroes and providing us with the comfort of narrative closure against our deep seated fear of accidental and sudden mortality.

The compulsions of 'Reality TV' cannot be divorced from the presence of voyeurism in camcorder culture, a theme which overlaps with the pleasures of home video viewing and which also informs our response to the TV screening of surveillance footage. Indeed surveillance footage represents one of the crudest satisfactions of the scopophilic drive, a sense of power at being privileged to see that which was meant to remain unseen: the point at which the private, connoted in the actual visual grainy texture of the wobblyscope camcorder image, goes public through TV transmission. Camcorder use in this context massively extends the potential for TV to function as cultural confessional. The *Video Diaries* format is the most obvious example.

Video Diaries have dealt with adolescent traumas, living with anorexia, dealing with death in the family, coping with cancer, watching your child die. Here is a voyeuristic loop, private pain becoming public pleasure in the domestic space of the private living room. It would be unfair to characterise all uses of this format as unremittingly mawkish; all kinds of subject matters have been dealt with, on a global and a local scale. However, they are essentially characterised by the sense of an intimate, private experience being packaged and structured for public attention. As such the diary certainly trades on our voyeuristic pleasures, the sense (again signified by the image texture itself) of the private, the intimate, and the domestic, entering into the public domain.

Again, this use of the camcorder cannot be isolated from other developments in the field of documentary. A great deal of the most interesting recent documentary film-making has been based on the development of reflexive techniques in which the film-makers themselves are made part of the story. I am thinking here in particular of films like Ross McElwee's *Sherman's March* or *Time Indefinite*, of Michael Moore's *Roger and Me*, of Nick Broomfield's films, *Driving Me Crazy, The Leader, The Driver, and The Driver's Wife*, and *The Selling of Aileen Wonours*. These films begin to mark the end of the direct cinema tradition as the dominant form of documentary practice. The film-makers deliberately put themselves into the frame. They deliberately construct narrative personae for themselves. These personae work to mobilise the audience's sympathy with the film-maker's point of view – they usually present themselves as anything but successful. This is the film-maker as klutz, the film-maker who makes mistakes, forgets things, retraces her steps, and, in the most significant figure, the film-maker who can't get the essential interview. If we are not terminally irritated by this refusal to assume the traditional authoritative point of view, then we will be recruited to the construction of the film-maker's subjective vision.

Video Diaries extend all these tendencies. The diarist becomes the subject, story, of the film whatever other issues may be under discussion. Subjectivity is the core of the form. Again we find in camcorder culture this insistence upon the individual, the particular, the specific experiences and vision of one individual testifying with his or her experience. The engagements on offer within this format are not the engagements of traditional factual programming; there is no balance, objectivity, or sense of arguments unfolding, research submitted in evidence; here is experience as evidence, raw and 'authentic'. Here the sense of audience construction is slightly different from conventional documentary or even 'Reality TV' programming. TV documentaries tend toward constructing an idea of an audience as normal, safe, middle class and secure precisely by foregrounding 'stories' that are extraordinary, dangerous, and from a world other than your own. They invite us to confirm what *we are* by looking at that which *we are not*.

Watching a *Video Diary* we are not asked to distance ourselves from the subject but to identify. We are offered a sense of intimate engagement with the otherness being portrayed. The totally subjective camera point of view, and the first person voice-over often spoken as live sync sound give us the chance to view the world through someone else's eyes. Not the usual opportunity to look at someone else looking at the world. Of course, at the end, we still step out of their world, with a 'there but for the grace of God' flick of the remote control.

Subjects and Subjectivity

One of the implications of the above is a new aesthetic of documentary truth: it is badly lit, subjective, wobbly; the more grainy it is the more it can claim truthful evidential status. This aesthetic should not be confused with merely a further development of the dominant direct cinema style. When we see the amateur video tag on TV news we are meant to read that the footage is even more truthful than it would have been had it been shot by the unlabelled 'professional' crew. However, this is very clearly *a* truth, not *the* truth. Whereas direct cinema sought to efface the presence of the film crew, to present unmediated reality, the new video gains its sense of authenticity precisely from the presence of the individual, precisely from the fact that it is personal, subjective, mediated. The video camcorder image is the mark of someone, a subject, having been there, an inscription of presence. This seems to me to constitute a major shift and one of the most interesting effects of video technologies. However it is an effect only distantly related to the predictions of the early video visionaries. The structures of power relations that regulate the mass media industries have remained completely unaltered by the challenge of democratic, accessible video media. On the contrary, every new stylistic development which video technologies suggested has been eagerly seized upon and recycled to further increase profit margins and audience ratings.

The utopian project of video failed because the political movements in which it was embedded failed. Nevertheless there is something in the early writings on video that does speak across the intervening years, a sense of how the technology might help the individual subject to have a different voice in the face of homegeneity. What nobody foresaw was that it would be the market mechanism that supported a culture of difference rather than a libertarian socialist regime. The effects of the technology have been played out within the dominant regime of realism, itself anchored in the forms of capitalism which developed during the last century. Whilst the globalisation and centralisation of media power has continued apace it has been accompanied by a seemingly contradictory fragmentation of cultures and political systems. The fragmentation has been reflected by the proliferation of subjective media forms such as camcorder video, which have served to undermine the citadel of objective realism. In an ironic way the traditional left critique of the TV documentary for the bias which lurks under the cloak of objectivity now gets its comeuppance – video-based forms that are anything but objective but which serve the needs of the market.

So the sudden infusion of camcorder truth into the mass media domain reflects wider cultural developments. Subjectivity, the personal, the intimate, as the only remaining response to a chaotic, senseless, out of control world in which the kind of objectivity demanded by grand narratives is no longer possible. A world where radical politics and critical theory are constantly defining and refining identity politics, the politics of the subject. A world in which the grand narratives are exhausted and we're left with the politics of the self to keep us ideologically warm. Video is playing its part in a wider process in which objective realism is slowly evolving into a different regime of truth. What is crucial here is that the technology can only be seen as one aspect of a complex set of wider cultural and economic shifts. The form which the technology adopts reflects and indeed embodies this wider context.

Postscript

I want to return finally to the digital, to the consideration of prediction with which this piece began. Part of me wants to reject the whole exercise. All the evidence of utopian prognostication for media technologies suggests that most cultural prediction is at best an inaccurate guidebook for the future. And the political crystal ball is no clearer: how many commentators fifteen years ago foresaw communism and socialism unravelling at such a rate?

But then again I can't quite shake some vestigial faith in history. There remains some intuition that there are fragments of my own cultural biography that I can salvage, and stitch together into some ragged map that could prove useful in the next fifteen years. So what do video histories have to say about digital futures?

What I have termed 'progressive' uses of video above have two characteristics. One is their assertion of the particular in the face of the homogenous. But the second is that they all occur within a political context, within a campaign, a struggle, a resistance movement. The kind of utopian manifestos which have become associated with New Media deliver the rhetoric but fail utterly on the organisation. They are without any sense of political context, of movement, of group. On the contrary the most critical fringe of digital culture defines itself around radical individuality – the hacker, the internet surfer, the garage graphics designer, isolated in the one-on-none screen matrix. If the utopian project of New Media is to progress, it will be because users rediscover some sense of individual identity within the group, some sense of collective resistance that is not defined by the technology but by the material conditions of life outside the net, the life that happens when you jack out. This tendency has already identified itself, as network communication systems like Greenet, defined around eco-action, begin to develop. (Fred Johnson deals elsewhere in this book with the kinds of political organisation that might form themselves within and around digital networks).

Camcorder culture might offer a couple of other entries for our guidebook. The surveillance connection between media and social control obviously becomes even more severe in networked communication systems. At least video has offered the possibility of counter-surveillance for some individuals and groups. I don't see much decentralisation of social control in a network system in which every communication is encrypted only by the US National Security Agency.[25] Where my every move within the net can be digitally tracked and used to define my consumer profile in ever more precise lines. As we have seen, a good deal of camcorder material deals with issues of personal safety and security in the face of a hostile world. Cable TV and phone companies already offer home security as a cable service, and it seems likely that this market will expand as we seek to ensconce ourselves ever more firmly into a digitally secured system that will defend us against the predations of an underclass whose power is the subject of endless media reduplication. Then there is voyeurism. What can we learn from

the recent exploitation of video within the market's regime of 'Reality TV'? Certainly that popular forms of digital media will be determined through market competition, rather than through the desire of the global entertainment and communications companies to foster a new age of enlightenment.

But more specifically the voyeurism of the camcorder cult offers us the vicarious experience of intimacy and intensity which is often missing from our human relationships. The network and, in the more distant future, VR, seem perhaps to offer all kinds of ways that this vicarious living could be extended. Multimedia pornography already offers a form of virtual sexuality that we are sure to see a lot more of. The live network bulletin board offers something like the telephone chatline but as yet without the same intimacy or sense of privacy. The idea that we could experiment with different kinds of identities in different kinds of communities suggests a whole realm of virtual relationships that seems in some sense to replicate the desire for the vicarious in camcorder culture. An entire, intense, various lifestyle that we can switch on or off. A virtual existence that perhaps offers the audience/player an even stronger sense of safety and security than TV.

What is not so clear are the market conditions that will determine what kind of experiences are to be sold to us. If 'Reality TV' is a response to the market condition of increasing competition within TV then can we foresee similar pressures in the digital communications marketplace? Presently the multimedia, VR and network fields all have slightly different market conditions, a survey of which is beyond the scope of this piece. However one only has to look at the Microsoft phenomenon to observe how monopoly tendencies are active across the distinct fields. It does not seem unreasonable to assume that if it is possible to market a digital version of tabloid culture then we'll be seeing it soon.

Finally, camcorder culture has diffused itself through consumerism, via the shopping malls and bargain basement electronic goods warehouses. Digital culture is disseminating itself through the same networks; Dixons and Argos will be the

site of propagation for the so-called information revolution. A digital utopia is predicated upon lots more shopping. Lots more money to circulate within the global systems that control production. Lots more profit.

Notes

1 Raymond Williams, *Television: Technology and Cultural Form*, Fontana, London, 1974, p135.
2 'Video: Shedding the Utopian Moment', Martha Rosler from *Illuminating Video*, Doug Hall and Sally Jo Fifer (eds): Aperture/BAVC 1991, p31.
3 *Postmodernism, or, the Cultural Logic of Late Capitalism*, Fredric Jameson, Verso, London 1991, p120.
4 Sean Cubitt, *Videography*, Macmillan, London, 1993, p3.
5 Frances Frith, 'The Art of Photography', in *Art Journals* [1859] reprinted in *Photography: Essays & Images*, Beaumont, and Newhall (eds), Secker & Warburg, London, 1981.
6 Albert Sands Southworth, 'The Early History of Photography in the US', *British Journal of Photography* [Nov 1871] reprinted in Beaumont and Newhall, *op.cit.*
7 Boleslaw Matuszewski, *Une Nouvelle Source de l'Histoire* [1898] quoted by Jay Leda, '*Films Beget Films*,' London, 1964.
8 W.K.L. Dickson, *History of the Kinetograph Kinetoscope and Kinetograph*, New York, 1895.
9 Ralph Lee Smith, *The Wired Nation*, 1971.
10 Marshal McLuhan with Quentin Fiore, *The Medium is the Message*, Penguin, Harmondsworth 1967, p63.
11 *Ibid.*, p68.
12 Michael Shamberg (ed), 'The Alternative Television Movement', *Radical Software*, Issue One, 1970. Reprinted in *Video in Community Development*, Ovum/Centre For Advanced Television Studies 1972.
13 Arthur C. Clarke, 'Everybody in Instant Touch', *Life*, 25 September 1964. Reprinted in *The Coming of the Space Age*, Gollancz, London, 1967.
14 People's Video Theatre, 'Proposal for Video Theatre', *Radical Software*, Issue Two, 1972. Reprinted, *op.cit.*, p.45.
15 New York University Media Co-Op, *Neighbourhood Video Workshop* 1971.
16 Dorothy Todd Henaut, *Challenge for Change Newsletter*, No.8, Spring 1972.

[17] *Tactical TV*, APT Film & TV to Channel Four. Transmitted 24.5.93.
[18] *Ibid.*
[19] *Satellite Dreaming*: APT Film & TV to Channel Four: Transmitted 3.5.93.
[20] Witness Project Press Release, 24 June 1993.
[21] *Videos, Vigilantes and Voyeurism*, director Fenton Bailey, World of Wonder Productions to Channel Four. Transmitted 27 April 1993.
[22] *Ibid.*
[23] *Ibid.*
[24] *Ibid.*
[25] Mike Holderness, *The Guardian*, 3 March 1994, p17.

Who Gets to Play? Art, Access and the Margin

Ailsa Barry

The Magic Box – A Future Fairy Tale

Once upon a time there was a poor artist. He had the most wonderful ideas but he didn't know how to express them. He tried painting, drawing, photography, writing, singing, and sculpture but they all lacked something, and no one could see what wonderful ideas he had. Every night he donned his magic beret and wished, 'Please find me a paintbrush that will express my ideas. I want the whole world to see them'. One morning after he had been particularly kind about the works of other struggling artists he woke up to find a computer at the end of his bed. Tied to it with ribbons were several plump manuals.

He quickly got to work and within no time he had produced magnificent work which explored the richness of his imagination. Everyone who saw the work was amazed and soon it was travelling along cables and networks to every home in the country (that had a computer) and was being beamed by satellite across the world.

Origins of Myth

This, like most fairy tales, is attributed to an anonymous author but one suspects that it could have been created by the marketing departments of any multinational computer company. Who started this myth and why do we all believe it? Its origins could lie with the computer gurus.

Steven Levy, Stewart Brand, and magazines like *Mondo 2000*, have all espoused the dream that computers and their networks will give access to information and they will become convivial tools in a cultural democracy. For groups that have traditionally been disenfranchised, not having access to the main economic and political channels of power and communication, there is a promise of a new digital voice. This chapter will provide an introduction into some of the issues and problems which arise when such concepts of 'access' are applied within the emergent field of digital media.

A convivial tool is one that is easily accessible and can serve the individual's needs and demands rather than those of society's managers. The computer, an expensive machine which is not simple to learn, is not an obvious contender for this role. Its promise lies rather in the unpredictable development of its use. Concepts such as shareware, where computer software is distributed free or for a minimal contribution to its authors, were hardly expected to emerge from the computer's military origins. Shareware allows software to gain wide distribution and be further developed, and is recognised as a contributing factor in software development. It epitomises a fundamental belief held by many in the computer community, that the building blocks of this information society must be free and that knowledge can no longer be a commodity controlled by a few.

The Internet offers a similar promise of distribution. Through bulletin boards or special interest areas users are able to access and distribute information for all to see, bypassing conventional methods of mass communication and distribution. The ideas, injustices and hopes of the world's population are available for anyone who has the time and inclination to view them. It is within this framework that computers are seen as potential convivial tools which will open up channels of information exchange to presently 'disempowered' groups.

Artists fall into this category even though their disenfranchisement might be self imposed. Within the past three hundred years artists have developed their position of muse in western society by gambling economic security. Their position on the fringe of society has been formalised and has given the artist a credibility to reflect and remark upon the society in which they live. However the very position of 'outsider' that has given them credibility has also made it difficult for them to be heard or listened to. The emergence of computers and networks, which make work easily reproducible and transportable, has suggested that work which can be made at home for a minimum outlay will then be easily accessible to a wider public, bypassing the moribund channels of galleries and museums. The artist's voice, as social critic and even 'shaman' will have found a more accessible channel of communication. This promise has been combined with the promise of the equipment itself, that not only is it 'the fastest route from imagination to reality'[1] but also that its use enhances the creative powers. The non-sequential element of computer data has facilitated the montaging and collaging of information in an unprecedented manner. There is a new collision of media allowing the artist to call on a wider range of expression. This new medium can be set in an artificial space, a vast conceptual world where the audience or viewer can interact or participate.

Dragons in the Tale

The reality is that accessing the equipment, let alone distributing the work, has particular difficulties and implications. This is compounded by the newness of the medium itself, which is confronting artists with issues of practice that are only realised as the technology is explored.

The nature of digital technology is challenging the artist's autonomy both in terms of economics and origination of material. The role of the artist as muse or social critic is implicated in these changes. As the role of the artist shifts we may have to face the possibility that although the dissolution of 'the artist' as a privileged and isolated position may be laudable, it could diminish any critique that the artist wishes to make. There is no guarantee that it will be replaced by more open channels of social criticism and commentary. New models of access and distribution may well erode the independent critical voice, merge it into a stream of digital bable. That such a wide range of issues would develop could not be foreseen in the fairy tale and the road to conviviality and new expression seems set to take a few unexpected curves.

The New Muse – Author or audience?

The promise has been that interactive new media will provide a 'powerful combination of interaction, graphics, sound and music'. The reality is that the use of new media and its interaction often disengages the viewer. This disengagement is inherent in the very act of interaction, and its dogmatic binary yes/no choice. No room for the enigmatic here, and audiences participate less for the promise of content and more for the concept of interaction. Interactive flow is becoming as important a consideration as content or narrative. This has re-opened theoretical debates, involving content versus process, that have lain dormant since the death of modernism.

It can be argued that the limited hierarchical choices on offer do not compensate for the rich and enigmatic layering of meaning and nuance that can be achieved in most arts medias. The counter argument to this is that interaction changes the way the audience engages with and receives the work. The work receives a greater proportion of its meaning from the audience itself and audience participation becomes vital to the content of the work. Interactivity is therefore blurring the distinctions between artist and audience. They are becoming co-creators in the work, breaking down the boundaries between the roles.

From the inception of the work the artist is now taking into account audience involvement. This subtly shifts the artist from the position of an individual muse and increases concern for direct public engagement with the work, challenging the traditions in mainstream and experimental art practices, in which the artist places herself outside of audience interaction.

Reproducibility – a Edged-double sword

If, as the gurus of the future predict, the artist's work moves away from a material commodity and into a realm of pluckable and reusable images, then the artist's role shifts again.

Digital reproducibility and manipulation of information has dovetailed perfectly into late twentieth-century deconstructivist culture, allowing both the artist and viewer to copy, merge and collage new images and sound from the old; resignifying material so that it has relevance now. This process has implication for authorship and copyright that are not easily solved. Copyright lawyers are working furiously to sew up loopholes in digitally copying, sampling and collaging images, and Microsoft is buying up digital copyright to thousands of works of art.[2] However the ability to infinitely reproduce information and images has brought us to a watershed in the concept of authorship being synonymous with ownership. The lack of an 'original' and the endless reproducibility of the work gives credence to the argument that if there is no authentic product there is no authentic producer. The role of the artist is again questioned.

Distribution on the network has compounded the problem. Images can be sent on-line to be exhibited, circulated and accessed. Artists are using this venue to distribute work, thereby ensuring that it is seen by a wider audience and not edited by a third party. Otis, a nominally managed electronic gallery, suggests that a copyright clause can be put upon the work and that the images should not be utilised without payment to the originator. The National Writers Union in the United States has also taken a firm view that work should not be circulated and utilised without payment.[3] But this is by no means a consensus view and the issue of ownership of digitally authored and circulated images remains contentious. The artist's position appears ambivalent: as producer the wish is to have the freedom to assemble and re-use images, and the legacy of computer shareware enforces this notion of freely distributing and re-purposing images and information. However, once work is created the same artist is likely to want it to have full protection and copyright.

Without copyright protection and payment for work created the artist loses a means to economic autonomy, and must increasingly rely on work that is commissioned for clients and patrons. Work that is artist devised and driven is less likely to be developed.

As 'art' becomes increasingly less tied to the material artefact and more reproducible the traditional forms of money spinning from the art market will be reassessed. If artist's work is impossible to own is it an investable or protectable commodity? The myth of the artist is in part tied to the unpredictable economy of the art work. If this shifts as art merges into everyday unpaid consumption then the artist loses economic and social autonomy.

The Cost of Collaboration

Further to this is the realisation that multimedia is a medium of collaboration. A work is generally a collaboration between visual artists, musicians, computer programmers and performers, more akin to film or TV than traditional fine art practice. This alters the perception of the artist as a single muse and shatters her economic autonomy. The production of multimedia work is enormously labour intensive and expensive; it requires technical support and fluency in several software platforms. The creator needs to gain funding and support from an institution or commercial body to support the project. Although some software may be freely available the equipment and training to use it is expensive. It is not enough to feed oneself, one has to feed a costly technical habit. The question is, who will be making these large economic ventures affordable?

Games production is where it is suggested that the money will be made, and the ability of the new interactive films to attract viewers will be dependent on their ability to have visually stimulating graphics. The artists of the future will have a protected niche in creating visions in a fantasy environment and will become 'experience designers'. Their long vigil in the cold seems set to be ending but what of the poor misfit who still wants a critical voice? As creative expression becomes more obviously confined to Nintendo games, interactive TV and market forces, will digital graffiti develop to shake us from our comfortable consumption?

These issues all have immediate implications for the place of the artist in society. Changing patterns of distribution and access further affect the nature of the medium and the role of the artist. However at present the uncertainty in gaining access to the production means and distribution mean that the critical body of work that is needed to assess the medium and the changes that it is creating is slow to evolve.

Current Access

Access to computers and the decoding of their information is still restricted to relatively few. The development of the games and entertainment market, the possibility of interactive television and of the promised digital highway has reinforced the belief that common access to the computers and new technologies is imminent. However easily affordable and easy to use consumption technology is not equivalent to having moderately priced computers capable of producing, outputting and receiving high level multimedia. It is simply giving easy access to another closed and controlled way to receive information rather than produce it.

Although the computer, like the telephone, is an encoder of information and a potential means of communication, the similarity ends there. You cannot learn to use it within an hour. Even computers which are known to have user-friendly interfaces require intense teaching to understand simple graphics programmes. Presently the average primary school child in Britain has access to 45 minutes a term of hands-on training on the computer. It is exceptional to leave school with any fluency

142

in a graphics software programme. In undergraduate art colleges it is a battle for students to gain hands-on experience with the computer and this is generally limited to those who are specifically learning 'new technologies' or computer-aided design. It is therefore not an easily accessible medium for creativity and unless there is a rapid increase and change in government priority it is not a medium that will allow a common fluency in its use for ten to fifteen years. The consumer market and commercial capabilities of the medium will have exponentially grown in this time.

So it is fair to say that within that timespan the work that will emerge will be from those artists who can gain exceptional access and knowledge of the technology. As it is a medium that is continually changing and updating it is not enough to have sporadic access; constant access is needed to maintain a fluency in the software programmes. Exceptional access to machines and training can at present be sponsored through a few educational institutions and public funding organisations. Support for such access is oversubscribed and artistic status and track record are generally criteria for being sponsored; artists with this status generally already have other channels of communication. This pattern of frustrated access blocks any potential of the computer to develop as a convivial tool. There is no evidence to suggest that current patterns of artist's limited access to hi-tech fields such as video will change in the emergent digital discourse.

The Independent Path: Access and Production

There are at present digital arts agencies, that are government funded, that make an effort to give independent users access and training. Artec in London, is a publicly funded body that specifically explores creative applications of digital technology. It produces creative multimedia projects on a non-profit basis and develops strategies to give artists access to digital media. Over the last three years Artec has found that one successful approach for access is through developing project work that artists can have hands-on participation in.

Giving access and training on machines only partially solves the problem of learning the new technology; the most expensive part of learning this technology is the time commitment that is involved in gaining fluency. Through developing projects in collaboration with artists and securing funding for them, the artist's time, training and access are built into the project costs. The artist can then work with a team of creative multimedia designers and learn the conceptual issues inherent in multimedia and software skills. Training in software skills is also available to groups on a non-profit basis and a successful year long training course in multimedia is run for unemployed adults.

Similar agencies are developing at Lighthouse in Brighton, Artimedia in Batley and Watershed in Bristol; others are developing in Cambridge, Newcastle and Liverpool. An arts network that will link these centres and allow for on-line collaboration is in the process of being developed. The difficulty with all these agencies is that the amount of training and access that they can give is miniscule when measured against the tide of interest and requirements.

Down Time

Another form of independent access that has been suggested is 'down time'. 'Down time' is when expensive digital equipment not being used by the commercial body or institution that owns it can be used by non-commercial groups to develop their work. The reality is that most multimedia industries are furiously driven by 'just in time management'. As they lurch from each creative crisis there is not much 'down time' left for those not fitting into the next production budget. This is exacerbated by the fact that most improvements in the technology are made to increase productivity and reduce time costs, and are advertised as such. The free access time that is left is limited to those with the ability to work in the remaining 'down time', usually at night.

Lo-Tech

The other way to solve frustrated access is through the artist procuring the most basic computer and a few photocopied manuals and hacking away. Is it necessary to make an impact within the medium to have the latest in powerful computers and digital technology? Like the development of the early days of video or performance art the newness and scarcity of the product guarantees a hearing. As the consumer and the critical bodies gain more choice these guarantees will fade. The ability of the games and entertainment industry to produce increasingly sophisticated graphics will widen the gulf between the small independent producer on their lo-end machines and the large teams working on high powered machines producing glossy graphics. The success of the medium will eventually work against independent lo-tech work getting distributed.

In a sense this is the failure of the promise of video access. Viewing and making videos has become common practice. There are, for example, 100,000 video outlets in India.[4] In Britain, British Telecom is developing an interactive video library: the telephone will allow videos to be accessed directly to your television. We are now swamped with cheap visual data. We need criteria to sift this data, and the paradox is that one of the criteria we still use to judge whether information is worth our attention is its apparent unavailability. While a medium is new and fairly rare it will receive attention and critical acclaim, but as it succeeds and becomes commonplace the standards by which it is judged increase. A pattern will emerge where marginalised groups will have to maintain increasingly higher standards to maintain their digitalised voice. Small groups will find it difficult to maintain independent development of an increasingly professional standard and will need to have access to expensive and specialised platforms that can only be supported by technical specialists in that area.

At this moment it is possible for marginalised groups to take advantage of the newness of the digital frontier. There is an eagerness to view the work and, like the exploration of frontiers of old, there is a willingness to fund the marginalised and the dispossessed to open up the area and pave the way for further development. Training is presently available to the unemployed, women and ethnic minorities. There is, therefore, a moment when the computer is a convivial tool, where it is accessible to serve the needs of the marginalised groups within the society. But this is a result of the newness of the medium rather than of any safeguards of the medium itself. As such it should be treated as a hiatus in a pattern of development rather than a prediction of a future trend. It is likely that, unless a common fluency in this medium is established across society and positive steps are created to develop continual access after the initial hiatus, digital technology will become increasingly inaccessible to marginalised or non-commercial groups.

Distribution Digital Highway Versus Digital Dirt Track

Access has two sides; one is the access of the artist or group to the medium, the other is that of the public to the work. Adequate distribution of work to a larger public is one of the main hurdles for much creative work. It has been a particular problem in the development of video work. The distribution of digital production is at present uncharted territory and can fall broadly into three areas: networks, CD-ROM or CD-1 publication, or exhibition format. All of these methods of distribution are not yet clearly defined.

Perhaps the main promise of the computer as a communicator is that the personal computer on your desk is not a closed system, and with relatively little expense can be converted to an access point on a global network of information transmission. The digital highway at present is only a digital dirt track, accessible to a few, in possession of the right vehicles; but its rate of expansion will probably outstrip the speed at which computers are taught in schools.

The Internet was conceived by the US Department of Defense. In the late 1980s it expanded to allow national

146

academic institutions to have simultaneous access to five super computers. Universities in other countries quickly set up links. Today there is access in 60 countries with an estimated 20 million users growing at 10 per cent a month. In the United States the expectancy of a telecommunication infrastructure as an inalienable right has led to a much faster development of the network and its use by non-commercial groups. In Britain the nature of the telecommunication system has led to a slower and more fractured development. However, within this digital dirt track the shape and potency of the medium is beginning to emerge. Until recently in both the States and Britain networks have been accessible only through commercial or educational institutions. Accessibility has therefore been confined to the individuals or groups which are party to those institutions. The networks that are available through such institutions, although generally slow, support a wide range of services and text and graphic images can be easily circulated and accessed.

The cost of linking onto a network and the Internet has in the past been prohibitive for the individual, but recently small commercial companies have given access to the Internet for a nominal hook-up and monthly rental fee. In England, Demon, a company with this policy, set up in 1992 and now has 4000 users.[5] For the user however there is little software support or easily understandable technical advice on how to access and circulate material. A degree of technical proficiency is therefore needed to move through the system. Setting up a modem to connect onto the Internet is also a highly skilled job and one needs technical help or a buddy system to achieve it. The network as a tool of accessibility and conviviality is therefore hampered by prohibitive costs or by the degree of specialised technical competence that is needed to use it.

The underlying question of the network is whether the promise of independent bulletin boards and virtual communities will remain or whether the control will come to rest with the mega corporations that own and control the channels of communication. As TV and telephone monopolies merge to control the highways of communication, they will have the power to enforce tighter restrictions on the users and to control the economy of access. Issues of authorship could be further muddied as it becomes unclear whether the information belongs to the sender, the receiver or the owner of the channel of communication. The digital copyright could end up being the prerogative of the networks.

ISDN

Presently the unco-ordinated way that the network has developed means that it can take a variety of forms, from fibre optics to copper wire and cable. These platforms can each deliver different quality and rates of information. However there are constant improvements made in the amount and quality of information that can be squeezed down the wire, and although work is presently predominantly text-based, it is likely that multimedia work will become available on the network in the near future.

ISDN is at the moment the most achievable way of sending real-time multimedia to separate sites. It offers two separate digital channels over a single telephone line to send or receive large volumes of data images or text at very high speed while discussing it on the telephone. Commercially it has been developed to increase productivity and reduce time costs while improving the quality of communication, and it is used primarily for video conferencing. For artists it gives rise to a new forum for the development of performance based art. The setting up and maintenance costs of ISDN links are presently prohibitive in England.[6] Sponsorship for specific events therefore needs to come through large, wealthy funding bodies who have their own agenda for supporting such events.

As the ISDN networks are only developed for specific events, the work created becomes performance and event driven. The performance of such new technologies becomes the prime attraction rather than the content of the collaboration. The work is developed on-line, the creation is the event and the successful event has the immediacy and vitality of good performance art.[7] ISDN links are being curated regularly by organisations such as Electronic Mural in the United States. But as one-off events they cannot be confused with a viable mode of access for marginalised groups.

The Medium Dictates

It is on the digital highway that our present concept of the artist and the production of artefacts is being most rigorously re-assessed. For those who have a gateway to the network the pure computer artist is not concerned with the production of artefacts, but in the contribution and initiation of ideas, and the accessing and collaging of images. The role of the artist shifts again and the work that they are creating changes to accommodate the medium.

The network was created for speed, by a society that is fuelled by speed and judged by its ability to create and maintain speed. In the end it is inevitable that this premise will affect the type and the way in which work is created for the network. The need to develop artefacts has in the past slowed down our incessant greed for new images and for storing and accessing endless amounts of material. There is a maximum speed at which any system can operate before beginning to decay. Perhaps there is a maximum velocity at which we can usefully sort and retain images. The more images we create and re-image the less time we have to reflect on what we are creating. Creative production assumes judgement and reflection.

Through its emphasis on immediacy and speed, and the dismissal of the necessity of real artefacts, the digital highway is in danger of dismissing vital critical attributes of the creative process. We are increasingly moving away from real sources of information to electric ones. The creation of digital work from purely digital information means that the work that is produced has even less contact with the reality around us. Instead of enriching the creative process, faster access to images and information may simply make us more efficient managers and harbourers of visual information.

Distribution Through Disk

An alternative distribution of digital technology is through the publication of work on a CD-ROM format, or through one of the interactive video formats of the future. At this time this form of distribution is more viable than trying to access similar data down a telephone line and through a modem. Large quantities of data can be accessed for a moderate initial outlay. The format offers potential not only as means of distribution but as a medium in itself. The ability to press onto this five inch disk multimedia software that introduces a time element, interactivity and the potential to collage sound, video, graphics and text, creates an attractive medium. It has rapidly moved from a cataloguing system of digitally produced and reproduced images to a new medium.

The production of multimedia work for a CD-ROM is again labour intensive and expensive. The funding available to gain fluency in the applications and access to the computers is negligible. Having gained access and funding for production there still remains the problem of publication and eventual distribution. The cost of pressing a CD-ROM disk is nominal and it is likely that small independent publishers will soon be able to press work that has been produced outside of the commercial or educational realm. But at present in Britain an adequate network for distributing and publicising such work is unavailable. Unless the commitment to fund the publication and distribution of such work is developed, the medium will again end up as a commercially driven commodity.

Exhibition

The new media are not limited to display on monitor either

through networks or CD and CD-1 format. Distribution and access can also be found through installation and exhibition. However, the development of sponsorship and funding for the mounting and organising of electronic and digital work is at the moment several magnitudes higher than an exhibition based on a traditional medium. This makes it extremely difficult for events to be mounted that cannot muster strong regional and national support. The logistics of locating and organising the expensive equipment required means that specialised agencies are developing to meet these needs. Although these organisations are often heavily subsidised, alleviating the actual economic costs, another layer is placed between the creator of the digital work and their ability to locate a path of distribution to a wider audience.

Another Wish?

Access to a computer and the development and distribution of digital work does therefore not necessarily have the fairy tale ending that has been suggested. The ways that it will change the manner and distribution of work, and the role of the artist in society, are fairly complex. The inaccessibility of the hardware and the difficulties in procuring training to learn software will create further difficulties for artists or any other group that does not have instutionalised access. It is likely that changes will occur before the majority of members from these groups have had a chance to partake in the digital world.

However, it becomes increasingly important that such groups do develop and maintain a digital voice. The computer is shaping the nature of our emerging information society. Its ability to access large amounts of data and reorder them is gradually affecting the way that we organise the fabric of our society. Increasingly finance, education, health, police, transport, and science and technology are becoming wholly reliant on digital technology, and these groups are reorganising themselves to be compatible with the technology. Survival skills

151

within the society are going to depend on being able to work with and understand electronic media. Access to the media and the networks of communication by only part of the society will inevitably lead to an Orwellian scenario of the future.

Beyond ensuring our own survival is the necessity for different components from the society to have the ability to play with the medium and to shape the way in which it might develop. This is crucial because of the powerful dual nature of the tool, both as a medium and a mediator of information. It is only through a broad range of access and distribution that we will safeguard that the medium remains a channel of communication and not just a channel of consumption. We have now recognised the necessity to safeguard access to information and protection of data in this information society; the need for broad access to computers, training and information networks must now also be recognised and ensured. At the moment there is the danger that a very powerful and creative medium will only be accessible to and controlled by a minority of the population.

Ivan Illich has suggested that there needs to be rational research on the dimensions to which a technology can be used to implement the aspirations of the society without frustrating equivalent aspiration of others.[8] Within the context of the development of electronic media that research should begin now.

Notes

[1] Benjamin Woolley, *Virtual Worlds*, Penguin, Harmondsworth, 1993, p35.
[2] William J. Mitchell, *The Reconfigured Eye*, MIT Press, Cambridge, Massachsetts, 1992.
[3] Points raised by Anna Couey in conversation with the author, 1994.
[4] Cited by Tony Fry, 'Art Byting The Dust', in Philip Hayward (ed), *Culture, Technology And Creativity in the Late Twentieth Century*, John Libbey, London, 1990, p160.
[5] Demon offers a standard service cost of £12.50 (plus VAT) and then a monthly subscription of £10 (plus VAT). There are no extra charges in

the UK. All their services provide a direct connection to the Internet and all services are available to corporate and home users. They advise on the best software to use and have a guest account that allows you to download the software needed. Email internet@demon.net.

[6] The cost of ISDN2 link as of 31 March 1994 is £400 per hook-up charge for each site and £84 (plus VAT) for quarterly rental. International charge rates on top of this are 76 pence per minute for each line and a minimum of two is needed.

[7] In discussion with Michael Eleftherides, who has been instrumental in setting up ISDN networks between Europe and the United States, he mentioned that the sense of time shifting and collaboration between participants is as important to the feeling of creativity as the work that is produced.

[8] Ivan Illich, *Tools of Conviviality*, Marion Boyars, London, 1990.

Playing with Yourself: Pleasure and Interactive Art

Beryl Graham

I'm beginning to worry about our bouncing new baby art form of interactivity. I think it might be in danger of being smothered at birth by the weight of critical, pop-philosophical and academic attention being heaped upon it. By the time it actually reaches its audience, the artwork often appears to be too flimsy to support this weight.

Whilst a certain occurrence of childhood diseases might be expected from such a young art form, it is perhaps time for the artists and exhibitors to begin to face some responsibilities if the art is to have any kind of a healthy future. If interactive art is not to be doomed to be a permanently marginalised freak-show alongside holography, then we have to start addressing more thoroughly the ways in which the audience relates to the art, and how audiences might get pleasure from it (or otherwise).

Bearing in mind that the discussions about artist-audience relationships for *all* of the visual arts tend to progress under fierce debate, there are nevertheless still reasons why the debate for interactive art is a particularly interesting, and a particularly difficult one: for a start, often we quite literally don't know what we're talking about. Because very few accomplished interactive artworks are touring or cheaply available, our primary experience of them is truly a 'virtual' one – that of reading second-hand descriptions or reviews. Whether the reviewers choose to maul or drool over them, either way the artworks reach us thoroughly dampened by the mouths of others. The particular nature of interactivity makes this a more than usually serious problem: as Robert Coover asks about hypertext[1] works, 'How does one judge, analyze, write about a work that never reads the same way twice?'[2] Whilst every good postmodernist knows that even a single, non-interactive photograph never reads the same way twice, the advent of interactivity has doubly exploded concepts of objectivity.

Whilst forcing critics to publicly acknowledge their subjectivity might be a useful by-product of interactive art, there is still a need for many more interactive artworks to be seen and thoroughly road-tested by 'real' audiences rather than virtual ones. At the risk of adding yet another blanket to the burden of critical attention (whilst acknowledging my views to be unashamedly anecdotal rather than scientific), it seems like a good time to look at the peculiar pleasures of interactive art, how the relationship between artist and audience is changed, and how this may affect the very structure of the exhibition form. Are you having fun yet?

Joystick Aesthetic: What Kind of Fun are we Having?

A primary question for those looking at interactive art is based upon a certain confusion about what kind of pleasures to relate this experience to: what *kind* of fun are we supposed to be having? Video pleasures? Installation pleasures? Cinema pleasures? Kinetic sculpture? Home computer? Game arcade? Happening? Picture gallery?

In many ways interactive art is 'the boundary-subject that theorist Gloria Anzaldúa calls the *Mestiza*, one who lives in the borderlands and is only partially recognised by each abutting society.'[3] Re-reading the critical theory of some abutting artforms such as video art, however, makes it clear that our bouncing baby art form is not of course sprung fully formed from Silicon Valley, but has many parent artforms claiming it, from Dada and kinetic art to video and community art, each bringing its own aesthetic values to bear.

The aesthetics of interactive art using computers is a difficult area to deal with critically at this stage of development; images on a computer screen still tend to look like, well, 'computer images'. Computer terminals themselves are still so loaded with cultural meanings of work, commerce etc, that it is difficult to override those meanings in order to see any content in what may be on the screen. In 1987 Vivian Sobchack characterised the computer screen in relation to cinematic space as 'spatially decentered, weakly temporalised and quasi-disembodied',[4] a character which must be critically addressed when thinking of the audience's first reactions. Just as video installation artists have struggled with ways of using the video screen which attempt to override the inherent reading of the object as a banal 'television', interactive computer artists have struggled with the problem of seducing the viewer close enough to those pale, gray, square boxes to be able to commune with the content on the screen (and once there, to engage the viewer sufficiently for them to want to explore the work).

Lucia Grossberger, for example, is an artist who was born in Bolivia, and who brings a range of sculptural and installation skills to her works using interactive technology. Her work *A Mí Abuelita* involves a series of Bolivian-style altars with sculpted items such as ceramic mummies, beer and religious imagery. The central image in each of the altars however is a computer screen, where the viewer can interact with HyperCard stories of the death of her great aunt, or screens which superimpose a video image of the viewer with 'day-of-the-dead' skull images. Although the content of the work concerns religion and death, the sculptural and textural qualities make the sites of interaction very approachable – much more so than a naked computer terminal.

When considering the aesthetic qualities of the screen-based images themselves, choices now range from the high definition to the deliberately coarsely pixellated. The extent to which the style of images and graphics is affected by mass-produced image-manipulation software is an interesting question –

certainly, I'm beginning to recognise when certain Photoshop 'filters' or Video Toaster effects have been used, not to mention the different styles of interaction which go with Director or Authorware software packages. To a large extent, artists who do not have access to the vast resources of tailor-made software, find themselves working within someone else's benchmark of style, or else tinkering with its peripheries.

Whilst images on a screen/monitor or video projection are not of course the only options for interactive artists, they are still the major options, and artists are still experimenting with their particular qualities of colour and space. One of the few pieces I have seen which managed to absorb me in a primarily visual pleasure is a part in Beverley Reiser's *Temple of the Goddesses*.[5] It is a piece where you as the viewer appear on a video projection to be moving within her graphics, and at one stage words and images of fire 'stick' to your hands and follow your movements. Although coarsely pixellated, the gestural graphics and rich, glowing colours managed to create an evocative and luminous space in which to juggle with fire (and other ideas). Given time, perhaps the 'pixellated aesthetic' may take on a quality of its own, and a reading beyond that of simply 'computer'.

Because of the newness of interactive art using computers, most of us will no doubt remain unsure of what kind of pleasures to expect from it, for some time into the future. Because of this fact, some of us are also destined to be disappointed if the work doesn't talk to our particular pleasures. If you are expecting pictorial pleasures then those images should be beautiful, if you are expecting televisual pleasures then the artwork has to override the other ambient stimuli, if you are expecting sculptural pleasures then the texture and installation are vital. On the other hand if you are expecting video-game pleasure then maybe you actually *want* your pleasures to be 'spatially decentered, weakly temporalised and quasi-disembodied'.

The advent of the video-game is just one of the recent cultural developments which have made some theorists question whether or not 'pleasure' within visual culture is in danger of being supplanted by 'fun'. It almost comes as a shock that Susan Sontag should have to point out so carefully that an aim of culture is: '... to produce food for the mind, for the senses, for the heart. To keep the language alive. To keep alive the idea of seriousness. You have to be a member of a capitalist society in the late 20th century to understand that seriousness itself could be in question.'[6]

This confusion of pleasures is certainly beginning to be addressed seriously. As Peter Lunenfeld says: 'To develop a strategy to theorize the products of the technoculture, we must draw from the traditions of aesthetic philosophy without holding computer-inflected media to a static and anachronistic set of "standards" – hybrid media require hybrid analysis.'[7] Lunenfeld also helpfully suggests a basic bifurcation of types of interactive art pleasure: the 'immersion' in the safe fakery of virtual reality versus the 'extraction' of narratives and information from hypertext.

The key pleasures of interactive art, including those of immersion and extraction, are of course not necessarily purely aesthetic or pictorial ones, but, unsurprisingly, the pleasures of interaction itself: as Allucquere Rosanne Stone argues in respect of Sobchack's 'spatially decentered' criticism of the computer screen, 'This seems to be true, as long as the mode of engagement remains that of spectator. But it is the quality of direct physical and kinesthetic engagement, the enrolling of hapticity in the service of both drama and the dramatic, which is not part of the cinematic mode.'[8] These qualities of direct engagement however differ greatly from artwork to artwork, for despite the hype of interactivity as a democratic wonder, there is a great disparity in the extent and quality of this engagement.

How Interactive?

The current romance of interactivity promises such things as being a better or more democratic art form and/or the art form of

*the future... Yet interactive videodisks do not empower the
viewer to create a wholly new work with the materials they are
given, and they only appear to eliminate the alienation of the
artist and viewer present in most avant-garde art.*[9]

As Ann-Sargent Wooster goes on to point out, there is an
existing history of 'happenings' and performance art in which
the interaction of the audience was of primary importance. The
kinds of interaction ranged from the 'pseudo participation' of
plants in the audience, through token involvement, to 'pieces in
which there were only participants-performers and accidental
spectators'.[10] In many of these, however, the relationship
between the artists and the audience was often a confrontational
one; challenging, tricking or simply frightening the bourgeoisie.
Now that the prevailing views of the relationship between the
artist and the audience are (perhaps!) different, it is the
'democratic' possibilities of interactivity which have been
receiving the most attention – the ways in which there can be
physical input and participation by the audience. However,
there are very many ways of interacting, and 'pseudo
participation' or token participation still seem to be present
amongst those ways. Interactive novelist Thomas Disch's
experience of hypertext is that 'As long as readers cannot add
new words to the story and change it ... the creativity of
interactivity fiction lies solely with the author.'[11] Obviously
though, there is a continuum of tactics which allows more or
less input from the viewer/participant, including the ultimate in
'audience input' – the ongoing freeform contributions to
electronic bulletin board systems, or networking events, which
have no director or controller but many 'equal' participants who
are equally their own audience.[12]

Art pieces such as Abbe Don's *Share With Me a Story*[13] are
sited at the more 'democratic', participative end of the visual
spectrum: it is usually shown alongside her *We Make Memories*
which is a HyperCard telling, with family snaps, of four
generations of Jewish women in her family. Viewers can get
ideas from interacting with that piece, and then, importantly,

Share With Me a Story enables them to scan in their own snaps and record their own story as a growing interactive archive. In her more recent piece *T.P.T.V.*, Don turned a 'photo-booth' into an interactive ideas terminal, where people could see artists work, record a moving image of their face with their opinions on specific issues and works, and interact with previous peoples' comments.

Not all artists choose such tactics however, and concentrate instead on ways of viewing rather than ways of contributing. Grahame Weinbren is keen to differentiate his 'interactive cinema' from the run of the mill 'point and click':

> In developing an interactive cinema, one of my primary concerns has been to retain the articulation of time. Without it, we quickly descend into the pit of so-called 'multi-media', with its scenes of unpleasant 'buttons', 'hot-spots' and 'menus', and the viewer is forced into a path-following, choice-making state of mind. 'Multi-media' leaves no room for the possibility of loss of self, of desire in relation to the unfolding on-screen drama.[14]

Weinbren's screen in the piece *Sonata* is 'continuously responsive' to touch, but maintains an 'articulation of time', so that the viewer is nudging and changing viewpoint rather than pointing and choosing different subjects.

Interaction is, of course, not a factor bounded by technology: in Gary Hill's *Tall Ships* piece, for example, the technical interaction is very passive and simple: video clips of single figures approaching are triggered by the viewer's body moving along a darkened corridor.[15] There is no choice or physical input from the viewer, but nevertheless, the 'emotional interaction' created is very strong, and because of the very simplicity of it all, the viewer must 'input' a lot of their own ideas.

Such hybridity of media and tactics means that each 'interactive' piece has to be judged individually on its degree of interactivity. However, there are some *particular* pleasures of interactivity which tend to be common across the range of works, from point-and-click to virtual reality.

Intimate Exchanges, Household Words

> *Our connection to the real world is very thin, and our connection*
> *with the artificial world is going to be more intimate and*
> *satisfying than anything that's come before.*
> Marvin Minsky, Toshiba Professor of
> Arts and Sciences at MIT.[16]

I'm in a crowded shopping mall gallery, and Pedro Meyer is
talking quietly into my ear. He has a rich voice, and speaks
thoughtfully and slowly in my headphones as he shows me
photographs about the death of his parents. Although people are
milling around me, I find myself absorbed, oblivious, and moved
to the point of tears by this ... computer.

Even simple interactive CD-ROMs like Pedro Meyer's *I
Photograph to Remember* are capable of an almost shocking
amount of intimacy.[17] Whilst one might have to be a Toshiba
Professor to actually find it 'more satisfying', it is certainly more
comfortable than, for instance, dealing with the real mortality of
one's own parents. Not that this is any very new reason for
moral panic; artists have been dealing in distanced and vicarious
emotional life as a popular recreation since before Charles
Dickens' serialisations in *Household Words*, and many a
relationship now takes place over the virtual voice of the
telephone. As Wooster comments, 'the current call for
interactivity on the part of video artists is part of a larger societal
development of machine-augmented simulacra of intimacy.'[18]

The physical situation of sitting close to a monitor designed
for one person, wearing headphones, controlling the images
which fill your field of vision, is an intense one. The performers
are performing for you alone, you are in control of something
bigger than yourself, but you are not responsible – the
advantages of being a child, but without powerlessness. We are
highly engaged and involved, and yet 'safe', because we know
we can switch it all off. Whether you are sitting in this computer
cocoon, or participating in couch-potato quiz games on your
future interactive TV, the 'comfort factor' of interactivity is very
high, there to be exploited by advertisers and artists alike.

However, while the pleasure of intimacy (even if it is a 'simulacrum of intimacy') may be a deeply engaging tool for the artist, it has counterpoints which could have serious effects on how that artwork may be able to be viewed.

Intimate Exchanges ... Selfish Pleasures?

I'm inside Gary Hill's *Tall Ships* piece at last. I've been looking forward to this, having had it described to me by several curators and reviewers: 'moving' they said, and 'haunting'. Actually, I'm currently more absorbed by the fact that the man behind seems to be standing closer to me than is strictly necessary in the darkened corridor. There's also someone in front of me talking very loudly at his girlfriend, in piercing Oxford accents. I can't tell whether Gary Hill's video figures are approaching *me*, or are just a little late to greet the previous viewers. Or maybe this isn't interactive at all? If only those other people would drop dead, then maybe I could tell. The piece may have brought tears to reviewers' eyes, but they (mutter grumble mutter) presumably had the luxury of private views (mutter grumble mutter). Sitting on the train later, I'm a little shamefaced. Even squeezing around the populous Pre-Raphaelite painting exhibition, I hadn't actually wished the other audience members wiped off the face of the earth.

I'm sitting in front of my computer, doing nothing in particular, when a colleague wanders over and makes a movement towards my keyboard. As an instant reaction, I grab his wrist, hard enough to make us both yelp in surprise. I would be happy to lend my camera to anyone of reasonably sound mind, so why do I start behaving like a dog over Meaty Chunks when it comes to my computer?

The powerful force of intimacy has a very important flipside for the exhibited forms of interactive art. Such intimacy is difficult to interrupt, share, or even gaze upon. The structure of much interactive technology is essentially one-to-one, and even when the physical structures allow for more than one person to view at a time, the members of the audience are often somehow *in competition* with each other, or at least confuse the reading and impact of the piece for the other viewers.

Are the primary pleasures of interactive art therefore necessarily *selfish pleasures* – more exclusive, more individualistic than viewing other visual arts? Those pleasures of choice which enable the viewer to choose paths, to go at their own pace, make it annoying or incomprehensible to anyone 'watching over their shoulder', and intensely irritating to have one's shoulder watched over. Does it change 'gentle readers' into snarling curs? The lonely pleasures of viewing interactive art could be seen as part of the increasing 'privatisation' of the body since the fifteenth century, when 'In particular, the subject, as did the body, ceased to constitute itself as public spectacle, and instead fled from the public sphere and constituted itself in text – such as Samuel Pepys' diary'.[19]

The theorist Frances Barker characterises such a privatised body as 'raging, solitary, productive'.[20] For the current circumstances, we could perhaps add 'consuming', for ideally we wish to buy and take home these pieces of art, to explore at our own leisure, uninterrupted. Compact discs, those glistening rainbow objects of desire, have never promised so much as their potential for intimate, headphone-cocooned, *personal* computer, private experience. The fact that a key area for commercial investment in interactive CD development is currently pornography, should come as very little surprise.[21]

Some theorists would go so far as to describe the privatised nature of interactive viewing as also being inherently narcissistic. Rosalind Krauss in her article 'Video: The Aesthetics of Narcissism' described the structure of many video installations as self-referential to the body of the performer/artists: 'The body is therefore as it were centered between two machines that are like the opening and closing of a parenthesis. The first of these is a camera; the second is the monitor, which reflects the performer's image with the immediacy of a mirror.'[22] In thinking about interactive works such as Beverley Reiser's, where the viewer appears on screen as animateur, for Krauss' 'body' we could perhaps read 'viewer'. Even if the viewer does not actually appear on screen, the machines obediently and immediately reflect their choices and actions, amplified and decorated. Some artists of course are aware of this nature, and use it within their work. *Rigid Waves-Liquid Views*[23] for example, which created a reflecting 'pool' that rippled when the user touched its screen, is described by Peter Lunenfeld as 'creating a model of VR fully aware not only of its oneiric but also its narcissistic underpinnings.'[24]

Narcissistic? Lonely pleasures? The fact that as a viewer of interactive art you are often effectively *playing with yourself* is simultaneously interesting, pleasurable and slightly worrying. The fact that when the artworks are displayed, you might be playing with yourself *in public*, makes these relationships even more complex.

Public Intimacy

I'm at an exhibition in Rochester, New York, one of four people standing in line to see Lynn Hershman's interactive piece *A Room of One's Own*. As it is a black box a foot or two square, on a pedestal, with an eye hole, the only indications of the content are the reactions of the current viewer, so we all watch that person intently, for want of anything more interesting to do. Most of the men look slightly embarrassed as they walk away. When it comes to my turn I bend down to peek in the peephole, and become aware that the piece is about voyeurism and privacy and gender. The video clips in this miniature 'woman's room' are actually being triggered by my eye movements, and I can see in part of the room my huge eyeball looking back at me. At the same time I'm also aware that I'm standing with my bum in the air in the middle of a public space, and that people are probably looking at me, especially those in the queue. As I leave the box, I hang around for a while to further study the reactions of the queuers and viewers, and realise that other people have done this too. Thus Hershman's small black box has become only the nexus of a room-size dynamic of voyeurism, in which awareness of your own body is inescapable.

The last century's 'privatisation' of the body, reflected in some modes of new technology interaction, is ironically turned on its head by presenting the pieces in the exhibition form. Although locked into an intimate experience, *the player/viewer also becomes a spectacle.* Especially when wearing VR helmets, the effect is rather like playing 'blind man's buff' and one's enjoyment of the experience rather tends to depend on one's level of trust in those who are surrounding, but invisible. The young and confident tend to have few problems with playing this game; those who have experienced the gaze as weapon tend to have problems with the idea of being an object as well as an audience.

As well as Lynn Hershman, there are other artists who are very aware of the complex position of the viewer as spectacle as well as spectator, and use this to add dimensions to their work. American artist Sharon Grace, for example, in her installation *Inversion*, ensures that viewers are very much aware of their own presence: in a bare, office-type room, you sit at a desk which has only a telephone on it.[25] If you answer its ring, then a video screen in the wall illuminates to show you the back view of a reclining female nude like a 'Vanitas' painting, only instead of holding a mirror, she holds a telephone handset, and looks at a live video image of your face, for you are being recorded by a hidden camera. She never turns towards you, but her telephone voice talks of how she longs to meet, how she wants to be remembered over this distance, and how she misses the world. The piece was first shown at *Cyberthon*, a twenty-four-hour-long Virtual Reality gig held at the studios of Colossal Pictures, in San Francisco in 1990. Timothy Leary was there, as was Brian Eno, William Gibson, and several hundred male adolescents who might have been wearing anoraks if it hadn't been California. Anticipating the preponderantly male audience, Grace set out in part to address the sad alienation, and the repressed physicality of 'computer nerds', not to mention challenging the voyeurism of art and technology. The feedback she got was dramatic: male viewers had to be helped out weeping, and William Gibson was quoted as saying that the experience made him 'as vulnerable as I had ever felt in art'.[26] This use of challenging and addressing that unfortunate 'body' which technology tries to forget, is an important factor if interactive art is to maintain any depth of relationship with its audience.

As well as artists who address the physical presence of the audience, there are also artists who make conscious use of interaction *between* members of the audience. The works of Sonya Rapoport for example tend to use 'deconstructive play' and a variety of physical interactions (as well as electronic) to involve her audience. In *Shoe Field*, for example, the participants have to remove their shoes and input their information into a computer rather like a corny automatic fortune-telling machine, in order to receive their highly technical-looking shoe character profile.[27] This tells the participant to place their shoes on a particular tile laid out on the floor like a giant board game, get a Polaroid taken, and then further interact with the 'shoe-personalities' of previous players. The piece is designed for several participants at once, and shuffling around with plastic bags on one's feet seems to have produced a sufficiently sociable atmosphere to enable the reviewer from *High Performance* magazine to go home with a date (Rapoport has also produced more recent pieces concerning sexual jealousy).

Perry Hoberman's 1993 *Bar-Code Hotel* is even more dependant on interaction between members of the audience for its full effect.[28] Participants 'work' the piece by running light pens over bar-codes stuck to a table on which real objects are arranged: run your pen over the bar code next to a bust of Elvis Presley, and a 3-D graphic of the bust appears on a big video projection screen. Run your pen over the bar codes marked 'rotate' 'fast' 'slow', 'bigger', etc, and you can produce your own animation. There are however several tables and several light pens attached to the same screen, so you either get very annoyed with the other participants, or work out some way of communication with them in order to create joint effects or stories. Thus Elvis can suddenly appear wearing a pair of graphic glasses from another table, but only if you can manage to coordinate the right size and position. It's fun to watch as well as participate, and so becomes some kind of social event which is actually better with more people, rather than being devalued by their collective presence.

There are obviously many more ways than tapping on a keyboard for interactive art to meet its singular or collective public. All this talk of 'viewers', 'participants', 'players', or 'audience', however, seems to have skipped a fairly important point: do we know more or less who these people might be, and how they look at art?

Who Do They Think They're Talking To?

In Montreal, Videotron *allows home television viewers to install, for a slight fee, a small computer that tracks choices and then discerns the viewer's age, sex, and socio-economic status and programs commercials that are personality-coded. For instance, a white woman in her forties would get different program choices (and commercials) than a teenage African-American.*

Lynn Hershman.[29]

I'm at a new technology trade fair in New York State, watching people play on a virtual reality game which combines the wearing of a VR helmet with being strapped into a gimbals-like circular cage whch tilts the victim every which way up. People are queuing for up to three hours for a go, and can watch what the players are seeing, on a video screen (the usual 'shoot 'em up' scenario). As people stumble off the ride, I ask a handful of people of each gender the same two questions: 'What did it feel like?' and 'Was it *you* in there?' Although hardly scientific, there is a marked difference in the responses: the men talk mostly about being 'out of body' and the women talk mostly of disorientation and discomfort. In answer to the second qustion, *all* of the men say 'How do you mean?' and *all* the women laugh and say 'Nooo'.

167

'What is your target audience for this piece of work?' – that's the question which always makes my students groan and wriggle uncomfortably. Not that I blame them, for it's a very difficult question. The current theory is that artists and funding bodies are terribly concerned about knowing who their particular audiences might be, but in fact the practice is that the arts, unlike advertising companies, are not very well-informed about exactly who they're talking to. The debate about audience is an ongoing one for all visual arts, but interactivity has some particular problems of its own.

One of the grand claims for interactive art was that it would have a broader possibility for pleasing different audiences, because people could, like browsers in a supermarket, choose paths within the artworks to suit their particular tastes. As Norman M. Klein says ...The "creative" consumer invents his or her own community. Instead of painting by number, the viewer buys in by menu.'[30] However, rather than letting interactive art off the hook of 'the audience problem' it seems that interactivity needs to be even more careful in this area than other artforms: different individuals have always, of course, read the visual art in very different ways, but if the art uses interactive technology, then different people seem to have a very different way of approaching, experiencing and *using* the technology, as well as reading its content (take, for example, the different reactions of men and women to the virtual reality game).

Although it isn't usually terribly useful to directly apply the ways in which advertising market research categorises its audiences to the art world, the fact that the existing market for commercially-produced interactive computer products is preponderantly male and adolescent is an interesting pre-existing condition for those seeking to define audiences and use. Even assuming that the artist has a 'narrowcasting' rather than a 'broadcasting' aim however, there is still the danger of stereotyping the perceptions of that particular target group.

The Small Body Part

Forgetting about the body is an old Cartesian trick, one that has unpleasant consequences for those bodies whose speech is silenced by the act of our forgetting; that is to say, those upon whose labor the act of forgetting the body is founded – usually women and minorities.[31]

The issue of 'the body' is a seminal one for computer interactivity, and one which is under hot debate by many contemporary writers.[32] Within the complex debates, many suggestions have been made that the male-gendered experiences of the technology tend to differ from the female, and that the reasons lie deep in psychology. Some say that the desire for 'immersion' in VR is to do with virtual space being female, some say the popularity of video-games with certain groups is because of desiring 'freedom from the sense of loss of control that accompanies adolescent male embodiment.'[33]

Whatever the reasons, the fact that the disembodied nature of computer-based 'simulacra of intimacy' is available has led to a rash of tales (some apocryphal) of 'computer crossdressing'. The majority of tales are of men adopting a female persona, such as the male psychiatrist who interacted for many months with women, through postings on a computer bulletin board system under the persona of 'Julie', an older disabled woman.[34]

This short excursion into the subject of 'the body' is really an adjunct to my musings on audience, in order to warn that even if artists think they have a good idea of how to define their audience, that may not be how the audience chooses to define (or redefine) itself.

Virtually There (In Which Our Heroine Rounds up Pleasures in Cyberspace)

I'm sitting in a sunny and tiny flat, as Pat and Jocelyn show me their interactive work in progress – a computer-based telling of their experience of being stranded for several days by a blizzard

169

whilst backpacking in the Californian Sierras. As they talk me through the unfinished sections, they laugh, interrupt each other, and give me different versions of the same event, swapping hiking anecdotes with me and scratching their Poison Oak rash from yesterday's walk. They've done a thousand different things in their lives, from bookbinding and textiles to American Sign Language and the study of wolf behaviour. Their interactive work manages to combine many of these pleasures, as well as reflecting their many-branching characters. Pat's design company has produced interactive CD-ROMs in collaboration with other artists from varous disciplines, and the company is called, she tells me, Convivial Design.[35]

Despite the fact that mass-produced software is such a strong aesthetic and structural controller of much interactive art, the medium can nevertheless still show the marks of the personality of the artist. Hence retentive boffins with few social skills are highly unlikely to produce a piece of work which is bursting with conviviality and the talent to engage a general audience.

It's hardly a new or profound comment to say that the interest of an artwork lies in its content, but the inherent pleasures of interactivity have tended to mask this salient point. The pleasures of 'extracting' ideas and information from an interactive CD-ROM, the pleasures of exploring the illusion of a virtual environment, the pleasures of having an environment respond to you, are all such strong medicine that we are willing to forgive a lot. Even those CDs that are so badly constructed as to be plodding, frustrating, confusing, predictable or simply dull, can at least keep me pushing buttons out of curiosity, or fear that I might miss something. Those pleasures of 'choice' can even start to dull the political acuity: seeing the CD-ROM *From Alice to Ocean*[36] for the first time, a long time ago, I was highly amused by the part where, as a subtext, you see a small picture of the woman who travelled by camel across Australia, and a small picture of the photographer who recorded the trip; click on him and he waffles on about light and atmosphere, click on her and she moans about what an immature pain he was, always getting in the way by taking photos. Great, I thought, this is polyphony, no more linear logic. You also get two different political views about Aboriginal Australians ... but what you don't get, of course, is the Aboriginal Australians' own viewpoints. The fact that you're getting two different kinds of white bread doesn't mean that you're getting any real choice, but it makes you *feel* as though you are. Our pleasures of choice are still small options within narrow boundaries: this means of production and distribution are still (surprise surprise) in the hands of the military or big business, and the artists getting access to the means are still predominantly white, and male.

Perhaps a primary pleasure of interactivity is that of *control*, which is why the thwarting of audience control, or the realisation of 'token' control, is a site of such *dis*pleasure. But if audiences get pleasure from control, then so do the artists, and the delicate balance between the two is surely one of the key skills of interactive art. All too often, having control of shiny new technology seems to inspire certain artists to huge abstract concepts which encompass god-like ranges of history, space, art, science and religiosity (sort of a 'Renaissance Man with a hard-drive' kick). Certainly, new interactive technology is capable of being very 'impressive' (as long as the audience is willing to 'take no notice of him behind the curtain'), but what then? The skills needed by artists if they are to truly loosen control over the audience, but still share their pleasure, are perhaps less like traditional art skills, and more like the social interaction skills of 'throwing a good party', or of enabling/community art. The pleasures of control for the audience also have to achieve a delicate balance within the work, in counterweight to those pleasures which need an absence of control: the pleasures of surprise, suspense, or chance. Exhibited works of the CD-ROM variety are often too concerned with plodding down pathways rather than letting imaginations branch. Often they provide much too much information and images, just because they can.

We should perhaps remember that, ultimately, the audience's final pleasure is in choosing *not* to interact, in total denial of the author's power. If passivity didn't have its own particular pleasures, then presumably television would have died out by now. There are times in life when you don't want to have to choose options, or input your own thoughts; indeed there are times when you might be bored to tears by your own ideas, and would much rather just receive somebody else's creativity.

So What Might This Mean for the Exhibition Form?

> *Once having discovered the touch screen, the dilemma faced by the viewer/participant is whether to keep making selections or to move toward the centre of the space in order to fully comprehend the results of his/her interventions. This, in effect, frees up the touch screen for others to participate in the selection process.*
> Peter d'Agostino, *Double You (and X, Y, Z)*[37]

I'm sitting in the chair in front of the screen of Grahame Weinbren's *Sonata*,[38] trying to get into its subtle and wandering structure. There's a 'corral' around my chair, with stretched nylon filaments on a frame, like I'm inside an aviary. My screen is connected to a tower with some monitors which face outwards, so that the people outside the aviary can see them ... but the people standing waiting for a turn aren't looking at those monitors, they're looking at *me*. And some of these people are tapping their feet. And drumming their fingers. And sighing, heavily. When a small child begins to turn from querulous to definite whine, I give up the effort and slink out apologetically. Some months later, the American curator of that show is at a conference, denouncing the fact that an arts reviewer had refused to look at Weinbren's piece because she 'didn't have time for that'. It seemed churlish to admit that the bashfulness of Brits may be a less contentious reason why the longer and slower interactive arts don't get a full viewing.

The particularities of the pleasures and dynamics of interactive art mean that certain problems arise when trying to view some of them in an exhibition form. Queues happen, some pieces are bypassed, some leave the audience's role unclear, some are paced too slow, some are too intimate to survive a group, some are read only on the first, surface level because of the lack of time to peruse, and (very, very often) they break down.

Assuming that the petulant technology can be cured, there still seems to be a need to rethink the exhibition form for interactive art, and examine carefully its audience dynamics. After all, interactivity has perhaps even more to lose than other visual arts: any analysis of how interactive art is looked at relates interestingly to an eternal problem for art in general – do the images visually communicate what it is that is expected of the audience? With a painting or an installation, the audience may move on having metaphorically 'failed to see the point' of the artwork. However, with interactive art which demands a response of the audience (an approach towards the active sensors, or a sitting down at a terminal, or a triggered moving through a series of images) this becomes a more practical question: if the image at the first point of contact fails to communicate, then the audience may move on having *literally* 'failed to see' the rest of the work. Whilst viewers rarely walk out of cinema presentations, the gallery has a context of 'the two-second glance', and the pleasures must be strong ones to keep the viewer long enough to see an extended piece of work.

Artists like Hershman and d'Agostino have obviously thought very carefully about designing their pieces to work with an existing gallery audience dynamic, but what of possible 'new' forms of disseminating the work, which interactivity might create or expand? At this stage, it is indubitably foolish to try and prophesy exactly what will happen to the public face of interactive art. The prophets of the 'camcorder revolution' were certainly quite definite about the utopian future of that medium, which in reality has ended up splattered messily somewhere between Jeremy Beadle[39] and Rodney King. Like video art however, the means of seeing interactive art may end up straddled over various tactics, from exhibition (sitting on hard chairs in galleries) and product distribution (buying CDs or renting from alternative distributors), to transmission (some-where on the margins of interactive TV or other networks). The particular means of reception for the artwork therefore depends very much on what you mean by interactive art: if you are talking about involved CD-ROMs then really the exhibition form can only act as a 'trailer', for ideally you buy those objects of desire to take home, and satisfy yourself in private. If you are talking about 'networking' art events, from humble computer bulletin boards to live international video link-ups then, although interesting to the direct participants, 'outsiders' (those with no direct physical or mental access to it) can only have a rather devalued relationship to the events.[40] Like 'fax art' the networking genre currently seems to proceed in some kind of permanent 'underground', with very little focus or documentation. If you are talking, however, about a virtual reality variety of interactivity, then the structures of theme park, video game, and timed, paid-for audience interaction seem to be the dominating context.

If we are alternatively talking about adapting the traditional 'art gallery' means of presentation (for a range of different genres of interactivity), then perhaps the structure of the walls and spaces may change. Perhaps splitting into 'brothel-like' private booths? Perhaps with audience access through tickets purchased by the hour? Indeed, perhaps some varieties of the artform might change the gallery in ways which are highly ambivalent: 'If interactive art simply mirrors the game – its themes and values – it becomes symptomatic of uncritical postmodernism where there is no difference between entertainment and art, where consumerism reigns. And when, loaded down as amusement, it knocks on the museum door, it insists on altering how and why museums function, further institutionalising art as consumer fun.'[41] Those 'selfish pleasures' of computer interactivity may indeed turn out to have a long-term effect on the commodification of artworks.

Although the spectre of populist or simplistic button-pressing is indeed a serious one, and although those enthralled by new technology have a tendency to dismiss the earthbound lessons of the past, some answers to the difficulties of audience relationships may in fact be found in closer attention to the experience of municipal galleries, or 'discovery museums' with their lower-tech interactions.[42] In support of lessons of the past (and in praise of older artists), it is also no coincidence that the artists who produce some of the most successful interactive work are those, such as Lynn Hershman, who have a long history of relevant work in video and performance, and who have spent years of applied hard work on the tender dynamics of interaction. Neither is it a coincidence that the artists producing some of the most effective virtual reality art are those, including Brenda Laurel, and Toni Dove & Michael MacKenzie,[43] who come to the field with a strong theatrical background, catholic interests and, very importantly, plenty of evolved social skills. Artists such as Bill Viola have been wrestling for much of their lives with the problems inherent in video installation, to get to a point where the medium has the power to seriously move and enthrall; it is a little soon perhaps to expect as much from our bouncing baby interactivity, and certainly too soon to discard the experience of the past. As Regina Cornwell emphasises, 'These explorations are crucial to how the world can be re-drawn and viewed in an art whose power is in its open-endedness and its polyphony. And for the participant, too, the interactive installation is hard work. To be meaningfully experienced, it demands time and serious attention.'[44]

Notes

[1] Hypertext has been defined by Ted Nelson as, 'non-sequential writing – text that branches and allows choices to the reader, best read at an interactive screen.' Theodore Holm Nelson, *Literary Machines*, Mindful Press, Sausalito 1990.
[2] Robert Coover quoted in Regina Cornwell, 'Interactive Art and the Video Game: Separating the Siblings', *Camerawork*, San Francisco, Spring/Summer 1993.
[3] Allucquere Rosanne Stone, 'Will The Real Body Please Stand Up? Boundary Stories about Cyberspace', in Michael Benedikt (ed) *Cyberspace: First Steps*, MIT Press, Cambridge, Massachusetts, 1991.
[4] Vivian Sobchack quoted in Allucquere Rosanne Stone, *op.cit.*
[5] The piece is adapted from the Mandala children's game, where a small

video camera records the player, and puts their image onto a video screen where they can trigger interaction with the on-screen graphics. The game includes scenarios where the viewer can be an ice-hockey goalie, or play the bongo drums.

6 Leslie Garis, 'Susan Sontag Finds Romance', *The New York Times Magazine*, 2 August 1992, quoted in Regina Cornwell *op.cit.*

7 Peter Lunenfeld, 'Digital Dialectics: A Hybrid Theory of Computer Media', *AfterImage*, November 1993.

8 Allucquere Rosanne Stone, *op.cit.*

9 Ann-Sargent Wooster 'Reach Out and Touch Someone: The Romance of Interactivity' in Hall and Fifer (eds), *Illuminating Video*, Aperture, New York, 1991.

10 Michael Kirby quoted in Ann-Sargent Wooster, *op.cit.*

11 Thomas Disch's views described by Ann-Sargent Wooster, *op.cit.*

12 Computer bulletin boards are systems whereby computers including home personal computers are connected via modems and telephone lines to each other, and can send and receive text messages, or browse a collective pool of data to which anyone can contribute (that is, anyone with the technology, the knowledge, and the money for phone bills/commercial subscription fees if they don't have access to College nets). See also footnote 40.

13 For a fuller description of this piece, see *Ten 8*, Volume 2 Number 4.

14 Graham Weinbren, 'Pointing at an Interactive Cinema', *Camerawork, op.cit.*

15 Shown as part of the one-person show, *Gary Hill: In the Light of the Other*, which toured to venues including the Museum of Modern Art, Oxford, 1993.

16 Quoted in Tim Druckery, 'Electronic Representation: Imaging beyond Photography', *Camerawork, op.cit.*

17 CD-ROM, produced by The Voyager Company (USA), which presents Meyer's black and white photography work, with commentary, as a simple interactive narrative/slide show.

18 Ann-Sargent Wooster, *op.cit.*

19 Allucquere Rosanne Stone, describing Frances Barker's arguments, *op.cit.*

20 Frances Barker quoted in Allucquere Rosanne Stone, *op.cit.*

21 My article 'The Panic Button: Interactive Pornography and Gender', in *Ten 8*, Volume 2 Number 2, explores this in more detail.

22 Rosalind Krauss 'Video: The Aesthetics of Narcissism' in Gregory Battcock (ed), *New Artist's Video*, E.P. Dutton, New York, 1978.

23 By Monika Fleishmann, Christian A. Bohn, and Wolfgang Strauss, 1993.

24 Peter Lunenfeld, *op.cit.*

25 A media artist based in San Francisco.

[26] *Village Voice* (USA), 12 March 1991.

[27] For further description see, *High Performance*, Issue 36, 1986.

[28] Work in progress seen at the Banff Centre for the Arts, 1993.

[29] Lynn Hershman, 'Art-ificial Sub-versions, Inter-action and the New Reality' *Camerawork, op.cit.*

[30] Norman M. Klein 'Audience Culture and the Video Screen' in Hall and Fifer (eds), *op.cit.*

[31] Allucquere Rosanne Stone, *op.cit.*

[32] Including: Donna Haraway, *Simians, Cyborgs and Women*, Routledge, New York 1990; Vivian Sobchack, 'What in the world: Vivian Sobchack on new age mutant ninja hackers', *Artforum*, Volume 29, April 1991; N. Katherine Hayles, 'Virtual Bodies and Flickering Signifiers', *October* Volume 66, Fall 1993.

[33] Allucquere Rosanne Stone, *op.cit.*

[34] *Ibid.*

[35] Convivial Design Inc, based in San Francisco and run by Pat Roberts, has created amongst other things the CD-ROM *Creation Stories*, with artwork by Jocelyn Cohen, Grace Chen and Hagit Cohen.

[36] CD-ROM created by Robyn Davison and Rick Smolan, Against All Odds Productions 1992. Produced by Magnum Design in co-operation with Apple Computer.

[37] Peter d'Agostino, 'Interventions of the Present: Three Interactive Videodiscs, 1981-90', in Hall and Fifer (eds), *op.cit.*

[38] For further descriptions see Grahame Weinbren, *op.cit.*

[39] Host of a comedy show of home videos.

[40] For descriptions of some image-based telecommunication arts events see: Steven Durland, 'Defining the Image as Place: A Conversation with Kit Galloway, Sherrie Rabinowitz and Gene Youngblood', in Arlene Raven (ed), *Art in the Public Interest*, UMI Research Press, Ann Arbor 1989; Artur Matuck 'Intercities Sao Paulo/Pittsburg', *Leonardo* Volume 24 Number 2.

[41] Regina Cornwell, *op.cit.*

[42] See *Museums Journal*, Volume 93, February 1993, for a special issue on the subject.

[43] Brenda Laurel is working with a team of other artists from Interval Research, at Banff Centre for the Arts (in Canada), producing a virtual reality piece using images 'sampled' from nature. Toni Dove and Michael MacKenzie also produced *Archaeology of a Mother Tongue* at Banff; a VR piece constructed as a theatrical interactive narrative.

[44] Regina Cornwell, *op.cit.*

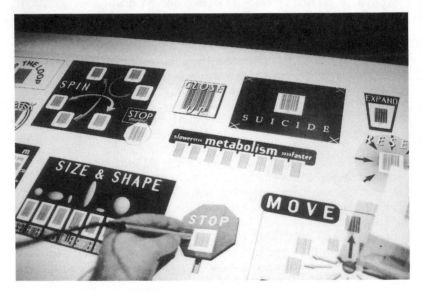

Bar-Code Hotel by Perry Hoberman, 1994.
Installation details. Photographer: Perry Hoberman.

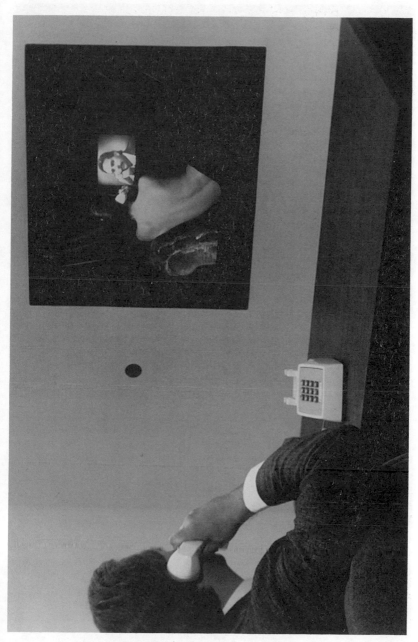

Inversion by Sharon Grace, 1990.

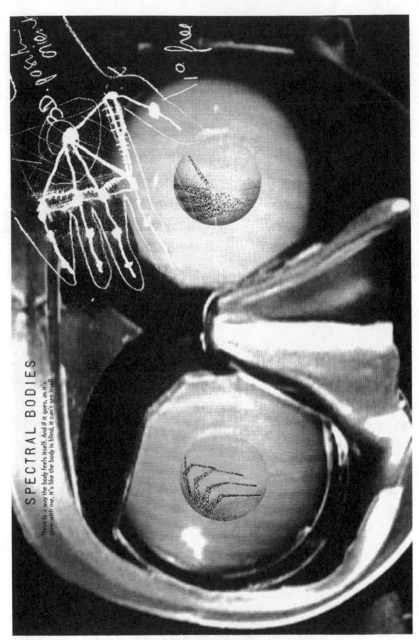

Spectral Bodies by Catherine Richards, 1991.
Videotape 5.30 minutes.

The Virtual Body by Catherine Richards, 1993.
Interactive Installation.

181

A Letter on Fungal Intimacy: Art, New Media and Feminist Tropes

Catherine Richards

It was the disturbance of conventional notions of the self I found most provocative when first introduced to Virtual Reality (VR) in 1985. Here, it seemed to me, was a technology which, in its very human-technical interface, creates a site to explore a new body, for the lack of another term, an entity that can no longer be defined as distinct. VR led to a notion of a subjectivity that has little to do with the image of boundaries normally associated with an individual subject.

Spectral Bodies and *The Virtual Body* are two recent works that have resulted from a long process to materialise an ambiguous relationship with contemporary technology. In this process, I side-step the role of artist as technological celebrant and humanist. Both pieces in their own way also encapsulate many of my preoccupations with new technologies:

- the body as site for new technologies;
- body illusions as a threshold to capture the body and couple with technology;
- the destabilisation of accepted notions and construction of subjectivity with the body/technology cyborg;
- the interpenetration of the material and virtual.

A Letter on Fungal Intimacy

This 'Letter on Fungal Intimacy' traces a parallel process to my art production, one that acknowledges the particularity of my time and place in North America. What follows are observations and rationalisations of a woman working with contemporary technology such as VR.

I saw VR as a site to try out the projects preoccupying postmodern debate: the project of inventing new images of the body where it could be seen as a threshold, a field of intensities rather than half of the mind/body dualism; and the feminist project of redesigning female subjectivity, a subjectivity well-disposed to dispersal in images of webs of connections, to functioning in a net of interconnections – artificial, abstract and perfectly operationally real.

VR technology and feminist research were simultaneously developing in the North American society in which I live. I relished the thought of metaphorically linking attributes identified as female (at least culturally and even traditionally) with key structural characteristics of the technology. This possibility seemed a richly humorous joke out of anyone's control.

Could a technology, built by and intended for the reinforcement of the stereotypical monadic, hierarchical, specialised subject position, be pushed to such an extreme that it would support the opposite, namely, characteristics reminiscent of the very attributes currently describing women? Women were seen as largely responsible for personal and social relationships and networks, non-specialised work open to interruption, and undefined or at least unclear ego boundaries. What is interactivity, I thought, but expertise in structuring and restructuring complex and shifting relationships; what is parallel processing but expertise in handling multiple simultaneous events, skilfully choreographing continuous and interruptable tasks; what is the cybernetic and surveyed body/self but one that can sustain integrity with blurred boundaries and even multiple bodies and identities as in the case of childbearing? What is networking, a *raison d'être* of the electronic environment, but an acknowledgement of mutual interdependence – complete with such vulnerabilities as viruses, which only confirm the mutuality?

183

Could it be that the very structural characteristics of a technology such as VR also describe the attributes of a subjectivity required for survival within that new technological sensorium? Would this mean that women could, in a kind of historical accident, in a moment of incongruity, feel at home.

Several years later I encountered Donna Haraway's influential text on cyborgs.[1] Her text seemed to suggest more twists in the contemporary technological condition. Haraway's notion of illegitimate offspring appeared to rationalise the dubious militaristic origins of the technology. It seemed to suggest that VR could be seen as ironically reversing its intended purpose. VR was first developed as the head-mounted helmet for fighter pilots. Even though these bio-fighting-machines first appear as all powerful independent entities these individuals are intimately linked into larger cybernetic systems which profoundly increase their vulnerability. Also important for me, Haraway created an image of the interdependent feedback loop of interactivity as the cyborg condition. Finally, she identified a feminist position as having the best chance for survival and living to tell the tale as a cyborg, creating a girls' own book of cyberadventures.

Perhaps such a technological environment could be described as 'feminised' but at the same time this seemed like an elaborate hidden joke. To reinscribe existing gender representations (of whatever order, reactionary or radical) seemed overly literal and already nostalgic. Conversely, to suggest as some technologists did that gender and race could be erased in a virtual world of shared communication seemed as questionable as any promise of a universalising, levelling, utopian or dystopian environment. Since then the joke seems less playful and ironic, now more painful.

What I considered to be obvious in VR environments – the fluctuating reversals of subject/object in a cybernetic system – was not part of highly visible VR narratives. The technology in these narratives is not seen as disturbing a centred sense of self/body. On the contrary, it is seen as strengthening the intact self. The discussion of the challenges to our sense of identity and body has largely been left aside. An influential scientist such as Marvin Minsky saw VR as part of the technological evolution of humans towards increased independent mastery.[2] Cyberpunks in cyberspace were a kind of nostalgic mix: Jack Kerouac on the road to the new virgin frontier. The technologists promised a kind of superhuman untouchable body able to intervene invisibly.

Though a cyborg entity is often postulated in these narratives, it does not transgress the notion of a separate, independent, wilful and hierarchical self – instead it evolves a more powerful version. Ironically this technological condition is also seen as capable of neutralising troubling experiences which might disturb a notion of autonomous self with intact boundaries. The narratives have centred on safe sex, safe drugs, safe transcendence and now safe feminism.

The media play of teledildonics and safe sex in cyberspace is familiar, so too is Timothy Leary's evangelical promotion of VR as mind expanding. An attraction of telepresence is the apparent transcendence of bodily limits in reaching out to places inaccessible for the material body. The body is seen in fictional cyberspace as meat, and cyberspace, itself, is characterised as a chance to leave the body behind. A distant mentor of cyberpunk, William Burroughs, would laconically say 'the body is obsolete'.[3] Jean-François Lyotard would mix evolution, technology and transcendence when he said the aim of all contemporary research, in whatever discipline, is to emancipate the human brain from constraints common to all living systems on the earth, or to manufacture a system, independent of those constraints.[4] More recently, cyberfeminism has been pictured by Sadie Plant as the natural matrix, collapsing identity into the cybernetic net: as she sums up, 'If the male human is the only human, the female cyborg is the only cyborg.'[5]

Why might these narratives of technological sex, drugs, transcendence or feminism be so recurring? In a culture centred on the autonomous individual these experiences in life are transgressive. Could this technology therefore be a means to simulate those experiences, control and annul them, to tighten the defences around an intact identity?

On the other hand there may be another way to look at a

common thread running through virtual experiences. All are experiences which challenge a conventional integrity through an out-of-body, out-of-identity, or at least, an intersubjective experience. It may not be sex, drugs, transcendence or cyberfeminism that the user experiences but an environment that shares some of their characteristics. These narratives are a way to account for a transgressive technological experience for which there is as yet no subjective position. That an autonomous, replete monadic subject is being decentred by the operations of the system itself, not from any critique or imaginative move on the part of feminists, or postmodern theorists or philosophers, gives pause for thought. Something about contemporary virtual technology may erase gender as articulated. It may well be that the technology is implicated in constructing a different position of subjectivity for all of us, a position which will accommodate and be appropriate to the new social economic order.

In cyberfeminism there seems to be an assumption that cyberfeminists will remain unscathed in these environments. Before rushing in to claim this territory I must ask to what ideological ends it might be useful to have a technological environment constructing a subjective experience closer to an alternative, female and postmodern position. I expect the most unexpected and taken-for-granted aspects of subjectivity to be modified. What if both cyberfeminism and lonely male heroic narratives are nostalgic content?

Let me indulge in some speculation and play with the cyborg for a moment. As a figuration it takes on powerful imaginative and political roles as a material and virtual entity that exists as flesh and information in a continuous feedback loop. Artists, however, intentionally manifest it as a lived condition, transforming metaphorical figure into material sign. In the process, some darker sides come to light. Pain. Though there are invisible and seemingly unnoticeable hybrids of machine and human, the material hybrids bring to the surface the price of transgressing embodiment. If one desires to transcend the material body it will be painful. One could suggest that this

186

physical pain is also the sign of psychic pain as we reorganise our psychic structures. Artists such as Orlan and Stelarc seem to place themselves in laboratories of pain, experimenting with ways to remain fully aware throughout cybernetic mutations of the body. Within this context Orlan's description of herself fully conscious on the operating table, performing for her interactive satellite audience, takes on a complex pathos. 'I was able, without feeling pain, to answer the people who were feeling their own pain as they were watching me'. Telepresence takes on a new meaning as does VR's relationship with drugs. Through Orlan the spectators experience their own pain indirectly and through telepresence; they are there and not there. Conversely they are acknowledged as part of the telepresence experienced by Orlan denying her own pain through drugs.

As much as the cyborg represents a transgression of boundaries, it also falls short of complex interdependence. As much as it pictures the hybrid of machine and human, the model of multiple humans and machines is unformed. The cyborg still suggests a solitary state reminiscent of bachelor machines, those artist machines modelling self-enclosed sexuality and repro-duction which have been a problematic subject for feminist artists. Haraway suggests as much. Her final imagery of cyborgs calls upon a salamander's ability to regrow as a new model and is suspicious of the reproductive matrix and of most birthing. 'We require regeneration, not rebirth, and the possibility for our reconstitution to include the utopian dream of the hope for a monstrous world without gender.'[6] Though this is a compelling image I wonder how it may parallel the technological agenda already in place: promises of transcending the body, the genetic code, the birth process, carbon-based life forms, gender, race (but not class), and enclosing and enlarging oneself within a fluctuating cyborg body. As the cyborg image seems to move closer to a feminine bachelor machine caught up in its own self-referential motor it increasingly appears as a mirror image of a too familiar condition.

Before throwing out the biological baby with the embryonic

fluid it may be useful to remember that part of our biological experience does illustrate deep interdependent relations with difference. Childbearing is one experience of complex and non-socially constructed metamorphosis; it involves an interrelation of fluctuating identities which must be navigated as the same system and differentiated at the same time; it is a process of uncontrollable events among two willful systems – and these are negotiated first in our own experiences as a child.

Sometimes, at night, when I start to picture the cyborg, I wonder if the popular narratives are right. Is it/will it be a more powerful intact identity but with all the other attributes as well: unclear boundaries, here and everywhere, regeneration over time (that is, a grasp on immortality), regeneration over birth (that is, assurance of replicating myself), a laterally displaced, nonhierarchical networked interior, multiform sexuality and reproduction?

I contemplate the fungus found in Michigan, ten thousand kilos replicating itself over fifteen hundred years, over fifteen hectares in one vast underground network, now and then discreetly showing itself above ground in the guise of an individual, and picking and choosing its form of reproduction.

Spectral Bodies (1991)

Spectral Bodies is a videotape that considers the issues at stake around simulation and subjectivity in contemporary technology. Specifically, it is concerned with virtual reality technology, which literally reads and writes our bodies. Using emerging technology, it traverses the boundaries between the imaginary and the 'real' in the realm of scientific metaphor, physiological testing and the construction of our own subjectivity – of our selves. *Spectral Bodies* could be seen as an approach to science fiction that disrupts the metaphors we have woven around ourselves and technology. Technology is treated as *instrumenting* (if I can use this word), or rendering instrumental our preoccupations and desires in today's culture.

As a result, this science fiction is as much a fiction of science as it is a fiction about contemporary subjectivity.

Through puzzles and short narratives, the tape describes how we may perceive a loss or change of body and, quite often along with it, a loss of personal self. The image of the body as an intimate part of perceptual and technological processes has been extended through the development of computer technological instrumentation, such as VR. The conceptual reinscription implied by this and the possibility of occupying other senses is explored in my recent works such as this one. *Spectral Bodies* focuses on narratives that explore one of these other senses – the sense of presence. It is a form of intimacy with our own bodies that is relatively unacknowledged in everyday life and yet enables us to function as a complex relation of parts, despite body changes. This sense is formally known as the proprioceptive sense. As a sense of presence it is, in many ways, how we know we are.

The *Spectral Bodies* narratives can be seen as equally fictional and 'real' testimonies to how we think we know where our senses and body boundaries begin and end. The tape begins with a reference to mid-nineteenth century scientists who discovered through the study of after-images how the corporal body is involved in the process of vision. At that time scientific activity in this area was so compelling and exhilarating that several scientists went blind experimenting with their own vision by staring directly at the sun. This new work on vision destabilised the earlier camera obscura model in which the observer was autonomous and sacrosanct. It marked a beginning: the body was seen subsequently as both influencing our perceptual process and as a site to read and to write upon.

Two stories in the tape from neurological histories poignantly testify to the loss of the sense of the body. The first is the most touching: a woman attempts to describe what it is like to completely lose, through neurological disease, any sense of where her body is at any moment in time. She is like a rag doll, incapable of motion or position. The proprioceptive sense is taken for granted to such a degree that both she and our culture lack words to describe it. It is like the body is blind, she says, it cannot see itself. This is part of the reason I play with images of blindness and sight, external and internal, throughout the tape.

We often assume our body limits are fixed, and the boundaries clear. Other stories in the tape tell how bodies can change in impossible ways, however, and very quickly. These testimonies are excerpts of physiological experiments, which I performed, creating body illusions with 'subjects'. The experiments suggest that our imaginary bodies (or are they our real bodies?) can be destabilised.

After destabilisation, 'bodies' are ready to be re-mapped. A segment of interactive work then begins the process of re-representing the body as a virtual body. Working with scientists at Brandeis University in Boston and the University of Alberta in Edmonton, I combined body illusions of impossible arm and hand transformations with VR technology. A spectral hand and arm are portrayed as spectral dots and skeletal lines in a virtual environment. The VR participant recognises this as a conventional schematic representation of his or her arm and hand. However, these initial representations of hand/arm begin to transform. The spectral arm and fingers lengthen, the palm spreads open and so on. Combined with body illusions, the participant's limb is mapped into an insect-like thing. As this mapping takes place there seems to be a physiological sense that this transformed virtual body is oneself.

VR computer technology can be approached as a kind of fiction made physical. At the same time it is a machine to create fictions of ourselves. This short excerpt of virtual reality (VR) work in the middle of the tape is one narrative among many – and one irony among others. As a whole, *Spectral Bodies* opens the door on the permeable and flexible mapping of the imaginary body with the material one, pointing to the role of technology as an instrument that intervenes in both the physiological and the imaginary.

The Virtual Body (1993)

The Virtual Body is a nostalgic material object. A first sight it seems to be a museum piece made of alluring, warm, fine materials, reminiscent of the column stereoscopes of the mid-nineteenth century. These innovative optical devices were part scientific instrument, part aesthetic object, and part perceptual media. *The Virtual Body* occupies this ambiguous ground of instrument and object. Evocative of nineteenth-century taste and world view, its reassuring distinction between the spectator and the object is still familiar. But it is just this familiar relation that is challenged; in new technologies and, once the spectator interacts with this piece, the familiar spectator/object relation is turned inside out.

The Virtual Body initially presents a rococo room as an object for the spectator. Then these relations are inverted, taking up the spectator within the simulation. Instead of the spectator being central to the room's perspective, standing under an interior sky, a model of order, the spectator is taken in, dispersed, positionless, yet everywhere.

Not overtly about technology, this quiet piece has a deceptive appearance. It mimics absorption of current technology into familiar material environments. But as technology seems to disappear, assimilated by objects, it remains ubiquitous, everywhere. As a consequence, the object, in effect, becomes simply a carrier, a host, a nostalgic remainder of materiality.

This work addresses a shift in the idea of self under these conditions. In the highly technological culture of North America the clear distinction between the spectator and object is changing so that the boundaries between the two are no longer clear. Shedding the comforting nineteenth-century perspective of the body as a self-contained organism, the body cannot now, in a sense, be distinguished from the information environment. Rather than a contained and independent self, we have a body that is intimately readable, a universally coded information event. Our boundaries seem porous, in a cyborgian condition.

This piece is about the moment of awkwardness as we recognise ourselves in this experience.

Interaction in new technologies is experiential, often crossing physiological thresholds and body boundaries. This is why a body illusion is at the centre of this piece. The illusion is experiential. Body illusions can modify the sense of body presence, impossible to describe as material or virtual. In this case they create the sense of motion without moving, a sense of the body travelling with the awareness that the body is still. One cannot stand back from the artwork and observe it. To experience it one must be taken in by it. Human physiology and the machine, spectator and object, the observer and observed are merged.

The great technological dream includes a wish to simulate experience. Will we attempt a direct technological link with our own body presence; will we intervene in the way we inhabit our own material presence? *The Virtual Body* brings these subtle shifts to the surface in seemingly innocent ways.

The wooden cabinet stands on a platform in the middle of the room. As spectators enter they see on top of the cabinet a miniature glass room. The walls are semi-transparent and illuminated. On approaching they see that the images in the handblown glass and liquid crystal mylar portray a rococo room. These richly coloured images glow with light from the patterned floor within – a computer-generated pattern on a monitor.

Steps to the platform beckon to take a closer look. Standing next to the glass room, spectators notice a brass peephole in the top/ceiling. Peering inside they see, momentarily, the rococo ceiling – in fact a reflection. But just as it appears, this ceiling image is interrupted by the floor image on the monitor, and this floor image in its turn is overtaken by the ceiling. The space in the miniature room destabilises.

On one glass wall of the room, where a knob on an instrument might be, is a hole in which to put one's hand – to enter the room. This intervention by the spectator is sensed and a third state begins. The glass walls of the miniature room suddenly become opaque and lose their transparency for anyone standing on the outside. Meanwhile the peering spectator stares down at his or her hand spread across the room's floor, the monitor. The floor pattern on the monitor begins to scroll. In a few moments the spectator begins to sense a body illusion: a displacement of the body, an illusion of motion. One's hand appears to be infinitely travelling away from the body. Then the arm begins to take the body with it. It is as if miniature space is folded into infinite space, as if stillness is folded into motion. The body loses all references: inside/outside, giant/miniature, spectator/object, part/whole. The spectator becomes an instrumental site of the technology, caught up by the dispersion of events.

As the spectator withdraws, the transparent miniature room reappears, glowing once again. This rococo room, which was the original installation site in Antwerp, Belgium, is an illusionistic box designed to surround, overwhelm and trick the spectator. In a similar way many new technologies are committed to creating a simulated sensorium, enveloping all the senses. But there is a significant difference. In the rococo space, the floor remains firm for spectators while the surrounding visual intoxication is oriented towards them. In the postmodern, virtual world the floor is no longer firm and stable. In *The Virtual Body*, as the floor destabilises it takes a sense of a separate self along with it.

Notes

1 Donna Haraway, 'A Manifesto for Cyborgs: Science, Technology and Socialist Feminism in the 1980s', *Socialist Review* 80 (1985), pp65-107.
2 Marvin Minsky, public presentation during Ars Electronica, Linz, Austria 1990.
3 William Burroughs, 'Is the Body Obsolete?', *Whole Earth Review*, Summer 1989, p54.
4 Jean-François Lyotard, 'Designing the Social', in *Virtual Seminar on the Bioapparatus*, Catherine Richards and Nell Tenhaaf (eds), Banff Centre for the Arts, Banff, 1991, p28.
5 Sadie Plant.
6 Haraway, *op.cit.*, pp65-67.

Fabulous Feminist Futures and the Lure of Cyberculture

Judith Squires

Cyberspace

> ... neither a pure 'pop' phenomenon nor a simply technological artefact, but rather a powerful, collective, mnemonic technology that promises to have an important, if not revolutionary, impact on the future compositions of human identities and cultures.
>
> David Tomas[1]

In her 'Manifesto for Cyborgs', Donna Haraway claims that she would rather be a cyborg than a goddess. What are we to make of this? Her manifesto is, she claims: 'an ironic political myth faithful to feminism, socialism and materialism.' But why, in attempting to create a vision of a materialist, socialist and feminist future, does she invoke the image of a cyborg – 'a cybernetic organism, a hybrid of machine and organism, a creature of social reality as well as a creature of fiction'[2]? And, more importantly, why has this image proved so appealing to so many since? Cyborgs are becoming pretty ubiquitous: our films, popular fictions and theoretical writings are littered with them. Clearly the cybernetic has gripped our imaginations. It increasingly structures our fantasies, phobias and political aspirations.

I want to take a sceptical look at the lure of cyberculture: to ask why it appeals, what it has to offer, and what the dangers of being seduced by its charms might be. In particular, I want to look at the interaction between cybernetics, cyberpunk and feminism, critically evaluating the forms of cyberfeminism that have developed, along with their detractors.

I shall argue that whilst there *may* be potential for an alliance between cyborg imagery and a materialist-feminism, this potential has been largely submerged beneath a sea of technophoric cyberdrool. If we are to salvage the image of the cyborg we would do well to insist that cyberfeminism be seen as a metaphor for addressing the inter-relation between technology and the body, not as a means of using the former to transcend the latter. Furthermore, although the appeal of the cyborg may reside in the challenge it poses to Enlightenment metaphysics, we need not accept the Enlightenment's myth about its own nature as a coherent, unitary project, which can only be accepted or rejected wholesale. Thus, we can jettison the rationalist and individualist assumptions of Enlightenment thinking whilst reclaiming its pluralistic and democratic political project. In short, we may want to use the cyborg as a positive icon in our political imagination, but we cannot also allow ourselves to take an apolitical stance with regard to the form and operation of developing technologies.

Blurring the Boundaries: The Fourth Discontinuity

Forgetting about the body is an old Cartesian trick …
Allucquere Rosanne Stone[3]

In an ironic anticipation of the cybernetic theorists of postmodernity, Descartes mobilises a comparison between the cyborg figure of the machine animal (or the 'natural automata') and the human, in an attempt to ratify the human/animal distinction. Unfortunately the criteria of distinction claimed by Descartes no longer hold true: feedback mechanisms and generalising reason can no longer be claimed to be exclusive to humans. Hence the re-awakening of the metaphysical question which Descartes believed he had resolved so categorically. The sharp discontinuity which he argued to be of such importance

195

looks increasingly fuzzy. Whilst there clearly are differences between persons and machines, these are increasingly a matter of degree rather than disjuncture. As Baudrillard and others have pointed out,[4] the boundaries between technology and nature are in the midst of a deep restructuring: the old distinctions between the biological and the technological, the natural and the artificial, the human and the mechanical, are becoming increasingly unreliable. The cybernetic visions of popular fiction and film, and of recent theoretical writings, can be seen as important psychic explorations of the blurring of these boundaries and the possibilities for new human continuities – explorations which have manifested both a frightened rejection and a touching faith in the image of the cyborg: both technophobia and technophoria.

However modish, the blurring of boundaries is not, of course, distinctive to our age. There have been other boundaries, in other eras, which have been subjected to the challenge of knowledges which questioned, and ultimately undermined, the assumed disjunctures in the phenomena of nature. Following Copernicus (who deprived us of the illusion that the earth was at the centre of the universe) and Darwin (who shattered our belief that man was quite distinct from animal), Freud placed himself at the centre of the third key stage in the gradual progression towards the elimination of all discontinuities and the creation of continuities, claiming that he was 'endeavouring to prove to the "ego" of each one of us that he is not even master in his own house'.[5] These three epoch-marking challenges to the ego resulted, he argued, in the notion that human beings are no longer discontinuous with the world around them, but are continuous with the universe, the rest of the animal kingdom and with themselves.

It is in this context that we can understand the claim made by Bruce Mazlish that man's pride, his refusal to acknowledge the continuity between the human and the mechanical, is 'the substratum upon which the distrust of technology ... has been reared.'[6] Yet, despite this distrust, Mazlish argues that: '... the fourth discontinuity must now be eliminated ... in the process

196

man's ego will have to undergo another rude shock, similar to those administered by Copernicus, Darwin and Freud.'[7] The rude shock which confronts us today, challenging the assumed discontinuity between man and machine, takes a cybernetic form. 'To put it bluntly,' Mazlish continues, 'we are now coming to realise that man and the machines he creates are continuous and that the same conceptual schemes, for example, that help explain the working of his brain also explain the workings of a "thinking machine".'[8]

This gradual elimination of discontinuities could be conceived as the erosion of clear limits to the self: the complication of the other. As apparently secure walls, delimiting our sense of self, prove to be but permeable membranes, our insecurity has mounted, allowing for both liberatory explorations of the nature of being and various forms of retrenchment. In the face of insecurity about our limits and the realisation of the possibility of continuity, we all too often witness, not the celebration of new possibilities, but a retreat into fortress identities, the strategic use of the massive, regressive common denominators of essential identities: '... it is,' says Kristeva, 'a rare person who does not invoke a primal shelter to compensate for personal disarray.'[9]

Understanding these cosmological, biological and psychological developments as successive blows to our desire to conceive of ourselves as autonomous, self-determining individuals, enables us to place the current concern with the cybernetic in a context of a persistent ontological concern with the nature of the self. The human, it may be argued, has always been constituted by its boundaries, the location of these boundaries being a site of contestation. Taking a Derridean notion of identity formation we can argue that any entity, to be an entity, has to exclude that which is not itself, thereby constituting otherness. The other (to use briefly that ubiquitous term) constitutes the entity by defining its limits.[10] Constituting the Good of this entity (taken here to be the human) always involves, theoretically and politically, projecting the negative on to the other. Thus (contra recent concerns about the apolitical

197

nature of deconstruction), I would claim that understanding the nature of these limits is always an ethical issue, and challenging the parameters of the limits always a political project.

Thus, the redrawing of the boundaries of the self is a political process: how they are drawn will depend on who has the power to set the agenda. In this context it is worth reminding ourselves, lest we had forgotten, that our society is still deeply patriarchal, and that – given that previous concepts of the self have been informed by patriarchal assumptions – we cannot assume that the current cybernetic developments will not also result in ontologies that, although redrawn, are nonetheless still highly gendered.

In order to uphold the fourth discontinuity, between man and his tools, Descartes distinguishes between mind and matter: the 'rational soul', he claimed, is 'that part of us *distinct from the body* whose essence ... is only to think' (emphasis added). This Cartesian dualism has been much theorised within feminist theory, for whilst Descartes upheld the 'fourth discontinuity' for *man* through the transcendence by the rational soul of the body, this rational soul was a gendered soul. The boundaries of the self were drawn with a patriarchal pen. Thus, any loss of discontinuity will have different impact upon the masculine and the feminine self, the feminine already having been constituted as more continuous with the material/mechanical, through a denial of the tools of limit-definition. One might even conjecture that cyberculture is a particularly masculine exploration of the new-found continuity between mind and machine, of particular import to the masculine notion of the self which had defined itself in terms of the mind as distinct from the materiality of both body and machine. The feminine, however, having been more clearly constituted as *embodied*, must address technological developments from a different starting point. Hence, to investigate new possibilities for understandings of the self which encompasses both masculine and feminine experiences, we must explore the boundaries of both mind and body. For the division between mind and matter, between that without spatial location and that which is firmly grounded, is not one which will necessarily be resolved by the acceptance of the continuity between the human and the mechanical.

The disembodiment of the political has posed a distinct dilemma for feminists of all persuasions, for whom difference has most frequently been experienced in embodied rather than purely cerebral form. Indeed, part of what was at issue in the development of an autonomous women's movement was an explicit challenge to the arrogance of those who thought that ideas could be separated from presence. For this move all too often resulted in an amnesia about embodied differences which served to transform man into a paradigm of humankind as such, obfuscating the ways in which the body itself is a cultural construct. Far from 'forgetting about the body' we would be better served by following Butler's injunction to explore the political significance of the formation of its boundaries.[11] Thus whilst cyborg imagery *could* potentially aid us in our exploration of the body viewed as a variable boundary, 'a surface whose permeability is politically regulated'[12], we should not be too optimistic that it will necessarily do so.

Dreary Dreams of Texan Boys

> ... patriarchy is more willing to dispense with human life than with male superiority.
>
> Claudia Springer[13]

I want now to briefly consider the phenomenon of cyberculture – the writing of cyberpunks and the images of cyborgs, exploring cyberculture's celebration of the continuity between man and machine, its hip acceptance of the loss of the boundary.[14]

'Eighties tech,' claims Bruce Sterling, one of cyberpunk's most able advocates, 'sticks to the skin, responds to the touch: the personal computer, the Sony Walkman, the portable telephone, the soft contact lens ... prosthetic limbs, implanted circuitry, cosmetic surgery, genetic alteration.'[15] For cyberpunks technology is inside the body and mind itself. Yet it is also global: the satellite media net, the multinational corporation both recurring as dominant literary tropes in cybernovels. Cyberpunk is characterised by its integration of these technologies with a hedonism and a counter-culture 'guerrilla' political conscious-ness which – in contradistinction to 1960s counterculture that was rural, romanticised and anti-science – takes the hacker along with the rocker as its cultural icon.

Yet, despite its oppositional image, there is little understand-ing of social process or political critique in these writings, just a mystical desire to leave it all behind. In an age in which there is so much perceived risk in living and so much information for both body and mind to contain and survive, it is not perhaps surprising that we are confronted with the desire to transcend and escape where and who we are. But here the desire for transcendence is coupled by a refusal to contemplate that in which we are grounded. Thus, whilst one of cyberpunk's strongest features is its rich thesaurus of metaphors linking the organic and the electronic, one of its weakest is the fact that it completely ignores the question of whether some political controls over technology are desirable, or possible. There is an electronic solipsism which clearly derives from the compelling but ultimately naive prognostications of Marshall McLuhan, and it is marked by the same refusal to acknowledge the political reality of power and its operations.

Furthermore, it is the fictional vision of a very particular group of people, the imagination of a small subset of youth culture in the wealthy 'First World', the sensibility of the technicians and artists working with new media (special effects wizards, mixmasters, tape effect technicians, graphics hackers …). This group is, to quote Suvin, 'a small, single-digit percentage even of the fifteen-to-thirty-years' age group, even in the affluent North (never mind the whole earth)'.[16] It should not be forgotten therefore that many of the engineers currently debating the form and nature of cyberspace are, as Stone reminds us, 'the young turks of comput-ing engineering, men in their late teens and twenties, and they are preoccupied with the things with which postpubescent men have always been preoccupied.'[17] It is this 'rather steamy group' who will generate the codes and descriptors by which bodies in cyberspace are represented.

One example amongst many of how this is playing out currently is to be found in Virtual Valerie 1 and 2 (two CD-ROM programmes produced by Reactor) in which, 'the aim is to check out Valerie's 3-D computer animated department, then Valerie herself. If you keep her happy by giving the right answers to the questions she asks, you can undress her then get her to enact different fantasies (eg. in Valerie 2 she clones herself, grows a penis and has sex with herself)'.[18] Looking for more positive uses of cybernetic technology one might turn to the fact that in virtual space, the phenomenon of 'computer cross-dressing' is rife. 'On the nets,' one critic claims, 'where warranting, or grounding, a persona in a physical body, is meaningless, men routinely use female personae whenever they choose, and vice versa.'[19] Yet we must recognise that, despite this exciting potential for degendering social interaction, gendered modes of communication have themselves actually remained relatively stable, only who uses which of the two socially recognised modes has become more fluid. Furthermore, the uses of computer cross-dressing are themselves politically circumscribed. Whereas such cross-dressing seems to offer a minimal thrill for some of the men on the internet, most of the degendering on the net is being done for purely defensive rather than politically exploratory reasons: women, wishing to use the net without being subject to the usual inanities of chat-up lines and sexual stereotyping, have found it useful to make tactical use of non-gendered internet identities. Interchanges on the internet do not (yet) live up to our radical imaginings of their potentialities.

One does not have to be an eco-feminist (let alone a goddess) to recognise that most of the cyberimagery and cyberfictions produced to date have done little to challenge patriarchal stereotypes of gendered bodily difference. Far from exploring an ungendered ideal, cyborg imagery has created exaggeratedly masculine and feminine bodies. As Claudia Springer notes,

'While popular culture texts enthusiastically explore boundary breakdowns between humans and computers, gender boundaries are treated less flexibly.'[20] And, although it is certainly true that in the case of some contemporary science-fiction writers, technology makes possible the destabilisation of sexual identity as a category, it has been noted that there has also been 'a fairly insistent history of representations of technology that work to fortify – sometimes desperately – conventional understandings of the feminine.'[21] We might reasonably conclude that cybernetics alone will not change power relations, they merely allow us to reinscribe existing power networks in new forms and media.

The acceptance of the continuity between man and machine does not inevitably involve the challenge to gender discontinuity. Despite its willingness to relinquish other previously sacrosanct categories and distinctions, patriarchy on the net continues to uphold gender difference. Most of the cyberfutures on offer are simply representations of contemporary cultural myths and prejudices disguised under heavy layers of futuristic make-up. Perhaps we find here a 'fifth discontinuity', the elimination of which will mark another 'great shock to man's ego'. The bifurcation of gendered identities into discrete male/female categories appears to be a more resilient discontinuity within the political imagination of cyberpunks than the bifurcation of man/machine: all around us we witness explorations of the continuity between the latter, but continuities between the former are still largely absent from the political utopias on offer.

Given this, should we understand these cyberpunk visions as critical and rebellious, or escapist and co-opted? Is it, as one commentator argued, 'at its best conservative and at its worst rebarbative – if not downright tedious.'[22] If so, it would appear to be an unlikely source for utopian visions and political manifestos for feminist theorists. And yet ... One could happily write cyberpunk off as the latest fad of a few post-pubescent rebellious Texan boys, a handful of novels by William Gibson and a couple of effective PR men, if it were not for the fact that cyberpunk taps into concerns which are of import to a much wider constituency.

For cyberculture provides us with a particularly timely set of images which help us to think through the key theoretical agendas of the moment. Where multimedia provided a visual metaphor for the concerns of multi-culturalism, virtual reality offers metaphors wonderfully resonant for the theoretical concerns of poststructuralism. Regardless of their actual manifestations, these technological developments offer a new vocabulary for our political imagination, aiding the task of forging innovative political myths. Let us therefore note that for many the development of cybernetics and virtual reality are of interest primarily as a source of resonant images and icons with which to construct radical philosophical and political visions.

Hopeful Monsters: The Tyranny of Biology[23]

> Why aren't there any women in cyberspace?
>
> Scott Bukatman[24]

This section looks at the more specifically feminist attempts to negotiate cyberculture and asks: in what ways have feminist theorists appropriated the latest manifestations of techno-culture, and with what intent? Are these feminist writers motivated by the same concerns as the cyberpunks, or is their agenda rather different?

Despite a long-standing tradition of feminist writing claiming that technology is encoded in masculine terms, and despite the blatantly sexist outpouring of the cyberpunks, the image of the cyborg has not proved to be just another toy for the boys. In allowing us, requiring us, to rethink the relation between consciousness and body, technological development impacts upon one of the central concerns of feminism, in all its forms. And, while some feminists read its impact as just one more patriarchal mechanism of oppression, others have seen potential for liberation in cybernetics and begun to envisage a cybernetic future.

So, if the tradition of science fiction writing permits a fusing of political concerns with the 'playful creativity of the imagination'[25], what can we learn of the political concerns of feminists who feel drawn to the image of the cyborg? To answer this question I shall look at the writings of three quite different 'cyberfeminists': Shulamith Firestone, Donna Haraway and Sadie Plant. Their versions of cyberfeminism are crucially distinct: the first of these is an explicitly modernist and materialist vision of social revolution and human emancipation; the second adopts a more ironic socialist feminist stance informed by the theoretical developments of a pluralist postmodernity. The last is a postmodern perspective which (I shall claim) shares the apoliticism of the cyberpunks but also invokes a kind of mystical utopianism of the eco-feminist earth-goddesses. However, what all three perspectives share is a desire to reformulate the relation between gender and the body.

One of the most exciting visions of cyberfeminism to date is still to be found in a text from cyberculture's pre-history, Shulamith Firestone's *The Dialectic of Sex* (1972). Unlike most visions that have followed, hers is an explicitly revolutionary project, steeped in the rhetoric of emancipation and progress. Adopting and adapting the Marxist dialectical materialist account of class struggle, Firestone offers her own account of the sex-class predicament:

> And just as the end goal of socialist revolution was not only the elimination of the economic class privilege but of the economic *distinction* itself, so the end goal of feminist revolution must be, unlike that of the first feminist movement, not just the elimination of male *privilege* but of the sex *distinction* itself: genital difference between human beings would no longer matter culturally.[26]

It is to cybernetics that Firestone looks to end both distinctions. 'It has become necessary,' she claims, 'to free humanity from the tyranny of its biology.' 'Humanity can no longer afford to remain in the transitional stage between simply animal existence and full control of nature.'[27] Firestone's work is, of course, characterised by a wholly hostile relation to the female body: 'childbirth *hurts*', she proclaims. 'And it isn't good for you.'[28] Women's liberation for Firestone involved the freeing of women from the tyranny of reproduction by any means possible. The technophoric desire to use – what Firestone broadly defines as – 'cybernetics' to escape the confines of the body is manifest. It is however, embedded within a (now deeply unfashionable) structuralist account of the dialectics of sex, class and culture: a scheme which predicts the inevitable progress towards the mastery of nature.

What Firestone calls for is 'cybernation' – the full takeover by machines of increasingly complex functions, machines which she envisages may soon equal or surpass man in original-thinking and problem-solving. Reflecting on the immediate impact of cybernation on the position of women, Firestone predicted the following: the erosion of the status of the 'head of household' particularly in the working class, which could shake up family life and traditional sex roles even more profoundly; massive unrest of the young, poor and the unemployed, and ultimately, revolution ...

The vision is prescient, but the theoretical stance is sadly dated. When, in the 1980s, Donna Haraway was asked to write on what socialist-feminist priorities ought to be in the Reagan years, she too turned to cybernetics. But in her definitive cyberfeminist text, Haraway claims that the cyborg image helps to express two crucial arguments: the first one is that 'the production of universal, totalising theory is a major mistake that misses most of reality, probably always, but certainly now'; the second is that 'taking responsibility for the social relations of science and technology means refusing an anti-science metaphysics, a demonology of technology, and so means embracing the skilful task of reconstructing the boundaries of daily life, in partial connection with others, in communication with all of our parts.'[29] Thus her claim is that cyborg imagery 'can suggest a way out of the maze of dualisms in which we have explained our bodies and our tools to ourselves.'[30] Thus, whilst the second argument of the 1980s Haraway has echoes of

Firestone's 1970s agenda, her first argument is clearly a sign of the post-universalising times.

One could, of course, accept the first of Haraway's two stated arguments without taking on board cyborg imagery: and many have done so previously. One can reject the homogenising strategies of grand narratives and challenge the universal pretensions of modernist thought; one can endorse a politics of difference which celebrates the local and the particular, one can reject binary dualisms and false polarities; one can explore the possibilities of flexible, transitory identities ... without ever making recourse to cyborg imagery. Cybernetics, of course, becomes of central concern to one's political vision if one seeks an androgynous, disembodied future in which the fleshy issue of physical difference is transcended, thereby rendering the reproductive, maternal, essential women absent from one's future utopia. But it also provides a useful lexicon for rewriting origin stories: 'cyborg authors subvert the central myths of origin of Western culture' writes Haraway.[31] Thus the cyborg is situated directly against the competing ecofeminist representative of political change – the mother-goddess who is located quite firmly in the distinctly embodied female self. This polarity is not new: there have always been those who wished to transcend the bodily nature of the female and exist purely in the cerebral realm of individual autonomy, and those who wished to celebrate physical difference as the basis for essential ontologies and epistemologies. Haraway, however, has the advantage of writing at a time when technological developments make the former ideal attainable as never before.

In distinction to the eco-feminist utopia which would have us return to an innocent, natural organic past in the name of protecting mother earth, cyborgs represent the more flexible mediation capable of incorporating, rather than repudiating, science and technology. The manifesto for cyborgs is therefore seen by Haraway as a statement to socialist feminists that they would do better to opt for the contradictions of everyday material life, than for the comforts of divine resolution. Interested in bringing together feminist, Marxist and environmentalist concerns, Haraway ironically reconfigures the cyborg as an exemplary postmodern figure which resists the conventional unifying utopian vision. Her motivation for constructing such an 'ironic political myth' is explicitly grounded in the political realities of contemporary society: she never loses sight of the nitty-gritty of lived social relations.

In a similar vein, whilst recognising that ' ... cyberpunk is a boys' club', Joan Gordon also argues that it does much that could enrich feminism by 'directing it away from nostalgia'.[32] The implication is that we can escape the confines of natural women and vegetarian, non-polluting earth-mothers only by embracing the attitude of the sleazy boys of cyberpunk. And, despite the polarity of this argument, one can see that if feminist science fiction offers only utopian dreams of a pastoral world, fuelled by organic structures, inspired by versions of the archetypal Great Mother, then cyberpunk comes to seem appealing. But, perhaps more importantly, Gordon argues that, 'Cyberpunk, with all its cynicism, shows a future we might reasonably expect, and shows people successfully coping, surviving, and manipulating it.'[33] In recognition of this fact, Gordon argues that feminists need to 'acknowledge that if we can control technology even as it increases its potential to control us, we will have a better chance for survival in the imperfect future which we can reasonably expect.'[34]

One can see the appeal of cybernetics: it radically decenters the human body, the sacred icon of the essential. Virtual reality works further to decenter notions of 'the real': the rhetoric is seductive. Yet, despite the political importance of engaging with developing technologies, the irony of this is that, in its extreme manifestations, cyberfeminism takes us full circle and frequently ends up sounding largely indistinct from the form of mystical maternalist feminism of which the technofems are so scathing. If the cyborg was, for Haraway, an ironical political myth which was created to symbolise a non-holistic, non-universalising vision for feminist strategies, it has been taken up within cyberfeminism as an icon for an essential female being.

> Women ... have always found ways of circumventing the
> dominant systems of communication which have marginalised
> their own speech. And while man gazed out, looking for the
> truth, and reflecting on himself, women have never depended on
> what appears before them ... On the contrary, they have
> persisted in communicating with each other and their
> environment in ways which the patriarch has been unable to
> comprehend, and so often been interpreted as man, or
> hysterical.[35]

These are the words of self-proclaimed cyberfeminist Sadie
Plant, but they could equally have been spoken by the
arch-goddess herself, Mary Daly. Though Sadie Plant claims to
celebrate the cyborg rather than the goddess, her writing reveals
a longing for precisely the 'quasi-religious communion' that we
find in eco-feminist writing, the rejection of which spurred
Haraway's cyborg vision. In a flight from the actual material
differences which demand complex political responses, the
cyborg offers the possibility of flexible diversity, whilst holding
onto the comforting notion of essential femininity. Note, for
example, Sadie Plant's assumption that women have 'their own
speech' with their own lines of communication which are never
linear but manifest 'flashes of intuitive exchange'.[36] In place of
the particularity and plurality stressed by Haraway we find in
Plant's writing phrases like 'women have always found ...'
which fit ill with Haraway's rejection of the assimilation of all
women's differences into an organic unity. And, whereas
Haraway sought to explore cybernetics as a means of realising a
more pluralist world, Plant argues that 'the female cyborg is the
only cyborg.'[37] Given this one must have some sympathy with
Catherine Elwes when she claims that the cybernetic future
that Plant describes represents an 'escape from the body, escape
from the difficulties of inter-personal relations, escape from
biology, escape from history and most significantly perhaps,
escape from difference.'[38]

Furthermore, where Haraway's manifesto was clearly
political in intent, seeking a more adequate realisation of
socialist feminist aspirations, Plant's version of cyberfeminism is

distinctly apolitical: 'no-one,' she says, 'is making it happen: it is not a political project, and has neither theory nor practice, no goals and no principles.' It is for this reason that some have reacted with such anger to Plant's vision, arguing that, 'Cyberfeminism means the death of feminism and a post-political world'.[39] We must therefore question whether current cyberfeminists are engaged in a political process of deconstructing old oppressive certainties, or whether they are simply seeking coherence where all is in a state of flux – in pursuit of the totalising experience which eclipses all other worlds, to be found in the internet and systems which still have their own limited and understandable – though strange – internal coherence.[40] These two stances both exist in Plant's work, in an uneasy alliance of cyberfeminism and cyberpunk. For whilst cyberpunk does nothing to persuade us that the world it describes is a good or better world, Plant *does* claim that her world is a better world for 'women', but offers no political or ethical basis for such a claim.

Firestone ends *The Dialectic of Sex* with a section called 'Revolutionary Demands'; Haraway writes her Manifesto 'to find political direction in the 1980s'[41]; Plant, writing in Major's anti-political 1990s, has no sense of political project at all. The cyborg has become a symbol of philosophical challenge rather than an icon of political change.

So it is my claim that whilst for Haraway cyborg imagery suggests positive new ways of negotiating complex material differences, for others it offers the option of transcending them altogether; of leaving the messy world of material politics behind and entering a post-political utopia of infinite possibility.

In this context, I argue that whilst cyberfeminism might offer a vision of fabulous, flexible, feminist futures, it has as yet largely failed to do so. Instead, cyberfeminism has become the distorted fantasy of those so cynical of traditional political strategies, so bemused by the complexity of social materiality, and so bound up in the rhetoric of the space-flows of information technology, that they have forgotten both the exploitative and alienating potential of technology and retreated into the celebration of essential, though disembodied, woman.

Cyborg as Political Paradox

> Cybernetics is already a paradox: simultaneously a sublime vision of human power over chance and a multinational capitalism's mechanical process of expansion.
>
> Istvan Csicsery-Ronay, Jr.[42]

By way of a concluding consideration of the potential for feminist cyborgs, let us reflect upon the relation between political myth and practice.

The cyborg myth has a certain seductive imaginative power, but it is a myth, as Andrew Ross has pointed out, 'that can swing both ways'[43]. What is more, the pendulum is heavily weighted by very material manifestations of power. The cyborgs as 'technofascist celebrations of invulnerability' are winning out in the cultural battle against the semi-permeable hybrid cyborgs of Haraways's lexicon. Predictable enough, perhaps, given that cyborgs are the illegitimate offspring of militarism and patriarchal capitalism. As both symptom and critique of the expansion of the military industrial complex, cyborg politics is a tricky business. Even Firestone acknowledged that: 'Cybernetics, like birth control, can be a double-edged sword. Like artificial reproduction, to envisage it in the hands of the present powers is to envision a nightmare.'[44]

Yet to recognise that technology is currently constituted and operated in pursuit of the interests of the powerful is not to relinquish all attempts to reappropriate its potential. Technological developments are taking place, and it is as well that we engage with them and try to negotiate a form which most suits our own ends. We cannot afford to underestimate the tactical manoeuvres of the relatively powerless when attempting to resist, negotiate, or transform the system and products of the relatively powerful.[45] These tactics *include* ways of thinking, inseparable as they are from everyday struggles and pleasures. One needs to find the metaphors that allow one to imagine a liberatory knowledge, to colonise discourses which operate to exclude and undermine. It takes a certain form of political irony to grapple with this ambivalence: using mimicry, mockery, pastiche and parody as ways of appropriating dominant images for one's own ends. Thus the appropriation of the cyborg for the mapping of possible feminist futures has the potential to be a subversive act. But let us not imagine that persuasive rhetoric alone is sufficient to shift the distribution of power.

At issue here is both the development of a political imagination which can conjure up an ideal role and use for developing technologies, on terms we have defined – the creative project; and also the development of political regulations and controls which actually govern the form and uses of these technologies. The former is a necessary, though not sufficient precondition, for the realisation of an adequate technology. Despite the frequently asserted claim that we now live in a world in which fantasy and reality are impossible to distinguish, we cannot afford to engage in political utopias alone: we still need to negotiate with the mechanisms of state and market. For most people, faith in the technological vision requires such practical safeguards.

Note, for example, the latest detailed report from the European Union's Eurobarometer poll about new technologies (1993, a repeat of a survey done in 1991), involving nearly 13,000 people across the member states of the European Union.[46] Whilst there appears to be a general feeling that new technologies 'will improve our way of life' over the next twenty years, when asked more specifically about particular technologies, there was a noted lack of trust that biotechnology would improve things in comparison to the perhaps more familiar telecommunications. Substitute 'genetic engineering' for biotechnology and the distrust mounts notably. What is more, the sense of optimism that these technologies will improve life has dropped significantly since the question was asked just two years ago. It would appear that the majority of people still distrust attempts to meddle in what they perceive to be 'nature': perhaps for the related reason that they also distrust government and industry as sources of information about what is going on. Across the European Union only 1 per cent of people chose industry as the best source of information on the subject, 5 per cent trust the public authorities, 16 per cent university teachers, 26 per cent consumer organisations and 30 per cent environmental organisations.[47]

The fundamental issue to emerge from this poll is that *trust* is the key condition of acceptability for these emerging technologies. The fact that so many people place their trust in the market above all else is a sad indictment of our current political malaise. The vast corporate bodies of state and industry no longer inspire us with confidence: we would far rather buy into new technologies as individual consumers than as political citizens, allowing us the 'choice' to engage with these developments or not. Technological developments which can be packaged and sold in the global market-place (such as Sky TV and CD-Rom) are gaining our trust and capturing our imaginations. Those developments, however, which still require regulation and operation at state level (such as nuclear power) continue to fill us with dread. Thus we might argue that our responses to new technologies are inextricably bound up with our faith (or its absence) in those who are selling it to us. It is worth noting therefore that consumer and environmental organisations are the only bodies that seem to have gained the power to be worthy of our trust in this respect. The fact that, in Britain, more people are now members of Greenpeace than of the Labour Party indicates quite clearly who has won our political imaginations.

It is crucial that we are attentive to these political realities if we are to have a role in shaping the ethical and legal issues currently being negotiated about the development of techno- logical advances – from the patenting of genetically engineered tomatoes to the enscription of e-mail messages. A hunting ground for litigious lawyers and aggressive companies, the only criteria currently used for negotiating the acceptability of such developments is the pursuit of profit, occasionally constrained by a rather dated parliamentary concern for social utility. We do not yet have the developed ethical imagination nor the social structures to deal with these issues in any other way.

It has been claimed that cybernetics would oust all metaphysical concepts – 'including the concepts of soul, of life, of value, of choice, of memory' – for it is these very concepts which have served to separate the machine from man.[48] Yet, I would argue that although cybernetics may undermine the scope for metaphysical thought, we cannot afford to jettison the ethical altogether. We need not conceive ethics as either metaphysical concepts free-floating in the biosphere, or timeless foundations under our feet. We do not discover them: we invent them. I am interested here in the example offered by Foucault in his later writings. For, although Foucault placed himself in the counter-Enlightenment tradition, in these writings he appears not only as a critic of the Enlightenment, but also as its heir. This rehabilitation of the Enlightenment – the perception of it (like our cyborg) as both disease and remedy – depends on the possibility of denying the Enlightenment's myth about its own coherence. For Foucault this requires making a distinction between two distinct Kantian traditions: on the one hand, what Foucault calls 'the analytique of truth' – the analysis of the condition of knowledge which has pretensions of truth; on the other hand, what he calls 'the ontology of the present' – the questioning of who we are and the nature of the moment that we belong to.

The potential of the cyborg myth is that it might offer a lexicon with which to challenge the self-foundation project of the Enlightenment without giving up on its self-assertion project; abandoning the rationalist and individualist assumptions whilst retaining the pluralist and democratic political structures.[49] This theoretical move is, I think, invaluable in that it signals the possibility of circumventing the Enlightenment's myth about its own nature as a coherent, unitary project, which can only be accepted or rejected wholesale, allowing us to hold firmly onto the political project of the Enlightenment whilst rejecting its epistemological underpinnings.

The implication of this for our exploration of cybernetics and feminism is that we can embrace the ontological challenges these technological developments pose for our notion of the self – exploring the potentiality for eroding the dichotomous gendering of selves – whilst nonetheless holding onto a democratic political commitment which requires us to remain attentive to the material and economic power structures which might deny the potential for self-assertion. What is required of cyberfeminism is thus both a vision of cyborgs that may help to heighten our awareness of the potentiality for new technologies, and the political pursuit of the practical manifestation of an appropriate technology: unintimidating, accessible and democratic. Cybernetics *is* both 'a dreary augmentation of multinational capitalism's mechanical process of expansion' and simultaneously 'a sublime vision of human power': as such we must be attentive to the political irony embedded in our mythic cyborgs.

Notes

1 David Tomas, 'The Technophilic Body: On Technicity in William Gibson's Cyborg Culture', *New Formations*, pp31-32.
2 Donna Haraway, 'A Manifesto for Cyborgs: Science, Technology and Socialist Feminism in the 1980s', in Linda Nicholson (ed), *Feminism/Postmodernism*, Routledge, London, 1990, p190.
3 Allucquere Rosanne Stone, 'Will the Real Body Please Stand Up?', in Michael Benedikt (ed), *Cyberspace: First Steps*, MIT Press, Cambridge, Massachusetts, 1992, p113.
4 See, for example, Jean Baudrillard, *Simulations*, Semiotext(e), New York, 1983, and Mark Poster (ed), *Jean Baudrillard: Selected Writings*, Stanford University Press, Palo Alto, 1988.
5 Ernest Jones, *The Life and Work of Sigmund Freud*, (3 Volumes), Penguin, Harmondsworth, 1987, Volume 2, pp224-6.
6 Bruce Mazlish, 'The Fourth Discontinuity', in Melvin Kranzberg and William Davenport (eds) *Technology and Culture: An Anthropology*, Meridian Books, New York, 1972, p218.
7 *Ibid*, p218.
8 *Ibid*, p218.
9 Julia Kristeva, *Nations Without Nationalism*, Columbia University

Press, New York 1993, p2.

[10] Drucilla Cornell, *The Philosophy of the Limit*, Routledge, London, 1994.

[11] Judith Butler, *Gender Trouble*, Routledge, London, 1990, p33.

[12] Ibid, p139.

[13] Clauda Springer, 'The Pleasure of the Interface', *Screen*, Autumn 1991, p318.

[14] The concept of 'cyberspace' was coined by science fiction writer, William Gibson in the pages of his novel *Neuromancer* (1984). 'An unhappy word, perhaps', reflects one commentator, 'if it remains tied to the desperate, dystopic vision of the near future found in *Neuromancer* and *Count Zero* – visions of corporate hegemony and urban decay, of neutral implants, of a life in paranoia and pain.' Benedikt, *op.cit*, p1.

[15] Bruce Sterling, 'Preface from Mirrorshades', pp343-349, in Larry McCaffery (ed), *Storming the Reality Studio*, Duke University Press, DurhaM, 1991, p346.

[16] Darko Suvin, 'On Gibson and Cyberpunk', in McCaffery, *op.cit.*, p363.

[17] Allucquere Roseanne Stone, *op.cit*, p104.

[18] *I-D* magazine, July 1993, p28.

[19] Stone, *op.cit.*, p84.

[20] Springer *op.cit*, p308.

[21] Mary Ann Doane, 'Technophilia: Technology, Representation and the Feminine', in Mary Jacobus, Evelyn Fox Keller and Sally Shuttleworth (eds), *Body/Politics* Routledge, New York, 1990, p163.

[22] Tatsumi, quoted by Darko Suvin, *op.cit.*, p364.

[23] This title is taken from Nicholas Moseley's novel of the same name: his hopeful monsters nearly always die young – born before their time when it's not known if the environment is quite ready for them.

[24] Scott Bukatman, *Terminal Identity*, Duke University Press, Durham, 1993 p314.

[25] Sarah Lefanu, *Feminism and Science Fiction*, Indiana University Press, Bloomington, 1989 p2.

[26] Shulamith Firestone, *The Dialectic of Sex*, Women's Press, London, 1979 p19.

[27] *Ibid*, pp183-4.

[28] *Ibid*, p189.

[29] Haraway, *op.cit*, p223.

[30] *Ibid*, p223.

[31] *Ibid*, p217.

[32] Joan Gordon, 'Yin and Yang Duke It Out', pp196-203 in McCaffery, *op.cit.*, p197.

[33] *Ibid*, p200.

34 *Ibid*, p200.
35 Sadie Plant, 'Beyond the Screens: Film, Cyberpunk and Cyberfeminism', *Variant*, p13.
36 *Ibid*, p14.
37 *Ibid*, p7.
38 Catherine Elwes, 'Is Technology Encoded in Gender-Specific Terms?' in *Variant*, Autumn 1993, p65.
39 *Ibid*, p66.
40 Gillian Skirrow, 'Hellivision: An Analysis of Video Games', *The Media Reader*, M. Alvarado and J. Thompson (eds), BFI Publishing, London, p326.
41 Haraway, *op.cit*, p21.
42 Istvan Csicsery-Ronay, Jr, 'Cyberpunk and Neuromanticism' in McCaffery, *op.cit.*, p186.
43 Andrew Ross, 'Interview with Donna Haraway', Constance Penley and Andrew Ross (eds), *Technoculture*, University of Minnesota Press, Minneapolis, 1991, p17.
44 Firestone, *op.cit*, p190.
45 Constance Penley, 'Brownian Motion: Women, Tactics and Technology', in Penley and Ross, *op.cit*, p139.
46 Jon Turney, 'Tasty, fresh and unnatural', in *The Higher*, 8 April 1994, pp16-17.
47 *Ibid*, p16.
48 Jacques Derrida, *Of Grammatology*, extracted in McCaffrey, *op.cit*, p194.
49 For an example of this approach see Chantal Mouffe, *The Return of The Political*, Verso, London, 1993.

Notes on Contributors

Jon Dovey is a writer, producer and lectures in Media Arts at the University of the West of England. His practice and theory has been with video and TV production, but he is currently developing multimedia production skills with a particular interest in narrative and interactivity.

Kevin Robins is Reader in Cultural Geography and a researcher at the Centre for Urban and Regional Development Studies, University of Newcastle Upon Tyne. He is the author, with David Morley, of *Spaces of Identity* (1995).

Sean Cubitt is Reader in Video and Media Studies at Liverpool John Moore's University. He is the author of *Timeshift: On Video Culture* and *Videography: Video Media as Art and Practice*. A member of the editorial boards of *Screen* and *Third Text*, he has published widely on contemporary arts, media and culture.

Nickianne Moody lectures in Media and Cultural Studies at Liverpool John Moore's University. She has research interests in narrative and popular fiction, cultural history and oral history. She is currently carrying out research into Boots Booklovers Library.

Fred Johnson is a TV producer and writer active in the US Community Communications movement. He has co-produced a number of programmes with the BBC Community Programmes Unit and is currently developing a community media literacy project in Beaverton, Oregon. He is a founding member of Media Working Group Inc., a media production, education and research group in the USA.

Ailsa Barry has directed and produced multimedia programmes for the Tate Gallery and the Victoria and Albert Museum. She is the Arts Programme Co-ordinator at Artec, a post supported by the Arts Council to develop awareness and training in digital technology amongst visual artists, museums and galleries throughout England. Within this capacity she develops on-line events with arts centres and organises conferences on arts and digital media.

Beryl Graham, formerly of Projects UK in Newcastle, is now a freelance arts worker based in San Francisco and Newcastle. She is currently researching interactive art for an M.Phil/Ph.d at the University of Sunderland, and is developing *Serious Games*, an exhibition of interactive artwork, for the Laing Art Gallery in 1996.

Catherine Richards' interventions in the territory of art, culture and new technologies span fifteen years of work which has deliberately crossed many boundaries of art practice, theoretical projects and primary research. She has exhibited widely throughout North America and Europe, including initiating the *Bioapparatus* artists' residency at the Banff Centre for the Arts in 1991, and she produced *Spectral Bodies* using the first VR system in Canada in 1991.

Judith Squires lectures in Political Theory at the University of Bristol and is the editor of the journal, *New Formations*. She has edited, with Erica Carter and James Donald, *Space and Place: Theories of Identity and Location* (1993) and *Cultural Remix: Theories of Politics and the Popular* (1995).